THE ULTIMATE
Clever Puzzle
BOOK

THE ULTIMATE
Clever Puzzle
BOOK

Edited by

**Olivia Carlton, Philip J. Carter, Kenneth A. Russell,
Dave Tuller, Michael Rios, and Michael A. DiSpezio**

Sterling Publishing Co., Inc.
New York

10 9 8 7 6 5 4 3 2 1

Published by Sterling Publishing Co., Inc.
387 Park Avenue South, New York, NY 10016
This book is comprised of the following Sterling titles:
Crosswords to Exercise Your Mind © 2002 by Dell Magazines, a division of Crosstown Publications
Challenging IQ Tests © 1998 by Philip J. Carter & Kenneth A. Russell
Mensa Math & Logic Puzzles © 2000 by Dave Tuller & Michael Rios
The Ultimate Lateral & Critical Thinking Puzzle Book © 2002 by Sterling Publishing Co., Inc.

© 2002 by Sterling Publishing Co., Inc.
Distributed in Canada by Sterling Publishing
c/o Canadian Manda Group, One Atlantic Avenue, Suite 105
Toronto, Ontario, Canada M6K 3E7
Distributed in Great Britain and Europe by Cassell PLC
Welligton House, 125 Strand, London WC2R 0BB, England
Distributed in Australia by Capricorn Link (Austalia) pty Ltd.
P.O. Box 6651, Baulkham Hills, Business Centre, NSW 2153, Australia

Manufactured in China

ISBN 1-4027-0479-8

CONTENTS

Puzzles

CROSSWORDS
TO
EXERCISE
YOUR
MIND

INTRODUCTION

This last section harks back to the 1950s and 1960s, as did the first section. Remember, in those simpler times there were no cell phones, no e-mail, and no music videos. And back then, crosswords tested your knowledge of words. To solve them, you didn't need to know the names of minor pop stars or second-string baseball players. You just needed a big vocabulary and the ability to recall classical knowledge. The puzzles are from magazines that originally appeared during this era, and none of the clues have been updated.

So when you encounter the clue "Mr. Murphy of the movies," you need to fill in AUDIE, not EDDIE. For "Tennessee Senator," the answer is GORE, but it's referring to Al Gore, Sr., not the recent vice president. "Actress Barrymore" is answered with ETHEL, not DREW. The clue "They will explore space" uses the future tense, since ASTRONAUTS hadn't yet gone up in rockets.

Despite not having any modern trivia in them, these puzzles are still quite tough. You'll definitely be exercising your mind when you solve them. But we bet that the workout you get from solving them will be a lot more fun than any workout you've done at the gym!

1

ACROSS

1 Sigh of woe
5 Georgia city
10 Location
14 Expense
15 Wear away
16 Salver
17 Threesome
18 Vocation
19 Stage part
20 Photograph
22 Imbibes
24 Farm tool
25 Happy
26 Bed cover
29 Goes before
33 Core
34 Pester
35 Uncooked
36 Dines
37 Casts off
38 Salary
39 High card
40 Steal: Slang
41 Santiago's country
42 Lifesavers
44 Pluto or Mars
45 Guide
46 Castle trench
47 Rumor
50 Uncertainty
54 What the earth
   turns on
55 Rub out
57 Gauzy face
   covering
58 5,280 feet
59 Wanderer
60 Blunders
61 Let it stand
62 Plant sources
63 Prickly flower

DOWN

1 Performs
2 Forsaken: Poetic
3 Large continent
4 Corks
5 Means
6 Dart
7 Winter garment
8 Unusual
9 Unnecessary
10 Long step
11 Golf club
12 Converse
13 "Peepers"
21 Bed board
23 Caucasian, for
   example

25 Classify
26 Cut, as wool
27 Tranquillity
28 Fixed charges
29 Looks slyly
30 Sewer
31 Bird of prey
32 Sugary
34 First, second, ___
37 Knitted clothes
38 Anything that
40 Petitioner
41 Applaud
43 Clothes storage
   room
44 Hard questions
46 Meditated
47 Male sheep

48 Way out
49 Heap
50 Conserve
51 Roman despot
52 Gentlemen
53 Otherwise
56 Fish eggs

ANSWER, PAGE 261

2

ACROSS

1 Cod or Ann
5 Peruse
9 Spring flower
13 Soldier's truancy: Abbr.
14 "___ Brute!"
15 Styles
17 Cry loudly
18 Telephoner's convenience
20 Cap
21 Retain
22 Lose
23 Everlasting
25 Obligation
26 Origin
27 FDR's "___ chats"
31 Station
33 Painful twinges
34 Mingle
35 Astringent substance
36 Scope
37 Animal protection agency: Abbr.
38 Britain's air arm: Abbr.
39 Droopy, as pants
40 Sultan's household
41 Upholds, as a law
43 Sheltered inlet
44 Foray
45 Forthrightness
48 Stay
51 A few
52 "Sweet ___" (song title)
53 Magic phrase in "Arabian Nights"
55 One of Columbus's ships
56 Spree
57 Ancient
58 Folk singer Burl ___
59 Stage aids
60 Cautious
61 Nuisance

DOWN

1 Overseas telegram
2 Expect
3 Make-up aid
4 Building addition
5 Iterate
6 Singer Waters
7 Upon
8 Ask for payment
9 Drinks
10 Perches
11 Graven image
12 Bristle: Latin
16 Bashful
19 Come out
21 Overhand or figure of eight
24 Space
25 Dirty and dark
27 Long teeth
28 Arousing solemn feelings
29 Gaming cubes
30 Test
31 Venture
32 Spirit
33 Called publicly
36 Wisconsin city
37 Rescue
39 Sears meat in fat
40 Sharpen
42 Juicy fruit
43 Amusing play
45 Greek poet
46 Melodies
47 Bread ingredient
48 Steal from
49 Heroic tale
50 Carte
51 Legend
54 Envisioned
55 Small bite

ANSWER, PAGE 262

3

ACROSS

1 Thick piece
5 Leisurely
9 Depart
10 A stopwatch is one
12 Nastier
13 ___ Kingdom (Great Britain and Northern Ireland)
15 Table support
16 Sgt. Friday's TV program
18 Small boy
20 Spoken
22 ___ up for (defend)
23 Corn-meal bread
24 Places to erect buildings
26 Ogle
27 Rainier's wife
28 Cooked in vapor
30 Ridiculed
32 Tier
33 Eli Whitney's invention
34 Slapped
38 Satisfied
42 Sieved pulp
43 Geological time division
45 Postpone
46 Imitated
47 Horse goads
49 Moist
50 Pliable metal
51 Shouted encouragement
53 Golf mound
54 Pond within a coral reef
56 Thinks
58 Rescued
59 Makes docile
60 Fewer
61 Killed

DOWN

1 Caribbean is one
2 Earth
3 Affirms
4 Scolded sharply
5 Dazed
6 Ruled, as paper
7 Leave out
8 Rainy
9 Pope's envoy
11 Fill again with ammunition
12 Deserve
14 The ___ (Arthur Murray's forte)
15 At a ___ (puzzled)
17 Cheerful
19 Good ___ (kind act)
21 Well-informed
23 Published
25 Cure, as meat
27 Crush into bits
29 Female sheep
31 Conceit
34 Petty quarrel
35 Scholar
36 Places for boxing matches
37 Is contingent (on)
38 Rabbit-food
39 Puts in good spirits
40 Titles
41 Write by machine
44 Regret
47 Sabots, for example
48 Outer leaf of a flower
51 Small bay
52 Thin coin
55 Young woman: Slang
57 Just bought

ANSWER, PAGE 264

4

1 Friend
5 Known fact
10 Extend over
14 Ready for harvest
15 Rub out
16 Sharpen
17 Fragrance
18 French cap
19 Vehicle
20 Strong inclination
22 Rush
24 Minute particle
25 Unit of electrical power
26 Smother
29 Baseball pitching style
32 Engage in a debate
33 Occult art
34 Spike of corn
36 Recline lazily
37 Devastation
38 Inkling
39 In addition
40 Engine
41 Drudge
42 Kind of muffin
44 Bent
45 Fruit drinks
46 Gloomy
47 Breed of dog
50 Pardoned
54 Dismounted
55 Semblance
57 Earth hollow
58 "This scepter'd ___"
59 Hitlerites
60 On the ocean
61 Sly glance
62 Welcome
63 Season of fasting

DOWN

1 Riding whip
2 Conceal
3 "Once ___ a time"
4 Compassionate
5 Argument
6 Boxing ring
7 Small fruit pie
8 Employ
9 Systematic
10 Mount ___, California
11 Look sullen
12 Poker stake
13 Kind of display light
21 Cavity

23 Actor Guinness
25 Energy
26 Seasoning
27 Body of cavalry
28 Eskimo house
29 Relish
30 Abate effort
31 Delicate purple
33 Companions
35 Actress Donna ___
37 Hanging fluttering in the air
38 Relating to office work
40 Manner
41 Counterfeit coin
43 Glib speech
44 Wooded tract

46 Motherless calf, in the West
47 Take a sea voyage
48 Otherwise
49 Piece of baked clay
50 Disconcert
51 Flower-vessel
52 Uniform
53 Orderly
56 Damage

ANSWER, PAGE 266

5

ACROSS

1 Be a sign of
5 Muscular contraction
10 Untidy clutter
14 Related
15 Forbidden
16 Wheel spindle
17 Speech fault
18 Flood
20 Wanes
22 In high spirits
23 Sound discordantly
24 Crimson
25 Beautiful, in Scotland
26 Sparing of words
30 "Mugs"
31 Tease
33 Moneyed
34 Inquire
35 Barber's speciality
36 Hawaiian dish
37 Expires
39 Beverage
40 Meager
42 Curved blades for cutting grass
44 House plants
45 Regret deeply
46 Seasoned
48 Leave
51 Choral compositions
54 Uneducated
56 Like (as)
57 Coin opening
58 More painful
59 Resound
60 Millinery
61 Very small
62 Move sideways

DOWN

1 Shiny-pated
2 Itinerant farm laborer
3 "Platter spinner"
4 Board an airliner
5 Tight-fisted
6 Door section
7 Mistreat
8 Male child
9 Temperate
10 Bullfighter
11 Way out
12 Wild plum
13 Transport
19 Actor Guinness
21 Highway hotels
25 Fundamental
26 Dwell
27 Neck and neck
28 Religious pictures
29 Pert girl
30 Temporary styles
31 ___ and that
32 Pale and drawn
35 Most lovable
38 Narrow waterways
40 Denomination
41 Wrinkles
43 Injured
44 Sunday togs
46 Frighten
47 Communion plate
48 Eloper in "Hey Diddle Diddle"
49 Girl's name
50 Scheme
52 Steady pain
53 Display
55 Caviar

ANSWER, PAGE 268

6

ACROSS

1 Jordan resident
5 American buffalo
10 Counterfeit
14 Fluid rock
15 Wear away
16 Professional tramp
17 Always
18 Innermost parts
19 List
20 "___ York"
22 Exchanged
24 Branch of service
25 Project
26 A country gentleman
29 Chirping insects
33 Curves
34 Fail
35 That
36 Outfits
37 Beside
38 "Eat" gum
39 Exist
40 Get up
41 "___ and Punishment"
42 Genealogy
44 Cut, as bread
45 Fleet-footed animal
46 Wild disturbance
47 Strain
50 St. Louis ballplayer
54 Locality
55 One more than once
57 Arrive
58 Shopping memo
59 Consumed
60 On the ocean
61 Carry
62 Treat wounds
63 Give for a time

DOWN

1 Malt drinks
2 Rant
3 Declare
4 Things you spend money on to save money
5 Grew to be
6 Sarcasm
7 Type
8 Poem
9 Very young bird
10 Became smaller
11 Gangster: Slang
12 Physically fit
13 Shape
21 Makes a mistake
23 Clothing stand
25 Dried plum
26 Thong
27 Set of 24 paper sheets
28 Impelled
29 Slam
30 Pertaining to morals
31 Topic of discourse
32 United by stitches
34 Pilot
37 Put in custody
38 Faultfinding
40 Grows old
41 Lump of earth
43 Form an opinion
44 Warning devices
46 Jockeys' jaunts
47 Sodium chloride
48 Singing group
49 Remainder
50 Quote
51 Durante feature
52 So be it
53 Bullets
56 Contest

ANSWER, PAGE 270

ACROSS

1 Keats creation
5 Relaxes
10 Bills and coins
14 Competent
15 Special edition of a paper
16 "Rio ___" (musical)
17 Fling
18 Construction metal
19 Russian mountain range
20 Gotten and spent quickly
23 Heavy hammer
24 Be in session
25 A story's setting
28 Nonsense: Slang
33 Very angry
34 London newspaper
35 Source of iron
36 Car accessory
37 Heathen
38 Walk in water
39 Garden tool
40 Excellent
41 Ascended
42 Imperil
44 French ___ (fancy dessert)
45 Convent-dweller
46 Foundation
47 Useless pursuit
54 Assert
55 Fire particle
56 Cut with shears
58 Highway division
59 Emblem of the United States
60 Hard to find
61 Recognize
62 Partly frozen rain
63 Water jug

DOWN

1 Lump (of butter)
2 Woodwind instrument
3 Party-giver Maxwell
4 Navy dining companion
5 Save
6 Praise to the skies
7 Stalk
8 Maple, for instance
9 Store employees
10 Bad-tempered
11 Light and graceful
12 Male deer
13 Angel "light"
21 New England university
22 Intentions
25 Supple
26 "The Hunter" constellation
27 Was concerned
28 Striped feline
29 Persian poet
30 Sunday's meat
31 Command
32 Very small
34 Binding strip
37 Short, turned-up "snoots"
38 A know-it-all
40 Cozy
41 Reckless
43 One of the twelve apostles
44 Small parcel
46 Milton ___ (comedian)
47 Hike
48 "The Terrible" czar
49 Curtain fabric
50 Lustrous gem
51 Wise
52 Cabbage salad
53 Irish Republic
57 For each

ANSWER, PAGE 272

8

ACROSS

1 Interlaced
5 Woody plant
10 Doctrines
14 Deception
15 Residence
16 Drudge
17 Singer Pinza
18 Kind of tree
19 Equestrian game
20 Feeler
22 Jungle king's small offspring
24 Black
25 Storage places
26 Bundle
29 Approve
33 Woman's secret
34 Ridges
36 Trigger, for instance
37 Loud, steady noise
39 Actress Bernhardt
41 Contest
42 Shore recess
44 Claw
46 Head of the family
47 Compassion
49 Puzzling questions
51 Lily plant
52 Gainsay
53 These fly from a forge
56 Commercial traveler
60 Poet Whitman
61 Clutch
63 Cloth made of bark
64 Summit
65 Impulses
66 The "windows of the soul"
67 Low; vile
68 Hangs
69 Crush

DOWN

1 Sharpen
2 Exude slowly
3 Peacockish
4 Strikingly unusual
5 Fetters
6 Foliage used for wreaths
7 Impolite
8 Benefit
9 German city
10 One who passes off as another
11 Before long
12 Distance unit
13 Aperture
21 Afresh
23 Move almost imperceptibly
25 Fundamental
26 Site of the Louvre
27 Great suffering
28 Kingdom
29 Wander
30 Sultan's decree
31 Movie award
32 Requirements
35 Workshop tool
38 Witty talk
40 Desperate
43 Chat
45 Not a bit
48 An even chance
50 Method
52 Stunned
53 Mop
54 Large rodent
55 Poor-box money
56 Put your "John Hancock" on
57 Central Amer. Indian
58 Copies
59 Make of auto
62 Prior to

ANSWER, PAGE 274

18

9

ACROSS

1 Barracks beds
5 Engine
10 Lean-to
14 Spread for bread
15 Useful
16 Volcanic product
17 Family scapegrace
19 Complete set
20 Poised
21 Puzzling question
23 Shakespearean king
24 Tropical tree
25 Writing pad
28 Tranquil
31 Prankish spirit in "The Tempest"
32 Bungle
33 To and ___
34 Obey
35 "Dixieland"
36 Den
37 Wooden pin
38 Easter symbol
39 Supply food
40 Attributed
42 Tacitly
43 Wanders
44 Fade, as flowers
45 Shirtwaist
47 Purifies, as water
51 Misplaced
52 Creates a noisy scene: Slang
54 French cleric
55 Donor
56 Author Ferber
57 Striplings
58 Corundum
59 Ooze

DOWN

1 Irvin S. ___ (American humorist)
2 Spanish jar
3 River duck
4 Known improperly by this term
5 Capital of Oman
6 Different
7 Bound
8 Aficionado's cry
9 Reprimand
10 Muddy deposit
11 Work of "Lady Luck"
12 Morally wrong
13 Palm fruit
18 Assume a position of prayer
22 Short distance
24 Author-entertainer ___ Comden
25 Florida city
26 Zodiac sign
27 "Der Bingle"
28 Sixteen ounces
29 Milton's "regent of the sun"
30 British truck
32 Dice: Slang
35 Inundate
36 Trellises
38 Prejudice
39 Sects
41 Courses
42 Severe distress
44 More judicious
45 Tattle
46 Timber wolf
47 Plunge
48 Burden
49 Wet-wash cord
50 Break suddenly
53 Goal

ANSWER, PAGE 276

19

10

ACROSS

1 Close-mouthed person
5 Strata
10 Bridge
14 Citrus fruit
15 Century plant
16 Sharpen
17 Consumes
18 Recording strips
19 Very small amount
20 Feast
22 Young actress
24 Disturbed
26 Frequently: Poetic
27 Lasso
30 Disturbs persistently
35 Readies for publication
36 Silas Marner was one
37 Hem and ___
38 Assistant
39 Potato bags
40 Foundation
41 Scotch river
42 "Woof woofs"
43 Was concerned
44 Feature of a Hitchcock film
46 Hen's sound
47 Stripling
48 Be grateful to
50 Idiotic
54 Naive
58 In a line
59 American emblem
61 Wind instrument
62 Sick-looking
63 Hand-warmer
64 Tennessee Senator
65 Snow vehicle
66 More ancient
67 Break suddenly

DOWN

1 Social group
2 Singer Kirk
3 So be it!
4 Thorny western shrub
5 Most recent
6 Playing marble
7 Shrill bark
8 Pre-holiday times
9 Returns (to use)
10 What gamblers often "lose"
11 Billiard game
12 Poker bet
13 Shipshape
21 Arrow poison tree
23 Distant
25 Dense grove
27 Shows the way
28 French "farewell"
29 Goes on horseback
31 Makes queries about
32 Dangerous fish
33 Artist's stand
34 Stockholm native
36 Red planet
39 California city
40 Surpluses
42 Comedian Orson ___
43 Jargon
45 Cultivated
46 One's life work
49 Divide equally
50 Charts
51 Verbal
52 Actor's part
53 Speak to on the phone
55 Jet black
56 Rail bird
57 Ooze
60 Deity

ANSWER, PAGE 261

11

ACROSS

1 First appearance
6 Tell secrets
10 Out of danger
14 Entertain
15 Subtle emanation
16 Pastries
17 Trifler
18 In Sunday best
20 Greek letter
21 Temper tantrum
23 Swift
24 Tooth part
26 Stylish
27 Skillful
28 Garments
32 Mama's boy
34 Routine job
35 Neither
36 Rhymester
37 Scowl
38 Bind
39 Piercing tool
40 Make a connection
41 Muscle
42 Discuss at length
44 Chop ___ (restaurant dish)
45 Seasonal song
46 Realtor's sign
49 Plant buds
52 Motion picture
53 Swear
54 Santa's home
56 Actress Dunne
58 Assist
59 Spoken
60 Inasmuch as
61 Roly-___ (chubby)
62 Minister to
63 Consumed

DOWN

1 Old-fashioned
2 Act with feeling
3 Do business
4 Employ
5 Frighten
6 Sheriff's star
7 Tempt
8 Exist
9 Tuba
10 Oration
11 Helper
12 Clan warfare
13 Discover
19 Annoy or thwart
22 Social insect
25 Dry run
26 Circus cut-up
28 Church group
29 Whatever happens
30 Opposite of "yep"
31 Got bigger
32 Petty quarrel
33 Tall-Corn State
34 Angler's basket
37 A "fin": Slang
38 Row of seats
40 Fang
41 Conjecture
43 Difficult, as a problem
44 Musical tone
46 Pasture
47 Time being
48 'Twixt
49 Cinch: Slang
50 Tramp
51 Russian city
52 Cream-filled cake
55 Native metal
57 Creek

ANSWER, PAGE 262

21

12

ACROSS

1 Mental abilities
5 Atomizer
10 Fellow
14 Pale tan
15 Wright brothers' machine
16 Latest fad
17 Laborer
18 Overwhelming election victories
20 Walking wearily
22 Instant
23 Joan of Arc is one
24 Strive against
25 "A" in AWOL
27 Flax cloth
28 Fish delicacy
29 Blunder
31 Sloping passageways
35 School-division
38 Actress Arden
39 Sailing vessel
40 Dixie's location
41 Feminine name
43 Wilder's "___ Town"
44 Creator of "The Thinker"
46 Hovel
49 Drudges
51 Begins, as a meeting
52 Venus or Earth
53 Went beyond (the mark)
56 Head of an unlawful group
58 Broad
59 Cobbler's tool
60 Whirls
61 Ceases
62 1957, for example
63 Rigid
64 Remainder

DOWN

1 Shed tears
2 Freezer
3 Bride's wardrobe
4 Ice-cream dish
5 Broken-bone supports
6 Factory
7 Resounded
8 Also
9 Human "echoes"
10 Outlaw
11 Satan's abode
12 Representative
13 Nuisance
19 Defeated ones
21 ___ and tonic (summer drink)
24 More mellow
25 Circle parts
26 Hacking knife
27 Brighten (up)
30 Denim trousers
32 Illicitly distilled liquor
33 Sulk
34 Nimble
36 Newcomer
37 Snow-removal tool
42 Slander
45 Hate
47 That girl
48 Reply
49 Glide smoothly
50 Singer Mario ___
51 Kilns
52 Supplicate
53 Norse god
54 Balance of probability
55 Examination
57 Monkey

ANSWER, PAGE 264

ACROSS

1 Manager
5 Poem
10 The Thin Man's dog
14 Slat
15 Advantage
16 Radar marking
17 Birthplace of President Grant
18 Favors one leg
19 Cloy
20 Panaceas
22 Refrigerator's predecessor
24 Hurries
25 Soon
26 Caricature
29 Plane-finder, in civil defense
32 Love greatly
33 Steady gaze
34 Sass: Slang
36 Omen
37 Make a touchdown
38 Farm building
39 Envision
40 Baseball, for instance
41 Daunted
42 Atomic-bomb element
44 Rots
45 Desire
46 Submerged
47 Leftovers
50 Coffee accompaniment
54 Peter Pan's enemy
55 Moleskin color
57 Locality
58 Top
59 ___ Island (former immigrant station)
60 Angler's throw
61 Tourist aids
62 Peruses
63 Otherwise

DOWN

1 Pressure group
2 Honolulu's island
3 Agitate
4 Dressing aid
5 ___ Forge, Pennsylvania
6 Iniquities
7 Los Angeles team
8 Taste
9 Locale of "Hamlet"
10 Away
11 Bacon chunk
12 Yugoslavian leader
13 Summit
21 Military assistant
23 Dove's home
25 Separated
26 Sentry's word
27 Farewell: French
28 O.K., in the Air Corps: Slang
29 Tempest
30 Heroine of "My Fair Lady"
31 James Whitcomb ___
33 Pack member
35 Seed-holders
37 "Bachelor girl"
38 Certain contest
40 Ginger cookie
41 Ward (off)
43 Rouses to action
44 Pressure
46 Tasty
47 Pretense
48 TV's Grindl
49 Frolic
50 Dance at 2-Down
51 Spoken
52 Minus
53 "Better ___ than never"
56 Pub drink

ANSWER, PAGE 266

ACROSS

1 Boutique
5 Slice, as a roast
10 Luminesce
14 Decant
15 Outsider
16 Scoria
17 Throaty voice
18 Smooth; suave
20 New: Prefix
21 Closed
22 Secret
23 Water is one
25 The "man for all seasons"
26 Heel over
28 Track choice
32 Notions
33 Impertinent
34 "Collegiate" vine
35 Spur
36 Strong point
37 Pas
38 Joan of ___
39 Cold symptom
40 Mother-of-pearl
41 Practice, as a play
43 Is pugnacious
44 ___ of life (arborvitae)
45 "Quilting party" lady
46 Brawl
49 Finished
50 Girl's name
53 Pharos
55 Related
56 Israeli seaport
57 Companion of "wiser"
58 Transmit
59 Gunpowder, etc.
60 Lean and lanky
61 Victim

DOWN

1 Bridge
2 Cavity
3 Unobtainable
4 Debate position
5 Redeem for money
6 Audible
7 Split
8 Animal doctor
9 Establish firmly
10 Fighters wear them
11 Actress Veronica ___
12 Finished
13 Desire
19 Folk opera character
21 Prosecutes
24 Heavy metal
25 Give ___ to (say)
26 A good one is "a smoke"
27 Worship
28 Spacious
29 Economical traveler
30 Opposite of 22-Across
31 Classifies
33 Drunkard: Slang
36 Predict
37 Legend
39 Gem weight
40 Number of Muses
42 Engraves
43 Best bib and tucker
45 Gave medicine to
46 Apartment
47 Fertility symbol
48 Taj Mahal site
49 Dandy
51 Eat "at eight"
52 Singer Williams
54 Aficionado's cry
55 Viper

ANSWER, PAGE 268

15

ACROSS

1 Lose color
5 Hominy ___ (Southern dish)
10 Animal tooth
14 Oil-producing nation
15 Broadcasting business
16 Scent
17 Scandal
18 Relative by marriage
19 Roster
20 Famous city in Tennessee
22 Violent dislike
24 "Return of the Native" author
25 Loafed (in the sun)
26 Push ahead
28 Slipper fabric
29 Attention
30 Mild oath
32 Entrances
36 Hazards
39 Item from 14-Across
40 Eject
41 Prepare to pray
42 Sherbets
44 Pod vegetable
45 Fool
47 Unimportant person
50 Inebriated: Slang
52 Show partiality to
53 Bursting with health
54 Repudiated
57 Actor Guinness
58 Luggage piece
60 Art item
61 Lone Ranger's trademark
62 Sword
63 Purposes
64 Victim
65 Urged (on)
66 Indian hardwood tree

DOWN

1 Dog's name
2 Diva's solo
3 "Surprise" nominee
4 Snare
5 Place to cook pancakes
6 Long-limbed and slender
7 Unemployed
8 ___ Juana, Mexico
9 Disdainful phrase
10 Site of the nation's gold deposit
11 Worship
12 Took heed of
13 Alumnus
21 Choler
23 Out of the way
25 "Tin star"
26 ___ up (become animated)
27 Pour
28 Impertinent
31 Crush
33 Timely
34 Slender grass
35 Murder
37 Location of 10-Down
38 Narrow openings
43 Ate lightly
46 Sting; irritate
48 Eggs
49 Easter hat
50 ___ bear
51 Overweight
52 Buyer of stolen goods
53 Slanted road
54 Ladder step
55 Norse legend
56 Office table
59 Old garment

ANSWER, PAGE 270

ACROSS

1 Competitor
6 He has the leading role
10 Loud, heavy impact
14 Originate
15 Animation
16 Large wolf
17 One who can do many things fairly well
20 Insect
21 Observe
22 Comic-strip dog
23 Sheeplike
25 Prevalent
26 Lock (of hair)
28 Fight between two
29 Homo sapiens
32 Equanimity
33 Reduce to dust
35 Plant yielding a bitter drug
36 Cone-shaped home
37 Italian royal family
38 Bunched
40 Renowned
41 Letter
42 Kinds
43 Robbery asea
44 Capably
45 Poetic "are you able to"
46 Wading bird
49 Formal dance
50 Licensed auditor: Abbr.
53 Almost weightless; buoyant
56 God's ___ (graveyard)
57 Attract
58 Relative
59 Envisions
60 Wanes
61 Pupils' seats

DOWN

1 Indian ruler
2 Shah Riza Pahlevi's land
3 Triumphant
4 Invite
5 Like a lion
6 Item once used by pupils
7 Roof slab
8 Meany's labor union: Abbr.
9 Recover
10 Serf
11 Rich vein
12 Egg on
13 Lichen
18 Loving
19 Ransack and rob
24 Flower holders
25 Governed
26 Interval
27 Rings slowly
28 Hoaxes
29 Pairs up incorrectly
30 Mexican Indian
31 Indigent
33 Jaunty
34 Brings up
36 Tattler
39 Everest's site
40 Helsinki is its capital
43 Colorless
44 Pains
45 Places to dine
46 Word of woe
47 Bad habit
48 Monster
49 Sharp projection
51 Eat like a bird
52 Greek war god
54 The Nautilus, for instance
55 Bond

ANSWER, PAGE 272

ACROSS

1 Elevator parts
5 Ill-tempered person
9 Game played on horseback
13 Portent
14 Pursue
15 Sleeping
16 Wall decoration
17 Large pieces
18 Thoroughfare
19 Big hit: Slang
22 Refuse stubbornly to go on
23 Regret
24 Wrinkle
27 Actor Hayden
32 "I love thy rocks and ___"
33 Pulsate
34 Mongrel
35 Morally wrong
36 Bundle of grain
37 Broad
38 Tit for ___
39 Indigent
40 Spree: Slang
41 Raises
43 Peril
44 Recede
45 Rich fabric
46 Looks at skeptically: Slang
54 Culture medium
55 Hot-water drink
56 Jazzman Brubeck
57 Stubborn animal
58 Nautical miles
59 Awry
60 Sower's need
61 Rational
62 Circus "big top"

DOWN

1 Concluding passage, in music
2 Oriental nursemaid
3 Fashion anew
4 Accumulate quickly
5 Substantial amount
6 Sounded, as a bell
7 Inquires
8 Feel certain about
9 Bundle
10 Wind instrument
11 Meadowlands
12 Chances
14 Santiago is its capital
20 Maiden
21 Rein
24 Grecian island
25 Strive to outdo
26 Choice part
27 Gets rid of
28 Serving platter
29 Frosting
30 Push gently
31 Actress Garson
33 "My country, 'tis of ___"
36 Unexpected reverses
37 Ignored purposely
39 Arrests: Slang
40 Indonesian island
42 Changed course suddenly
43 Opera stars
45 Struck
46 Berets' kin
47 Chills and fever
48 Type of cabbage
49 Spanish lady's title
50 Religious picture
51 Carry on, as war
52 "Hot" spot
53 Distance measures

ANSWER, PAGE 274

18

ACROSS

1 Stuffs
5 Charity
9 "Venerable ___"
(English historian
and monk)
13 Harmful
14 Off ship's center
15 Work animals
16 "Keystone corner"
18 Refrigerated
19 Circus equipment
20 U.S.N. members
22 American poet
23 Actor Jose
24 "Portentous" bird
27 Famous English
cathedral
28 ___ Kringle
31 Barren
32 Barnyard sound
33 Used-car
transaction
34 Chess pieces
35 Chased
37 Marble
38 Chaplains: Slang
40 33rd U.S.
President's initials
41 Lavish party
42 More artful
43 Spy
44 Gave up
45 Spice
47 Author Clemens's
nickname
48 Devilish
50 Delayed
54 Departure
55 Make modern
57 Tear apart
58 Praises highly
59 Harrow's rival
60 Extorted money
from
61 Tree branches
62 Farm animals

DOWN

1 Musical sign
2 Declare
3 Isinglass
4 Spilled water
5 French ecclesiastic
6 Meadow
7 Ilona or Raymond
8 Malicious attack
9 Furnace parts
10 Censured
11 Caribou is one
12 Terminates
14 Cutting tool
17 Red-glowing gas
21 Annoyed
23 Glitters
24 Sloping roads
25 Of a region
26 Retaliatory
27 Audience
29 Candidate list
30 Hemmed
32 Streetcar
replacement
33 Soak, as flax
35 Former dictator
36 Employ
39 Reported
41 Girls
43 Area of military
action
44 Phlegmatic
46 Long view
47 Salty expanses
48 Balkan native
49 Stem-branch angle
50 Wagers
51 Yugoslav V.I.P.
52 Enough: Archaic
53 Cozy rooms
56 Liquor from
molasses

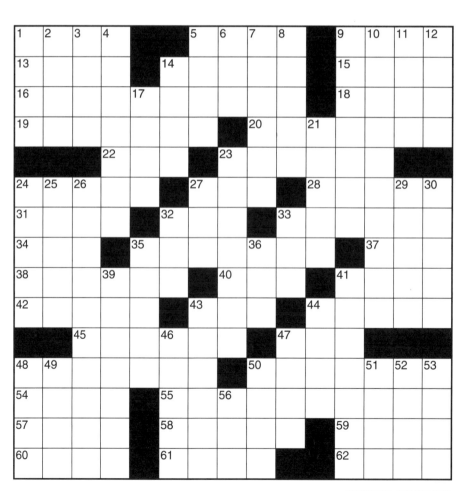

ANSWER, PAGE 276

ACROSS

1 Unscrupulous flirt
5 Composure
10 Mouth or gullet
13 Construction-work piece
14 Haile Selassie's capital
17 "Or ___" (threatening phrase)
18 Natty Bumppo epithet
19 Cakes and pies
21 The "boot" of Europe
22 Cravats
23 Wise
25 Odd-looking South American animals
28 Novelist Marie Henri Beyle
32 A cosmetic
33 Burns
34 The "Lion of God"
35 Egg (on)
36 Underworld god
37 Incision
38 Summer, in Paris
39 Sluggard
40 Dig
41 Jonathan Swift was one
43 Container used in religious services
44 Rhythm
45 Beer ingredient
46 River bank
49 Eastern, American, etc.
53 Throat projection
56 Felix Arndt song of the Twenties
57 Compels
58 Wicked
59 Print measures
60 Church parts
61 Final

DOWN

1 Competed (with)
2 Competent
3 Church service
4 Renown
5 Spanish priests
6 Playwright Clifford ___
7 "Beware the ___ of March"
8 Knight's title
9 Alphabet letter
10 Guatemalan Indian
11 Cain's victim
12 Cautious
15 Forms in a row
16 Restrained
20 Ireland
23 Aver
24 Of planes
25 ___ up (adjusts)
26 Main artery
27 Washington's ___ Sound
28 Sidetrack
29 Corridors
30 Animated
31 Metric measure
33 Nearby
36 Decorous
37 Guard
39 Most arid
40 Small valley
42 Bits of news
43 Fondle
45 Author A.A. ___
46 Fine fabric
47 Esau
48 Moving trucks
49 Sacred bull
50 New star
51 Yalemen
52 Mariner
54 Constellation
55 Baby food

ANSWER, PAGE 261

20

ACROSS

1 Courageous
5 Journal
10 Pretense
14 Type of lily
15 Over
16 Air
17 Close tightly
18 Country bumpkin
19 Arm bone
20 Person of importance
22 Ben-Gurion's country
24 Strong wind
25 Stated
26 Northern neighbor of the U.S.
29 Odd-job doer
33 Variety of quartz
34 Astaire's field
35 Specific period
36 Make pies
37 Arrogance
38 Courage
39 Untruth
40 Every 24 hours
41 Boneless steak
42 Approves
44 Beautiful
45 "___ in Boots"
46 Meadow mouse
47 Small person
50 Neckerchief
54 Wading bird
55 Small egg
57 Cold-weather fabric
58 Competent
59 Bright star in Orion
60 Mighty particle
61 Sorrows
62 Short-tempered
63 Desires

DOWN

1 Male voice
2 Margarine
3 Rich soil
4 Representative
5 Radio bribery: Slang
6 Dwelling
7 Slow
8 Actress Arden
9 Confidence
10 Strong and robust
11 Hawaiian dance
12 Prince Charles's sister
13 Repast
21 Commanded
23 Aspect
25 Gritty
26 Heavy wire
27 Once more
28 Nude
29 Greets
30 Actress Oberon
31 Shakespearean sprite
32 Smart-looking
34 Loses moisture
37 Traveler's document
38 Unintentional betrayal
40 Krupa's instrument
41 Sheep enclosure
43 Thinks
44 Desolate
46 Manservant
47 Type of salad
48 Tramp
49 Actor's part
50 Insects
51 Memo
52 Midday
53 Charity
56 Compete

ANSWER, PAGE 262

ACROSS

1 Reporter's "catch": Slang
6 Book of maps
11 Not "hep": Slang
12 Speaks monotonously
14 Talk confusedly
15 Green, as foliage
17 "Easy as ___"
18 A Model T, for one
20 Pod vegetable
21 Heraldic bearing
23 Entranceways
24 Keats product
25 Authoritative statements
27 Pen point
28 Evergreen shrub
29 Celestial
31 Easy gallop
32 Iranian coin
33 Vended
34 Upright piano
37 Ceiling window
41 Flat, white beans
42 Hawaiian delicacy
43 Scatter, as seeds
44 Angle between branch and leaf
45 Verity
47 Hindu garment
48 Fragment
49 Property administrator
51 Thick mist
52 Pacific coast animal
54 Prison-dwellers
56 Go hungry
57 Wading birds
58 Fencing swords
59 Detested

DOWN

1 Suppress completely
2 Sever
3 Vow
4 Mountain nymph
5 Private
6 Part of speech
7 Forest plants
8 Forsaken: Archaic
9 Also
10 Marseilles, for one
11 Ghost
13 Cold symptom
14 English china
16 Lion-trainer
19 Simmer
22 Perpetual
24 Hindu scholars
26 Zodiac sign
28 Victoria ___ (African landmark)
30 Consume
31 Demure
33 Capricious
34 Thick pieces
35 Fairies
36 Copy
37 French coins
38 Joined, as tree limbs
39 Villains' nemeses
40 Small branches
42 Trims, as 7-Down
45 Treasure ___ (pleasant discovery)
46 Shade of brown
49 Fatigue
50 Give forth
53 Fold (over)
55 Mimic

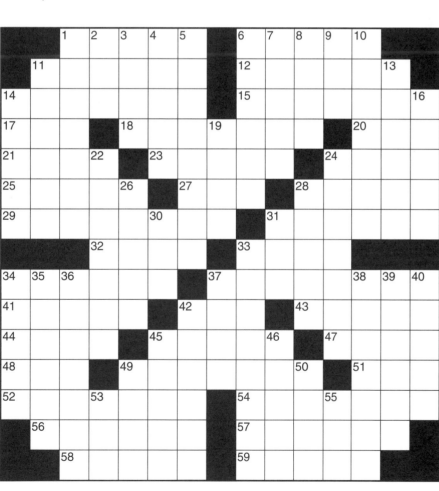

ANSWER, PAGE 264

22

ACROSS

1 Beat to a froth, as cream
5 Force
10 Framework for displaying merchandise
14 Hawaiian seaport
15 Audacity: Slang
16 Wind instrument
17 Unemployed
18 19th President
19 Surfeit
20 Piquant
22 Coins
24 Alcoholic drink
25 Purloined
26 Child's chum
30 Designer Rosenstein
34 Outfit
35 Methuselah's father
37 Non-flowering plants
38 Russian John
40 Committed a faux pas
42 Fathers
43 ___ out (allots)
45 Closed car
47 "The ___ is cast"
48 Dresses carefully
50 Of Innsbruck's province
52 Careful selections of food
54 Fifth sign of the zodiac
55 Seller of overpriced tickets
58 Talk about
62 Excavation
63 Pieman's questioner
65 Leg joint
66 Pindar's specialties
67 Imitating
68 Poetess ___ Millay
69 Changes the color of
70 Shoe parts
71 Toddlers

DOWN

1 Excellent one: Slang
2 Conceal
3 Misfortunes
4 Keats's medium
5 Brutal
6 Repast
7 Inquire presumptuously
8 Track-meet feature
9 Injury
10 Traveled by space ship
11 Competent
12 Self-possessed
13 Florida's isles
21 Rage
23 Musical symbol
25 Mysteries
26 Array nicely
27 Basis of pâté de foie gras
28 Mib
29 Pinnacles
31 Commerce
32 Nehru's nation
33 Chief city of the Ruhr
36 Actress Lamarr
39 Unnecessary
41 Wendy, Michael, and John, friends of Peter Pan
44 Quick cut
46 Negative answers
49 Playground item
51 Keepsake case worn around the neck
53 Nonsense: Slang
55 Fitted with footwear
56 "Buffalo Bill"
57 On the sheltered side
58 "___ give up the ship"
59 Bring to ruin
60 Dispatched
61 North and Mediterranean
64 .001 of an inch

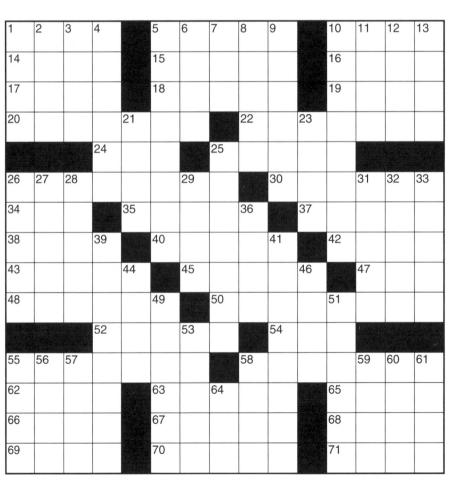

ANSWER, PAGE 266

23

ACROSS

1 Potato ___ (party food)
5 Precipitous
10 Prison room
14 Learning
15 Long for
16 Region
17 "Once ___ a time"
18 Poe's bird
19 Hazard
20 Ecclesiastical living
22 Dairy product
24 Gallop slowly
25 Prejudice
26 Taste
29 Practical
34 Figure of speech
35 Wharf
36 Girl's name
37 Ceremony
38 Chide
40 Swing loosely
41 Peer Gynt's mother
42 Part of a necklace
43 French river
44 Actor
47 Printer's need
48 Wrath
49 Death notice
51 Elf
54 Riches
58 Cry of sorrow
59 Similar
61 Wander
62 Elephant's tooth
63 Water wheel
64 Famous garden
65 Catch sight of
66 Fabric
67 Fender damage

DOWN

1 Cudgel
2 "Ski-nosed" comedian
3 Press
4 Ulysses's wife
5 Paper currency
6 Inquiry form
7 ___ trough (roof gutter)
8 Former resident of 64-Across
9 Sketched lightly
10 Gesture of endearment
11 Buffalo waterway
12 A smaller amount
13 Body of water
21 Golf term
23 "Crowning glory"
25 ___ out (jump from a plane)
26 Leather thong
27 Wake up
28 Elector
30 Lyric poem
31 Holland's flower
32 Senseless
33 Prance
38 Non-commissioned officer
39 Arrived
40 Made prominent
42 Sailing vessel
43 Barbecue pole
45 Lively
46 Raw recruit
50 "Staff of life"
51 Surfeit
52 In addition to
53 Scrape roughly
54 Dismiss from a job
55 Protuberance
56 Level
57 Dispatched
60 Having small elevation

ANSWER, PAGE 268

24

ACROSS

1 Bullet for TV Westerns
6 Yield
10 Corset "bone"
14 Mr. Murphy of the movies
15 Norse god of war
16 Elephant-sized
17 Fort ___, North Carolina
18 ___-sized (tiny)
19 God of love
20 Sound of sadness
21 Up and about
23 Dissuade
26 Take surreptitiously
27 Overlay the "overhead" with plaster, etc.
29 Jewel
30 Name
33 Ocean-dwelling puffer
37 Snapshot
39 Forbidden
40 ___ Allen (Vermont hero of 1776)
42 Eagerness
43 Sun-dried brick
45 Thought transference
47 Dramatist-poet Jonson
48 Buddy
50 Produced, as an egg
51 Penalized
53 Remnant of the past
56 Caustic criticism
59 John, in Russia
61 Vast waters
62 Singer Horne
63 Positive electrode
64 Solemn promise
65 Dines
66 Goddess of agriculture

67 Occupied
68 Journey
69 Rendezvous

DOWN

1 Barbara's nickname
2 Sensational
3 Proverb
4 Evening dance spot
5 Beer container
6 Policemen
7 Runs a newspaper
8 Banquet room
9 Main meal course
10 Masterful, romantic man: Slang
11 Revolve

12 Wide-eyed; excited
13 I agree!
22 Slanted walkway
24 Long thin fish
25 Abounding (with)
28 Ursa Minor constellation
30 Dunce
31 Mormon State
32 Scrawny
33 Knife wound
34 Walk in water
35 Very black
36 That woman
38 Star attraction
41 Close to
44 Film with 10,000 extras, for example

46 Large tart
49 Bobbysock
51 Not easy to believe
52 "Inferno" poet
54 Elephant tusk
55 Junipers
56 ___ Brummell (early "dude")
57 Rodents
58 Chore
60 Cozy home
61 Weep loudly
63 Pretend

ANSWER, PAGE 270

25

ACROSS

1 The "food of love"
6 Malice
11 Fully-developed
12 Tantalizing
14 Perfumes
15 Symbol of the U.S.
17 Mr. Van Winkle
18 Relate
20 Billiards stick
21 Cut quickly
23 Small ones of the litter
24 ___ cracker (thin, crisp biscuit)
25 Vital organ
27 Be untruthful
28 Visited briefly
29 Consumed
31 Flinches
32 Lariats
34 Weld
35 Conceit
36 Egg-protector
37 Dwell
38 Hawaiian dish
39 Shoe parts
43 Indefinite amount
44 Point of an antler
46 Ripped
47 Historic age
48 Moves unsteadily
50 Dairy beast
51 Expound
53 Enter for conquest
55 Bring together again
56 Dirty
57 Sarcastically
58 Woolen fabric

DOWN

1 "Leatherneck"
2 Ideal place
3 Total
4 Teheran is its capital
5 Actor Romero
6 The Upper House
7 Agreements
8 Atoll
9 Cravat
10 Settle snugly
11 Swamp
12 Go to bed
13 Flashier
16 Methods
19 Regulations
22 Act as chairman
24 Kind of baseball
26 Flavor
28 Brooks
30 Plaything
31 Sorrow
32 Unskilled worker
33 Lively
34 Gleam
35 Flower receptacles
36 Placate
38 Kind of girl who's "like a melody"
40 Site
41 Worn away
42 Stitched
44 Danger
45 Ground grain
48 Singer Bennett
49 Christmas "white"
52 Pelt
54 Compete

ANSWER, PAGE 272

26

ACROSS

1 Outline
7 Burning
13 Concerned
15 Sang softly
16 Instructive discourse
17 Rest interval
18 Wedge-shaped piece
19 Tableland
21 Isle of ___
22 Singer Logan
24 Bang!
25 Corporal or sergeant: Abbr.
27 Witty retort
31 Vipers
34 Glimmers
37 Philippine city
39 Male cat
40 Mrs. Nixon, to friends
41 Small in number
42 ___ out (dress)
43 Expose, as a fraud
45 Printer's machine
47 Vegetable for borscht
48 Defraud
50 Morning moisture
52 Mr. President
53 Pale beige
57 Capuchin monkey
59 Truthfulness
63 Haunch
64 Elusive
66 Year divisions
68 Pine-tar derivatives
69 Expand
70 Beermaker
71 Despise

DOWN

1 Ointment
2 Genuflect
3 Surpass
4 Small bird
5 Brilliant stratagem
6 Pitch
7 Scope
8 Ship's petty officer
9 Prune, as branches
10 Ill will
11 Greek "Z"
12 British Prime Minister
14 Harbor city
15 Crawled
20 Same as 6-Down
23 Branch
26 Is able to
28 Little devils
29 Highest points
30 Correct
32 Fall with a splash
33 Wise
34 Short pencil
35 Whet
36 Instantaneous
38 It describes a soldier in trouble: Abbr.
41 Delicate skill
44 Dined
45 Similar to
46 Golf gadget
49 Beverages
51 Peevish cry
54 Task
55 Tinkles
56 Worried
57 Croat
58 Affirm
60 Finished
61 Care for
62 Men's college
65 Darn
67 Convened

ANSWER, PAGE 274

ACROSS

1 Skirt part, in Civil War days
5 Spouse
9 Bakery items
14 Competent
15 Russian czar
16 Native of India
17 Loud burst of laughter
18 Weeps aloud
19 Old saying
20 Octopus
22 Was wildly enthusiastic
23 Assistance
24 Cloth fragment
26 Before
27 Acquiescence
31 Sly tricks
33 Prop (up)
34 Monk's home
38 Impoverished
39 English ladies
40 Historic times
41 Young misses, in Spain
43 Babble foolishly
44 Glossy black bird
45 Good-natured teasing
46 Tavern
49 Viscous liquid
50 Distress signal
51 On high
53 Exactly alike
59 Stately
60 Barren
61 Italian port on the Adriatic
62 Beast
63 Short letter
64 Spring flower
65 Range animal
66 Ran swiftly
67 Location (of authority)

DOWN

1 Unyielding
2 Double-reed instrument
3 King of Norway
4 Fairy, in Persian mythology
5 One who doesn't "belong"
6 Keep away from
7 Flaps
8 Holds sacred
9 Accusations
10 Verdi opera
11 Tricky rascal
12 Finishing machine
13 Napped leather
21 Country road
25 Cry of distress
27 Vipers
28 Oxford or pump
29 In the near future
30 Misplay, in baseball
31 Eve was one
32 Austere
34 Fabrics
35 Quod ___ demonstrandum (which was to be proved)
36 Degree of speed
37 Belgian river
39 Callas or Peters
42 Poisonous snake
43 Bygone days
45 Mortgaged
46 Arrow points
47 Watchful
48 Scoundrel
50 Large fishing net
52 Destiny
54 Fall in drops
55 Sacred bird of the Nile
56 Anxiety
57 Solo for 39-Down
58 Roster

ANSWER, PAGE 276

ACROSS

1 Actors in a play
5 Equips for war
9 Embarrass
14 Thorough
16 Small, close-fitting hat
17 Nearness
18 More factual
19 Short, shrill bark
20 Stack
21 Worry repeatedly
22 Nimble
23 Type of palm tree
24 Tiny person
27 Avid reader
31 Bitter
32 Ridicules
33 Menagerie
34 Stop up
35 Hoarse
36 Sullen
37 Youngster
38 Meticulous
39 Dialect
40 Furtive
42 Lean to one side
43 Frilly
44 Love to excess
45 Scabbard
48 Tremendous
49 Name
52 Most unpleasant
53 Strike a blow in passing
55 Similar
56 Exactly the same
57 Nut used in candy
58 Annoying person
59 Poor student's bane

DOWN

1 Replica
2 Distinctive air
3 A sojourn
4 Assess
5 Regard as beautiful
6 Muddy; turbid
7 Silent
8 Dirty hovel
9 Assails
10 Accept a loan
11 Bluish-green
12 Prosecutes
13 His and ___
15 Bit
21 Play ___ (go AWOL from school)
22 Gulp down
23 Jauntily conceited
24 Agreements
25 Renown
26 Wear away
27 Domineering
28 Air: Slang
29 A cosmetic
30 Person of low IQ
32 Overly sentimental
35 Rabbit cage
36 Dreadful
38 Crush
39 Most recent
41 Mt. McKinley is here
42 Convincing
44 Fops
45 Trade
46 Pit
47 Norwegian explorer
48 Secrete
49 Cut in small squares
50 Javanese tree
51 Girdle
53 Drink little by little
54 Clever humor

ANSWER, PAGE 261

ACROSS

1 Treble or bass
5 Clump of grass
9 ___ Rapids, Iowa
14 Listen to
15 Over 1 billion people live here
16 Mrs. Hobby
17 Demanding
19 Trousers
20 One receiving money
21 Short, simple song
23 Tree juice
24 Annoying fly
26 Raincoats
28 Ruffian
31 Dash
32 Inventor Whitney
33 Go swiftly
35 Full amount
39 Optical glass
41 Work, as dough
43 South Pacific island
44 Witches' forte
46 New fabric
48 Born
49 Short breath
51 Legislated
53 It's good with steak
57 Rail bird
58 Everything
59 Rand McNally book
61 Public walks
64 Acquire weapons over again
66 Ready insight
68 Infuse
69 Enthusiasm
70 ___ Pound (poet)
71 Canvas support
72 Border
73 Profound

DOWN

1 Poker "money"
2 ___ the Hyena of the comics
3 Even-tempered
4 Quaker
5 Tit for ___
6 Second-hand
7 End of a book
8 Informer
9 Mimic
10 1954 Best Supporting Actress winner
11 Opaque
12 Rose perfume
13 Grates
18 Animals that "clap their hands"
22 Plant sesame
25 Cover snugly
27 Handle
28 Tiller
29 Olive genus
30 Have exclusive control of
34 Poetic "above"
36 Tease
37 Away from the wind
38 Meant to deceive
40 Weary breath
42 Puts on
45 Chewy candy
47 Ruth's mother-in-law
50 Drunkard
52 Boxed
53 Madame Curie
54 Moslem scholars
55 Thick stones
56 Having long hair
60 For men only
62 Learning
63 Take quick pictures of
65 Street: French
67 Rubber tree

ANSWER, PAGE 262

ACROSS

1 Garbage-carrying boat
5 Baby deer
10 Talk idly
14 Prepare (the way)
15 Fool
16 "Knight of the road"
17 Iridescent gem
18 Poke
19 Revolve
20 Revealing
22 Push forward, as a boat
24 Engage in a tournament
25 Wander
26 Took long steps
29 Bits of festive paper
33 Intoxicating
34 Characteristic
35 Take first place
36 The "A" in A.D.
37 Root for
38 Crooner Crosby
39 Morse code signal
40 Holy man
41 Latin dance
42 Complete costume
44 Day's ending
45 Playthings
46 Flock
47 Expressive gestures
50 Boxed and wrapped
54 Burden
55 Wrathful
57 Temporarily bright star
58 Prince Charles's sister
59 Recorded on ribbon
60 Fasten securely
61 Asks alms
62 Card suit
63 Unite by treaty

DOWN

1 Locality
2 ___ Canaveral, Florida
3 Egg-shaped
4 Prosperous
5 Concluding part
6 Mature
7 "All wool and a yard ___"
8 Egg drink
9 Hurry up!
10 Word element meaning "color"
11 Ring of wood
12 Competent
13 Bridge tax
21 Shipshape
23 Makeshift boat
25 Bake
26 Protection from the sun
27 Wood projection forming a joint
28 Talks wildly
29 Old woman
30 Look-alikes
31 Slight color
32 Metal bar
34 Labors
37 Stands in for Mother
38 Large handkerchief
40 City haze
41 Ankara native
43 Piano pieces
44 Withdraw (from)
46 Abhorred
47 Thick slice
48 Sharpen
49 Sounded, as a phone
50 Mama's mate
51 Aim and ambition
52 Wicked
53 "What's My Line?" moderator
56 Knock

ANSWER, PAGE 264

31

ACROSS

1 Bridge bid
5 Smooth
10 Bed: Slang
14 Ford or Buick
15 V.P.
16 Author Ferber
17 Sacred image
18 Bring into agreement
19 Lounge
20 Party member
22 Rise (from)
24 Soft mineral
25 Petty quarrel
26 To the other side of
29 Cut of pork
33 Holy person
34 Digging tool
35 Single unit
36 Weak
37 Toni ___
38 Hawaiian dance
39 Letter
40 Sharp sound
41 Metal plate
42 Unnecessary
44 Omission marks
45 Dash
46 "Crowning glory"
47 Nursery character
50 Pat's real name
54 Large-mouthed jar
55 Angry
57 Debatable
58 Prevaricator
59 Carpenter's tool
60 Lowest female voice
61 Singer Martin
62 Wants
63 Kind of tide

DOWN

1 Stated
2 Clare Boothe ___
3 Tiny particle
4 Sameness
5 Tangles
6 Pale purple
7 Way out
8 Period of time
9 Players' protection
10 Cross out
11 Smell
12 Catch
13 Unharmed
21 Set of players
23 Female horse
25 Paddle
26 Poplar tree
27 Reason
28 Wash lightly
29 Twirls
30 Road
31 Small bay
32 Lima ___
34 Rustle
37 Actor
38 New York's Governor
40 Hint
41 Husband and wife, for example
43 Gloomy
44 Provides food
46 Detested
47 Sliding bar
48 Medley
49 Scheme
50 Boy servant
51 Composer Porter
52 Greek letter
53 Upon
56 Regret

32

ACROSS

1 Swamp
6 Saddle horse
11 "Frontier" fabric
12 Bone centers
14 Wholehearted
15 With other people
17 Large tub
18 Remove air from
20 Title
21 Patronage
23 Shelf
24 Ballot
25 Women: Slang
27 Washington and ___ University
28 Reminders, of a sort
29 Robert Kennedy, for one
31 Bishops' headdresses
32 Look-alike
33 Biblical weed
34 Beams, as of light
37 Middle
40 Forbidden
41 Tight spot
42 Drags, as to court
44 Above
45 Peace ___ (foreign assistance program)
47 Church part
48 Trawler's gear
49 Carry away
51 Kitten's cry
52 Interweaves
54 Repair shoes
56 Sowing machines
57 Classified
58 Feats
59 Finished

DOWN

1 White grapes
2 Record-breaking
3 Brazilian city, for short
4 Run before the breeze
5 Hilton edifice
6 Direct
7 Declaim
8 Impulse
9 Companion of neither
10 A couple
11 Fell (in)
12 Less harsh
13 "Serious" boyfriend
16 Fourth Estate
19 Criminal
22 Summoned
24 Ex-soldier
26 Took care of
28 Glee
30 "My country, ___ of thee"
31 ___ Friday (factotum)
33 Andante is one
34 Pebble
35 Places of refuge
36 Incited to wrongdoing
37 Loving touch
38 Stylish
39 Razed
41 Playing cards
43 Stitched
45 Wove a chair seat
46 Strong rush
49 Cause of surf
50 Gull's relative
53 Tiny
55 Melancholy

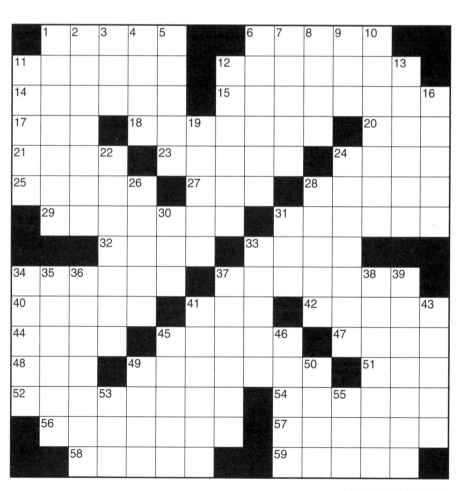

42

ACROSS

1 ___ leaf (Canadian emblem)
6 Insecticide dispenser
10 Lose color
14 Edgar ___ Poe
15 Iridescent gem
16 Dollar bills
17 Shore
18 Not in accord
20 Indefinite amount
21 Decays
23 Thin, as a liquid
24 Ermine source
26 Learning
27 "Wind in the Willows" character
28 Menu item
32 "Jack ___ could eat no fat ..."
34 Bees' homes
35 Look at
36 Bear's retreat
37 Less coarse
38 Successful actor
39 Circle part
40 Burn slightly
41 Tote
42 Treat gently
44 Palm starch used in puddings
45 Scolds constantly
46 Jimmy ___ (big-nosed comedian)
49 Place of safety
52 Transported
53 Goal
54 Exaggerate
56 Small egg
58 Nip
59 Dutch cheese
60 Saltpeter
61 Belly whopper's toy
62 Feet: Slang
63 Impertinent

DOWN

1 Large parrot
2 Unaccompanied
3 Be a prankster
4 ___ Vegas
5 Beg earnestly
6 Cowboy's footgear
7 Musical composition
8 Wrestling surface
9 Be dissipated as a storm
10 He wrote "Old Black Joe"
11 Poker stake
12 Fleet animal
13 Catch sight of
19 Transportation charges
22 Venerable
25 Fly high
26 Presidential reception
28 Game of chance
29 They will explore space
30 Equipment
31 Weird
32 Thick slice
33 Shave (off)
34 Clues
37 Moved nervously
38 Adventure story
40 Stocking mishaps
41 Boxes
43 Hardened
44 Solar body
46 Judges
47 Holders for hot plates
48 Corundum
49 Steals from
50 Wicked
51 Celebration
52 Party for men only
55 Commotion
57 By way of

ANSWER, PAGE 270

34

ACROSS

1 Baking powder ingredient
5 Shock; dismay
10 Sea bird
14 Skin blemish
15 Unsophisticated
16 On the ocean
17 Buzzing
18 Silent, as from shock
20 Rope-pulling contest
22 "To your health" drinks
23 Murdered
24 Piece of china
25 Penniless one
28 Prophecy
33 Greek letter
34 Be economical
35 Grass-skirt dance
36 Dry, as dishes
37 Was a secret agent
38 Verbal
39 Always
40 Bits of thread
41 Sudden outburst, as of words
42 Worthless person
44 Foremen
45 Mimic
46 Put to flight
47 Trouble, as with cares
51 Sightseers
55 Conquered
57 "___ off the old block"
58 Thailand
59 Greased
60 Japanese harp
61 Whirlpool
62 Girl's toys
63 Smoke residue

DOWN

1 Hit sharply
2 Place for 35-Across
3 Narcotic
4 Surrounding air
5 Reply
6 Tropical fruit
7 Wharf
8 Hail!
9 Gave an instructive speech
10 Festive
11 Purposes
12 In case
13 Maiden
19 "Where there's life, there's ___"
21 Dog's "foe"
24 Desire ardently
25 Mauled
26 Alert
27 Higher
28 Indistinct
29 Oriental "forks"
30 Emanations
31 Blackboard
32 Stories
34 Food seasoning
37 Generally careless
41 Tart
43 Endure
44 Leaps
46 Spur wheel
47 Stockings
48 Very eager
49 Peruse
50 Ike's former "employer"
51 Bridge tax
52 Scat!
53 Yugoslav ruler
54 Locality
56 ___ de Janeiro

ANSWER, PAGE 272

ACROSS

1 Called by the loudspeaker
6 Greek letter
9 Slide
13 Colorful shrub
15 Coal scuttle
16 Telegram
17 Awkward
19 "Hooky," army style: Abbr.
20 Great Lake
21 Modernize
23 Foxes' home
24 "Three strikes, you're ___"
25 Frivolous gal, of song
26 Lovingly
29 Roamer
33 Hunting expedition
36 Devour
38 Was clad in
39 Most short-spoken
41 National Guard
43 Mormon State
44 Make lace
46 Inability to carry a tune: Slang
47 Traveler's rest
49 Possible result of rickets
51 Fabulous bird
53 Puree vegetable
54 Plague-carrier
57 He says "good luck"
61 Kind of ranch
62 Chills and fever
63 Merchant
65 Puts up, as fruit
66 Coolidge nickname
67 Rets
68 ___ and ends
69 Be indebted
70 Mountain crest

DOWN

1 Walked the floor
2 Blue
3 Street urchin
4 German river
5 Actress Sandra ___
6 Kind of laugh
7 Domicile
8 Notions
9 Gulping
10 New Zealand bird
11 Old World age
12 Erase print
14 Firebug
18 Kind of poker
22 What the child is "father of"
26 Minus one parent
27 Mined matter
28 Sweet potato
30 Speck, as of dust
31 Diva's song
32 Start of a letter
33 Dross
34 Ingredient of a traffic jam
35 Collegiate brotherhood: Slang
37 Pipits
40 Actor Hunter
42 Stretch the truth
45 Excellent: Slang
48 "Swing ___ sweet chariot"
50 Bend, as a willow
52 The "Kid" of Mexico
54 Coin of India
55 Very able
56 Concise
57 Texas city
58 Mild oath
59 Actor John ___
60 "Pygmalion" author
61 Hunter's prey
64 Greek E

ANSWER, PAGE 274

36

ACROSS

1 Precisely neat
5 Savage's weapon
10 Platform for the "honored guest"
14 Crazy: Slang
15 Marry secretly
16 Open, as a package
17 Kitchen "hot spot"
18 Beats with a stick
19 Social climber
20 Pies or cakes
22 Blossom parts
24 Catalpa or birch
25 Figure
26 Abandon
29 "Morning after" reaction
33 Declares
34 Curve
35 Prepare (the way)
36 Allow
37 Boasts
38 Humble
39 Cupid
41 Refreshments: Slang
42 Penniless: Slang
44 Summary
46 Flew
47 Ring-tailed animal
48 Poses for the artist
49 The "S" in P.S.
52 Peddler's vehicle
56 Canal, city, or lake
57 For rent
59 On the ocean
60 Main idea
61 Wear away
62 Chain segment
63 Follow orders
64 Prevent
65 Cloy

DOWN

1 Trudge
2 Wander
3 Cooling desserts
4 Frankenstein's creation
5 Hidden
6 Flat dish
7 Eternities
8 Mimic
9 Answers
10 Floor cleaner
11 "___ and the King of Siam"
12 Heathen image
13 Weeps passionately
21 Is wrong
23 Unit of work
25 Serpent teeth
26 Glens
27 Each
28 Famous naturalist
29 Warms
30 Courage
31 Call forth
32 Marry again
34 Seat of intellect
37 Drunk
40 "The four hundred"
42 The pair (of them)
43 Scamps
45 Soft drink
46 Eva, to Zsa Zsa
48 Soft leather
49 State flower of Utah
50 Baby bed
51 Get up
52 Scheme
53 The Far East
54 Lease
55 Capture
58 Mineral rock

ANSWER, PAGE 276

46

ACROSS

1 Agreements
6 Sodded
12 Laborious
14 Makes possible
16 Attraction at a movie
17 Mediterranean playground
18 Chairman pro ___
19 Big ___ football conference
20 ___ Anne de Beaupre: Abbr.
21 Wine: French
22 City in Oklahoma
24 Tries for the 4-minute mile
26 Said, as a greeting
27 Reslant
29 Rocky hill
30 Tops of heads
31 Venerated
33 Dislike heartily
34 Son of Seth
35 Gossip
36 Unplentiful
39 Scarabs
42 Result (from)
43 Dance step
44 Jinxes
46 Shipping peril
47 He wears a light on his cap
49 Fender mark
50 "Blame ___ for Adam's fall"
51 Confused noise
52 Zodiac's "Aries"
54 Small inlet
55 Arranged in succession
57 Benedict Arnold, for example
59 Sulky-racer
60 Dispatchers
61 Shows scorn
62 Scans the paper

DOWN

1 Egotist
2 Human being
3 Mow
4 Race-track spy
5 More certain
6 More concise
7 Ones
8 Talk wildly
9 Government's sleuths: Abbr.
10 Raise in rank
11 Ridicules
12 Following
13 Legislative bodies
15 Most rational
23 Varied
25 Fish that provides oil
26 Skirmished
28 British small change
30 ___ Amboy, New Jersey
32 Sturgeon ___ (caviar)
33 Stamping device
35 Mojave and Gobi
36 Wisest
37 They have strong yearnings
38 Hinged part of a plane wing
39 Prohibit
40 Exercised, as influence
41 High-school bigwigs
43 Those who languish
45 They're in the limelight
47 Bishop's cap
48 Less frequent
51 Engagement
53 Lion's "crowning glory"
56 Follower of: Suffix
58 Mrs. Cantor

ANSWER, PAGE 263

38

ACROSS

1 Fastening for a door
5 Kind of vise
10 Operates
14 Operatic prince
15 Gun-pointer
16 Dueling sword
17 Undraped figure
18 Ruth's mother-in-law
19 With every hair in place
20 Cooperative effort
22 Steep slopes
24 Vexes
25 Male deer
26 Primitive dwellings
29 Wild fancies
33 Nut
34 Sycamore
35 Hasten
36 Cracow native
37 Santiago land
38 Wrong: Law
39 Building extension
40 Search blindly
41 Impressionist painter
42 Meetings
44 Ohio city
45 Scotch Gaelic
46 Poem: Poetic
47 Tams
50 Ringlings' winter quarters
54 Latin poet
55 Animal
57 Demeanor
58 Distribute
59 Seraph
60 On the ocean
61 Brought up
62 "Cloister and Hearth" author
63 Snug abode

DOWN

1 Intimation
2 Type of fever
3 Soft drink
4 First public performance
5 Watercraft
6 "Munchausens"
7 In a murderous frenzy
8 13th Hebrew letter
9 Primitive and uncorrupted
10 Household
11 Mimic
12 Lowest level of high tide
13 Tennis sessions
21 Small bird
23 Arrived
25 Kind of rock
26 Winning milers break them
27 School: French
28 Voting place
29 Desk items
30 European river
31 Ventilated
32 Fight
34 Call up
37 Transverse strip
38 Extra juror
40 Bound round
41 Actress Freeman
43 Did farm work
44 Marine reptile
46 Leveled
47 Atom ___
48 Always
49 Ceremony
50 Heroic tale
51 Tributary of the Seine
52 Golf pegs
53 Medical-school course: Abbr.
56 Compass point

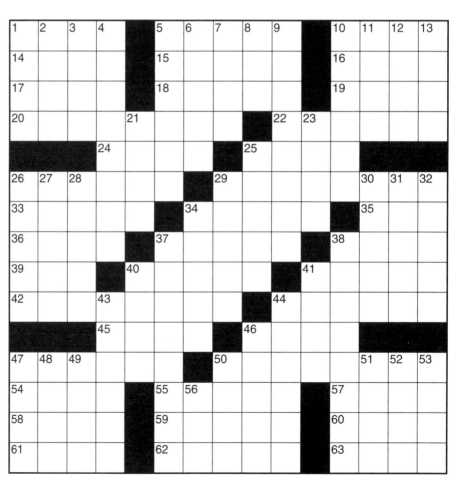

ANSWER, PAGE 265

ACROSS

1 Party for men only
5 Wight and Man
10 Thick slice
14 Impulse
15 Inflexible
16 Dainty trimming
17 Composition for two
18 Merchandise
19 Distinct air
20 Investigate
22 One behind another
24 Chimney accumulation
25 Thaw
26 Paid, as a bill
29 Renown
30 Plant seeds
33 Unbiased
35 One example of 5-Across
37 Lupine retreat
38 Hollywood statuette
40 Terminal appendage
41 Tobogganing slope
43 Sang romantic songs to
45 Amateur radio operator: Slang
46 Tense
48 Door parts
49 Take heed
50 Group, as of pretty girls
51 Short-distance race
54 Finished-basement area
58 ___ it (walk)
59 On a par
61 ___ Mater
62 Came to rest
63 R.N.
64 River duck
65 Sacred
66 Meted (out)
67 Columnist Wilson

DOWN

1 Beer: Slang
2 Factual
3 Crooked
4 Marrying the boss's daughter is one way to do this
5 Treats kindly
6 Overweight
7 Plunder
8 Finish
9 Method
10 Viewpoint
11 Praise
12 Land measure
13 Smile radiantly
21 South African Dutchman
23 Fish sauce
25 Cheek bone
26 Steal
27 Nebraska city
28 A narcotic
29 Jewel surface
30 Shovel
31 Bay window
32 Wildernesses
34 Emit
36 Whatever happens
39 Revoked, as a law
42 British school
44 Fleet
47 Be present at
49 Stylish: Slang
50 Indifferent to the pleasures of life
51 Iran's ruler
52 Equestrian game
53 Stir up
54 Knitting stitch
55 Olive genus
56 ___ Khayyám
57 Shaded walkway
60 "___ Vadis" (1895 novel)

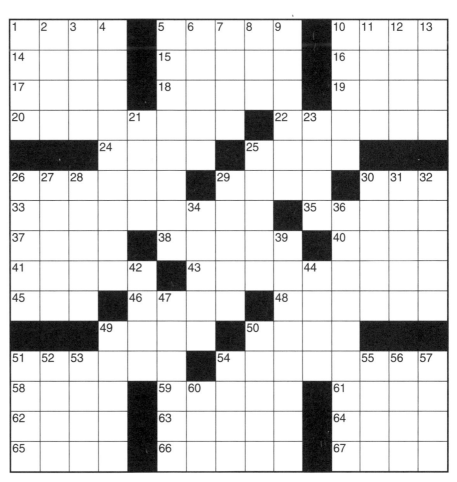

ANSWER, PAGE 267

40

ACROSS

1 Accident
7 Declares
13 Unfeeling
15 It's "from sea to shining sea"
16 Height
17 In a frenzy
18 Male turkey
19 Deep
20 Dodge, for example
21 Owing
22 Tillers
24 Punishment: Slang
26 Circuit
29 And so forth: Abbr.
31 "Who steals my ___ steals trash"
35 Emporium
36 Excessive
38 Black bird
39 Belief
40 "Humbug!"
41 Artlessness
43 Vigorous walk
44 Impudent
45 Single thing
46 Alpine song
47 Demon
49 Illustrious
51 Energy
54 Bear's "hand"
56 Printing liquid
57 Fabrication
60 Greed
62 Vent
64 Diminished
65 Chosen candidate
66 Impose tax on
67 Most recent

DOWN

1 Foggy dew
2 "Come ___ my parlor"
3 Pretense
4 Crude cabin
5 Good-luck charm
6 Legally "by word of mouth"
7 Daub
8 It goes into turtle soup
9 ___ longa, vita brevis
10 Made knots
11 Unbleached hue
12 Purpose
14 Taos is here
15 Broadcasting chain
22 Strike
23 Paving with rocks
25 Place
26 Pile up
27 Obsession
28 Edges of bowls
30 Standard
32 Fanatical
33 Rattler
34 Actress Barrymore
36 Finial
37 "Little ___ Blue"
39 International athletic meets
42 Greek letter
43 Right off the griddle
46 City in Washington State
48 Strides back and forth
50 Register
51 Brazilian rubber
52 Pre-holiday periods
53 Expands, as an expense account
55 Espouse
57 Payment for offense
58 Frozen desserts
59 Sugar source
61 Regret
63 Physically well

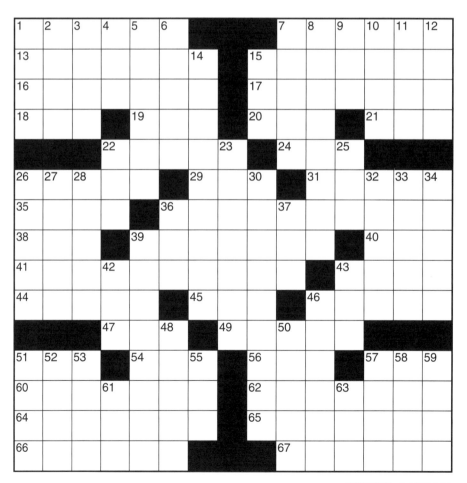

ANSWER, PAGE 269

41

ACROSS

1 Bundle
5 Makeshift floats
10 Fellow
14 Incite
15 ___ Stevenson
16 Cereal grain
17 Scoundrel
19 Taj Mahal site
20 Yearning
21 Badly
22 Actress Williams
24 Annoying insect
25 Swamps
26 Allot
29 Unmarried lady
32 Plays Ben Hogan's game
33 Spirit
34 Ham on ___
35 Came to rest
36 Steeple
37 Check
38 Father: Slang
39 Titan is one
40 Spirit
41 Settle securely
43 Thick club
44 Color slightly
45 Charity
46 Goes in waves
48 Piece of sugar
49 Petition
52 Out of port
53 Having a rainbow-like play of colors
56 Equipment
57 Entitled
58 Aural
59 Weapons
60 Wanderer
61 Shower's cousin

DOWN

1 ___ Snooks
2 Competent
3 Spare
4 And so forth: Abbr.
5 Type of sleeve
6 Mature
7 Censure
8 Sticky stuff
9 Gridiron edge
10 Shipping boxes
11 Nervous
12 Land measure
13 Fleshy fruit
18 Monarchs
23 Went under
24 Talent
25 Gush
26 Wide open
27 Lawmaker
28 Propeller wash
29 Backbone
30 Eagle nest
31 Revolt
33 Room
36 Prison at Ossining, N.Y.
37 Give up
39 Departed
40 Swallows
42 Tobacco rolls
43 Farce
45 Dandies
46 Norse tale
47 Utilizer
48 Wilted
49 Bristle
50 Single thing
51 Engrave
54 Dancer Bolger
55 Male swan

ANSWER, PAGE 271

42

ACROSS

1 Ambush
5 Church official
10 Pitcher's plate: Slang
14 First-class
15 Spread the news (about)
16 Size of type
17 South African gold district
18 Gaits
19 Kiln
20 Perfidy
23 Neither
24 Drudge
25 Poem of four lines
30 Quiver
34 In the past month: Abbr.
35 Arm joint
37 Torment
38 Tree of India
40 Italian money
42 Attacks
43 Composer Schubert
45 Lady Senator
47 Singer-pianist Cole
48 With increased tempo
50 Pittsburgh pro-footballers
52 Jacob's twin
54 Epoch
55 Machines important to editors
63 Lively tune
64 Fence steps
65 Touchy
66 Make eyes at
67 Sea duck
68 Or ___!
69 Football play
70 Legal papers
71 Demand

DOWN

1 Kind of pastry
2 Bellow
3 Queen ___ furniture
4 Narrow-minded teacher
5 Fascinate
6 Knowledge
7 Fashion leader
8 Prevent legally
9 Math answer
10 Poetic feet
11 Full of energy
12 Tennis points
13 Prohibits
21 Nucleus
22 Genus
25 Drink freely
26 Extreme
27 Greek giant
28 Wading bird
29 Standards
31 Home state of 45-Across
32 Coveted movie award
33 Pauses
36 Remain
39 Governmental agreements
41 Guides
44 Relish; flavor
46 "From ___ to Eternity"
49 Reared
51 ___ Peak (California volcano)
53 Unfasten
55 Drop in water
56 Capital of Latvia
57 Troubles
58 André ___ (novelist)
59 Besought
60 Boot part
61 Gaelic
62 Do farm work

ANSWER, PAGE 273

43

ACROSS

1 Roughen, as skin
5 Town in Panama Canal Zone
10 Jockey's hat
13 Author Victor ___
14 Suppose
15 Peel
16 Secret nuptials
18 Wading bird
19 Teamster
20 The "Moor of Venice"
22 Namely: Abbr.
23 ___-Lorraine
24 ___ with (sympathized with)
27 Days of yore: Archaic
28 Famous French painter
31 Assert
32 Misery
33 Sir ___ Hardwicke (actor)
34 Insect egg
35 Polite ways of behavior
37 Pother
38 More concise
40 Coral reef
41 Hebrew measure
42 Adjust (to)
43 "Bosh!": Slang
44 Out of date
45 Bizet opera
47 Go astray
48 Withdrawal
50 Hard-hitting tennis player
54 Drug-yielding plant
55 Put to trouble
57 Postal ___
58 At the back
59 Concludes
60 Halves of ems
61 Pithy
62 Tidy

DOWN

1 Masticate
2 Hawaiian dance
3 In a pother
4 Puffy muffin
5 Giant pitcher
6 One who mimics
7 Metal for cans
8 Countless
9 Homes in trees
10 Messages from across the sea
11 Seed covering
12 Mexican money
15 Put (together), as parts
17 Geraint's wife
21 Underworld
23 ___ lace, from France
24 ___ Claus
25 Vine-covered
26 Disparagers
27 Vast period of time
29 Military assistants
30 ___ card (tally)
32 Conflict
33 Weep
35 Unit of length: British
36 Devour
39 Saved
41 Boat crew
43 Go to bed
44 Baby carriage
46 Title for a woman
47 University in Georgia
48 Speed contest
49 Ardor
50 "Shoo, Kitty!"
51 Whet
52 Icelandic literary work
53 Repose
56 Navigable water

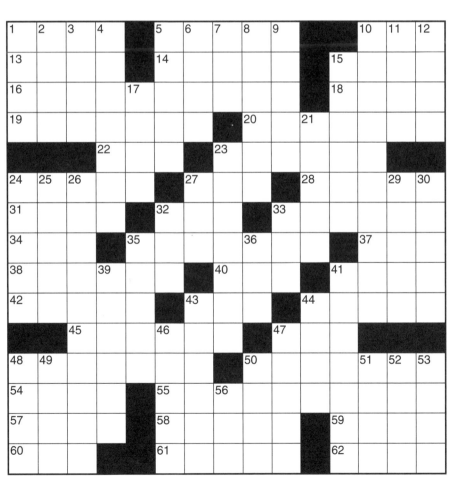

ANSWER, PAGE 275

44

ACROSS

1 Smoker's accessory
8 Conquer
14 Not conscious (of)
15 Exacts satisfaction for
17 Women's club
18 See him twice a year
19 Bushy clump of ivy
20 Nuisance
22 Fist fight
23 Heroic
25 Fathers
28 Complain bitterly (at)
29 Fast dances
31 Brooks
33 Alphabet letter
34 Wandering
36 Serving dishes
38 Ocean's noise
40 Box
41 Daydreams
45 Overloads
49 Mimic
50 Make happy
52 Uncanny
53 Cummerbund
55 Gush
57 Declaim wildly
58 Act the clown
60 Performance by two
62 Hoodlum's gun: Slang
63 Nutriment
66 Side view
68 Heir
69 Home on wheels
70 Became taut
71 Melancholy

DOWN

1 Grave; somber
2 Keyhole-peeper
3 More robust
4 "It takes ___ to tango
5 Grate
6 Zodiac sign
7 Polite affirmative
8 Head of house
9 Actress Arden
10 Swamps
11 Start upon (a profession)
12 Fluster
13 More irritable
16 Fur scarves

21 Vacation journey
24 ___ Boothe Luce
26 Building wings
27 Rebuffs
30 Breathe noisily in sleep
32 Condition
35 Follows stealthily: Slang
37 More honest
39 Get, as a reward
41 Scoundrel
42 Shoulder ornament
43 Trace
44 Stiff-shirt button
46 Delicate
47 Endings for musical compositions

48 Hunting dogs
51 Bursts forth
54 ___ being
56 ___ cotta
59 Favorites
61 Amphibian
64 Born
65 Radio's Mr. Husing
67 Fish "oar"

ANSWER, PAGE 277

ACROSS

1 Wed
6 Mrs. Truman
10 Chops
14 Texas landmark
15 Russian mountain range
16 Go out
17 Resemblance
19 Church recess
20 Pay for extra working hours
21 Nursery rhyme shepherdess
23 Edward's nickname
24 Mrs. Cantor
25 Filleted
26 Peer Gynt's mother
27 Thrive
30 Popular person
33 Contests
34 Also
35 Talk violently
36 Golfers' cries of warning
37 Distribute the cards
38 Sea eagle
39 Less
40 Convey
41 Metallic element
43 Hudson ___, Canada
44 They live on the banks of the Vistula
45 Expression of disgust
46 Water barrier
49 Pilfered
51 Feminine name
53 G.I.'s favorite reporter
54 Wicked actions
56 Dry
57 Location
58 Joyce Kilmer's subject
59 Mediocre
60 Hurried
61 Sorrowfully

DOWN

1 ___-Dixon line (famous boundary)
2 Active
3 Domesticated
4 Arabian prince
5 Stupid
6 Rangoon is its capital
7 Great Lake
8 Was in session
9 Cunning person
10 Person who amasses
11 Timesaver
12 Sage
13 Pace
18 Assistant
22 Burden
25 "St. Louis ___"
26 Deed
27 Tribunal
28 Fly
29 Sacred
30 Pre-college school
31 Countess's mate
32 U.S. Naval Academy
33 Extra payment
36 Delicacy
37 Actress Doris ___
39 Measure of distance
40 (In) partnership
42 Ohio city
43 Poet
45 Bundled
46 Had a meal
47 Spiritual being
48 Sloppy
49 Resorts
50 Novice
51 Quote
52 Italian coin
55 Bigwig

ANSWER, PAGE 278

46

ACROSS

1 Leander's lover
5 Strip of wood
9 Cavort
13 Admit frankly
14 "Whatever ___ Wants"
15 Shakespearean hero
16 Backwoodsman
18 Factor
19 Wholly
20 Remnants
22 Digits
23 Publicize
24 Hobgoblins
27 Beds
29 Knowland's party: Abbr.
32 Wagons
33 Roof dwelling
35 Seaweed
36 Sullenly rude
37 Futile
38 Genuine thing: Slang
40 Harbor
41 Devotee
42 Acorn trees
43 Turning around an axis
44 Done by us
45 Soggy earth
46 Cheat: Slang
51 Rank below a corporal: Abbr.
54 Thing of value
55 Gangster
57 Hallow
58 Long (for)
59 Division indication
60 Painful
61 Necklace part
62 Boil slowly

DOWN

1 Laughter sound
2 Depraved
3 A register
4 Bird of prey
5 Microscope plates
6 Contains
7 Troubles
8 Yucatan Indian
9 Pilot's "O.K."
10 Portent
11 Patch
12 Metal vessels
15 Salad plant
17 Anthologies
21 Well-groomed
22 Whole
24 Neckpiece
25 Flower leaf
26 Musical instrument
27 Mackerel-like fishes
28 Merely
29 Kind of jelly
30 Willow tree
31 Small coin
33 Ice hockey disk
34 Egg-shaped
36 Frighten
39 Sheds feathers
40 Nashua is one
43 Hazarded
44 Corpulent
45 Coffee-flavored
46 Pats
47 Norway's capital
48 Consumer
49 Grouchy person
50 Olympic event
51 Held in
52 Celebration
53 Exult
56 "My country, ___ of thee"

ANSWER, PAGE 263

ACROSS

1 Close-fitting
6 Trade
10 Flat-topped hill
14 Brass is one
15 Type size
16 Wicked
17 Building plans
19 Semester
20 Employ
21 Writer for hire
22 Views
24 A few
25 Flashy person
26 First-rate
29 Chinese-restaurant dish
32 Deadly pale
33 ___ be! (cry of surprise)
34 Southern constellation
35 Poky
36 Gibe
37 Be radiant
38 Showman Murray
39 Salt solution
40 Throb
41 Pilfering
43 Cried like a donkey
44 Low spirits
45 Swarm
46 On, as a ship
48 Wrinkle
49 Wrath
52 Weaver's frame
53 Receptive to new ideas
56 Female voice
57 Impulse
58 Dinner course
59 Ordinal number suffixes
60 Spree: Slang
61 Abrasive substance

DOWN

1 Forbidden
2 Woes
3 Mucilage
4 Garden tool
5 Tropical storm
6 One "ingredient" of little girls
7 Blink
8 Perform
9 Traveler's document
10 Measuring instruments
11 Sooner or later
12 Father
13 Charity
18 Inclined passageway
23 Facsimile
24 Simmer
25 Glistened
26 Chores
27 Small island
28 Small structure for callers
29 Adhered (to)
30 Worn away
31 Steered wildly
33 Advances
36 Tested
37 WW II battlefield in the Pacific
39 Become indistinct
40 Basis for an argument
42 Los ___ (A-bomb lab)
43 Shine
45 Belief
46 Wings
47 Lock part
48 Utah state flower
49 Unemployed
50 Raise, as children
51 Whirlpool
54 Golf teacher
55 Businessman's group: Abbr.

ANSWER, PAGE 265

48

ACROSS

1 Saloons
5 Smooth
10 City health problem
14 Origin
15 Sacred book
16 ___ sapiens
17 Look forward to
19 Region
20 Tradesmen
21 Lands east of Italy
23 Explosive
24 Small ball
26 Founder of a French royal house
29 Norman ___ Geddes (noted designer)
30 Metal waste
33 Employed
34 Strip
36 Poor thing to be in
37 Title
38 Marcher
39 Cold cubes
40 Invalid food
41 Playing marbles
42 French cleric
43 Noted golfer
45 Boston Red Sox star
46 Greek poet
47 Armistices
49 One of the Trinity
50 Outcast
52 Walked heavily
56 Poison tree of Java
57 Writing desk
60 Distribute
61 Fire a gun
62 Extreme anger
63 Greek god
64 Dispatches
65 Spill untidily

DOWN

1 Nail
2 Excellent
3 Roster
4 Stiffly formal
5 Dress part
6 Cuts (off)
7 Notable period of time
8 Corrode
9 Ring slowly
10 Small boy
11 Period of delay
12 Portent
13 Farm animal
18 Coin
22 Church official
24 Lares and ___ (Roman household gods)
25 Dodged
26 Tooth points
27 Man from Cathay
28 Commit, as crimes
29 Upbraid
31 One of Bolivia's capitals
32 Ranch animal
34 United Nations V.I.P.
35 ___ Moines
38 Italian city
42 Vultures
44 Begins
46 Owl's cry
48 Indoor game
49 Openings
50 Cougar
51 One who mimics
52 Goad
53 Telephone
54 Therefore
55 Profound
58 That lady
59 Study

ANSWER, PAGE 267

49

ACROSS

1 Swing gently
5 Knitting stitches
10 Omaha's state: Abbr.
14 Heap
15 Edible bulb
16 Pin on which a wheel turns
17 A continent
18 Popular dance
19 Pair of horses
20 Draftees
22 Dispatched again
24 Before
25 Short letter
26 Tendencies
27 Baseball team
28 Juicy fruits
29 Strong ale
32 Approaches
34 Skating surface
37 Look sullen
38 Smells
39 Terrible czar
40 Still
41 Occurrence
42 Mingle
43 Prepared (the way)
45 Heathen god
47 One who tallies
49 High cards
50 Distress signal
53 Landmarks of heaped stones
54 Having the most shrubbery
56 Miss Baxter
57 Useful
59 Musical group
60 Plots of land
61 Electronic detecting device
62 Always
63 Nuisance
64 Exercise (power)
65 Pure and simple

DOWN

1 Bowling score
2 More prudent
3 "___ in Wonderland"
4 Period of time
5 Medicinal drink
6 Alone
7 Wash lightly
8 Ship's diary
9 Boisterous laughers
10 Egyptian leader
11 Costly
12 Urbane
13 Leases
21 Single item
23 Epochs
27 Foolish person: Slang
28 Fastidious
29 Secret watcher
30 Foot part
31 Has a higher score than
33 Age
35 Is able to
36 Finish
38 Too certain
39 ___-mannered (rude)
41 Level
42 Nonsense
44 Apprehend
46 Abandon
47 Sell overpriced tickets
48 Small boat
49 Endure
50 Wait on
51 Willow
52 Shop
55 Short newspaper article
58 Income or luxury ___

ANSWER, PAGE 269

50

ACROSS

1 Rubbish
6 ___ jacket (sailor's coat)
9 Apostle and saint
13 Orleans river
14 Dixie metropolis
16 More mature
17 Attacker
18 Consumes, as fire
20 Passport endorsements
21 Officeholders
22 9 inches in length
24 Chinese silk
28 Roofing materials
32 Assumed name
33 Set limits to
34 Skill
35 Racing boats
36 Pygmy
37 Greek meeting place
38 "The ___ of St. Mark" (play)
39 Marks that remain
40 Shabby
41 Angels
43 Gazes fixedly
44 Garden pest
45 Proper
46 Junto
49 Bulwarks
54 Excessively burdened
57 Braid
58 Magnetic ore
59 Slur
60 Football players
61 Conceit
62 Hawthorne locale

DOWN

1 Dolt
2 Dungeon
3 Assists
4 Mandolin part
5 Water "buses"
6 Football play
7 Feminine noun suffix
8 Exclamation
9 Pier support
10 Exclamation of sorrow
11 Arm bone
12 Permits
14 "No" votes
15 Bon ___ (gourmet)
19 Single number
22 Metal strips
23 Covered with evergreens
24 Knight's aides
25 Yellowish-green color
26 African river
27 Fuel
28 Rage
29 More recent
30 Wear away
31 Remains
33 Sedate
36 Yearn (for)
37 Vast amount
39 Charms
40 Treeless plains
42 Bestows
43 Total (up)
45 Victor Borge, for example
46 Mr. Porter, composer
47 Name of three English rivers
48 Ornamental ball
49 Marital separation center
50 ___ Nazimova (famous actress)
51 Sora, for example
52 Current
53 Check or stop
55 Consumed
56 Hound

ANSWER, PAGE 271

51

ACROSS

1 Mitt
6 Felines
10 Coaster
14 Less frequent
15 Neglect
16 Stratagem
17 Indignation
18 Eat the main meal
19 Natural manner
20 Beetle-shaped gem
22 Wearing "three-cornered pants"
24 Prison: Slang
25 Acme
27 Discharge
28 Kind of moth
30 Glowing coal
34 Discarded
37 Armor for the lower leg
38 Raw metals
39 Avid
41 Not up
42 Overlooked
44 Adjusting contrivances
46 Penetrate
47 Women in white
48 Face part
50 A beverage
51 Fiery, as a temper
54 Criminal
58 Embarrassing situation
60 South African plant
61 ___ jacket (short jacket)
63 Flutter (over)
64 Employer
65 Singing voice
66 Levels off
67 At a ___ (puzzled)
68 For fear that
69 Meaning

DOWN

1 Take hold of mentally
2 Spear
3 Musical instrument
4 Shift
5 Eccentric
6 Food fish
7 Among
8 More minute
9 Water vapor
10 Candies
11 Fibber
12 If not
13 Legal document
21 Darted
23 Landing place
26 Defendant's statement
28 Western Union boys
29 Mr. Bergen
31 Infant
32 At any time
33 Bright colors
34 City on the Tiber
35 Land of "the green"
36 Witticism
37 Degrees
40 Govern the policy of, as a newspaper
43 Greek god of love
45 Fruits
47 Winged insect
49 "Swipe"
51 Refuge
52 Expands
53 To the point
54 Ancient European division
55 Likewise
56 Refusals
57 Spoils
59 Ramble
62 To no degree

ANSWER, PAGE 273

52

ACROSS

1 Pennant
5 Knights' wives
10 Garden walk
14 Judge's gown
15 Rouse from sleep
16 Century plant
17 Again
18 Household gods
19 Fully grown
20 Clanging in sound
22 Sampled
24 Tidy
25 Texas plant
26 Wood markings
29 Feign illness
33 Branch
34 ___ down (modulated)
35 Hatchet
36 Eve's mate
37 Vinegar bottle
38 Deceive
39 Coal mine
40 Avoids
41 Loafed
42 Exacting
44 Desert animals
45 Singing bird
46 Frolic
47 An account for publication
50 Vies
54 Nomad
55 Run off to get married
57 Alaskan city
58 Isinglass
59 Metal fastener
60 ___ the Red (Norse explorer)
61 Pare
62 Sows
63 Small arrow

DOWN

1 "___ Here to Eternity"
2 What "makes the world go round"
3 Encourage
4 Flower
5 Texan metropolis
6 Expect
7 ___ Connelly (author)
8 Supplement
9 Musical sextuplet
10 Minister
11 Dismounted
12 Drink to excess
13 Mind
21 Eyeglass
23 Sour
25 Ship's courses
26 Vine fruit
27 Root
28 Famous violin
29 Ascend
30 Bandage material
31 Dismiss
32 Stalks
34 Large suitcase
37 Hires
38 Moistened
40 Scorch
41 Lantern
43 Universal
44 Halley studied these
46 Lassoed
47 Runway
48 Great Lake
49 Steady step
50 Sheltered nook
51 Pentateuch
52 Arabian prince
53 Religious denomination
56 Former U.N. Secretary-General

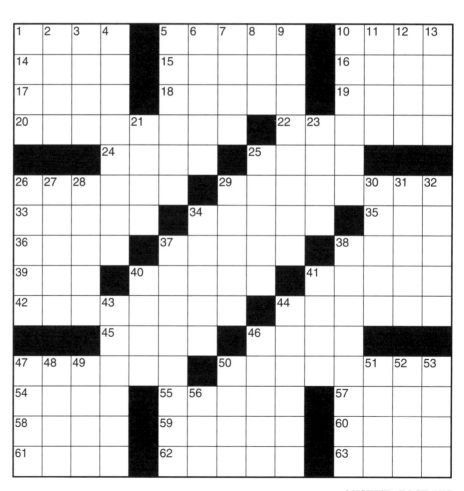

ANSWER, PAGE 275

53

ACROSS

1 Menu item
6 Special ability
12 Lady ___
13 Algonquian Indian
15 Eloper's aid
16 Beauty lovers
17 "We ___ Seven"
18 Washington, D.C. notable
20 Make lace
21 Metal
23 Mythological sea nymph
24 Location
25 Concluded
27 El ___ (Spanish hero)
28 Ranch animal
29 Biblical sea
31 Beets
32 Evil glance
33 Its capital is Vientiane
34 Elf
37 Sets up (a tent)
40 Laborers
41 Container
42 ___ Atatürk
44 Small case
45 Nostrils
47 Tebaldi, for example
48 "Live and ___ live"
49 Peerage member
51 Girl's nickname
52 West Indies island
54 Oregon college town
56 Old age
57 Factories
58 Hinders
59 Irish clans

DOWN

1 Rising to the heights
2 Appendixes
3 Hinged top
4 Prayers
5 Challenges
6 Examined
7 Illinois town
8 Bert ___
9 Farm animal
10 Sprucer
11 Handled
12 Coating, as on pottery
13 Humorous fond name
14 Acid salts
19 More pleasant
22 16th century Italian sculptor
24 Stored (away): Slang
26 Reducing plans
28 Scandalize
30 Famous West Pointer
31 Persian ___
33 Fabric
34 Kinds of wheat
35 ___ out (disappeared)
36 Fixed method
37 Comical imitation
38 ___ domain
39 Scholars
41 Weight units
43 Runners' paths
45 Lowest point
46 Trickles
49 Ill humor
50 Large bulrush
53 Insect egg
55 Delaware Water ___

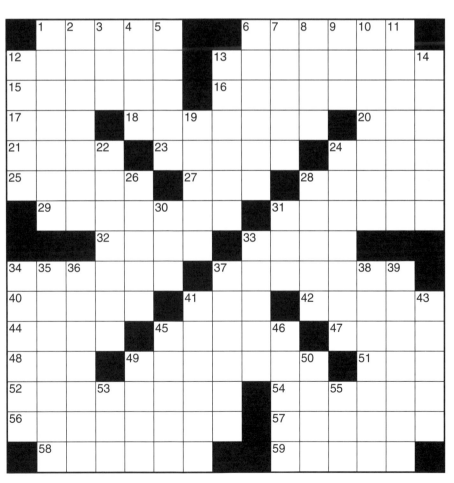

ANSWER, PAGE 277

54

ACROSS

1 Choir recess
5 Recedes
9 Vows
14 Monk's room
15 The ___ (Chicago business area)
16 Dart
17 Early settlers' ship
19 Itinerary
20 Historic age
21 Puccini works
23 Employed
24 Rescued
26 Sound of surprise
28 Lamented
30 Put
31 Hungry
32 Farm area
33 Tilt
36 Barge
37 Edge
38 Extensive
39 Bewitch
40 Held fast
41 "Ship of the desert"
42 Cannon sounds
43 Least colorful
44 Liberty
47 Bank safe
48 Hurry!
49 Morning prayers
51 Mature
54 Group of eight
56 Swing music fan: Slang
58 Push
59 ___ Khayyám (Persian poet)
60 Mexican jar
61 Wigwam
62 Depend (on)
63 Fuse

DOWN

1 High point
2 Juicy fruit
3 Wily
4 Fairy
5 Ran away to marry
6 Curtsied
7 Afrikander
8 Spreading awkwardly
9 Paddle
10 Incite
11 Faith
12 Inn
13 Bergman or Garbo
18 Was very fond of
22 Man-eating fish
25 Once again
27 Frigid
28 Eskimo's command
29 Formerly
30 Aches
32 Parading bandleader
33 Train schedule
34 Fresh-water fish
35 Animal skin
37 Blossom
38 Room enclosure
40 Food fish
41 Reason
42 Act
43 Kitchen closet
44 Ice
45 Dress trimming
46 Prevent
47 Essential
50 Use a stopwatch on
52 Sea bird
53 Minced oath
55 Scotch river
57 Tier

ANSWER, PAGE 278

ACROSS

1 Give
7 Cornered
14 Speak monotonously
15 Valorous female
16 Well-formed
18 Violent behavior
19 Product of Detroit
20 Majestic
22 ___ and tuck
23 Untie
25 Stuff
26 Have supper
27 Sacred image
28 Visit by phone
29 "Tightwad"
30 Boldness
32 Highest quality
33 Cry of disgust: Slang
34 Temperature
35 Reproduce
36 Conspires (with)
40 B.S.A. member
42 Immodest
43 Say "th" for "s"
44 Preserves
45 Locate
46 Opposite of 45-Across
47 Newspaper features
48 Ask advice of
51 ___ Meriwether (current Miss America)
52 Spotted cat
54 Foretell
56 Expand
57 Husband-to-be
58 Loud-voiced person
59 Walk unsteadily

DOWN

1 Small, soft cake
2 Intensify
3 Sought-after status in Filmland
4 Highest part
5 Individuals
6 Whip mark
7 Menace
8 Kingdom
9 Great multitude
10 Soft drink
11 Liberace is one
12 Train-puller
13 More profound
17 Private boats
21 Salver
24 Burdensome
26 Vaporize and condense
28 Metropolis
29 Contemptible
31 Spellbound
32 Curve
34 Street robbery
35 Comfort
36 Pros and ___
37 Extreme
38 Perfume
39 Reckless driver
40 Symbol of justice
41 Rhythmic
42 Cover for loose papers
45 Do without
48 Wagon
49 Attic
50 Musical group
53 God of flocks
55 Make lace

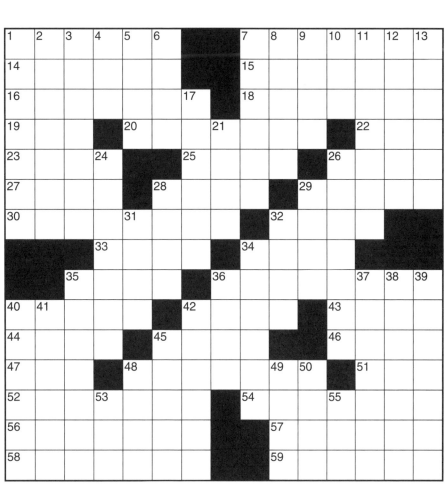

ANSWER, PAGE 263

56

ACROSS

1 Bored with life's pleasures
6 Captain Ahab's vessel
12 Make ready
14 "To Have and ___"
16 Dancer's garb
17 Former First Lady
18 Viper
19 Rascals
21 Head: Slang
22 Mollusk
24 Tear apart
25 Storage compartment
26 Auriculate
28 Places to preserve fodder
31 Conducted
32 Steering device
34 Evil persuaders
36 ___ tea (summer drink)
38 Auction
39 Devices for piling up hay
43 Sustaining wall of stones
47 "Ode on a Grecian ___"
48 Short comedies
50 Dowager's headdress
51 Decay
52 Norse god of strife
54 Studies hard
55 Sticky substances
57 Statement of grievance
59 Be in session
60 Gourmet
62 Uneasy
64 Member of the Upper House
65 Educated
66 Restores
67 Lock of hair

DOWN

1 City on the Oder
2 Jungle beast
3 Naturally fit
4 Controversial Basin
5 Mistake
6 Cajoles
7 Dutch painter
8 Hail!
9 Heavy metal
10 Make finer
11 More capacious
12 Gold source
13 Borders
15 General directions
20 Single group
23 Army doctor
27 Card packs
29 Persian poet
30 Acrobatic trick
33 Strong smell
35 Lukewarm
37 They dig for oil
39 Swelling waves
40 Cavalryman
41 New Orleans restaurateur
42 Greek portico
44 Dried grapes
45 Greeks of Argos
46 Glued
49 Suit part
53 Sluggish
56 Study closely
57 Front part of a ship
58 Former ruler
61 One of an Indian tribe
63 Gift for Dad

ANSWER, PAGE 265

57

ACROSS

1 Small splotch
5 Remove (the hat)
9 Cheats: Slang
13 Hawaiian isle
14 Common vines
16 Genuine
17 Broad smile
18 Disagreeable
19 Eskimo hut
20 Unpleasant animal of fable
23 On the sheltered side
24 Porker
25 Less fresh
28 Promises to marry
33 Garden flower
34 Philippine natives
35 Football fan's cry
36 In a line
37 Pleasingly plump
38 Measure of distance
39 Representative of the new
40 ___ out (apportions)
41 Kitchen tool
42 Senator Estes ___
44 Water-soaked
45 Employ
46 Shock severely
47 Ragged fellow
54 Western state
55 Rabbit fur
56 Brightness of color
58 Former pitcher ___ Newsom
59 Surrender
60 Brave man
61 Goad
62 Observes
63 Large book

DOWN

1 Marsh
2 Cooking fat
3 Buckeye State
4 Cottage
5 Evening meal
6 Egg-shaped
7 Mackerel
8 Lavish feast
9 American, to a Mexican
10 Robber: Slang
11 Colorless
12 Insult
15 Accompanying phenomenon
21 Holly
22 Tunes
25 Paddle
26 ___ bagger (triple)
27 Distant
28 Pugilist
29 Cupid
30 Attempted
31 Cut in two
32 Gloss
34 Silent
37 ___ Hills (Hollywood suburb)
38 The "witching hour"
40 Clio or Thalia
41 Man's spiritual part
43 Ferber or Hemingway
44 Kiosks
46 Amused look
47 Clumsy boats
48 Upon
49 Forbidden
50 Raised platform
51 Fencing sword
52 Type of shortening
53 Standard
57 Sorrow

ANSWER, PAGE 267

58

ACROSS

1 Fragment
6 Thick slice
10 Distant
14 Artless
15 Opinion sampling
16 Sociology word
17 Not perceptible to the touch
19 Sherbets
20 Pod vegetable
21 Desirable
22 Sagest
24 Infant
25 Envy
26 Burning
29 Becomes exhausted
32 Male honeybee
33 Sheltered inlets
34 To and ___
35 Artificial manners
36 More cunning
37 Legend
38 Cushion
39 Incline
40 Entwined
41 Insignificant
43 Amusing play
44 Journeys
45 Sensible
46 Steers clear of
48 Warble
49 Polite gesture
52 Plunge
53 Harangues
56 Tied
57 Spoken
58 Elliptical
59 Fragrant ointment
60 Stupid person: Slang
61 Synthetic fabric

DOWN

1 Cut quickly
2 Walking stick
3 Girl's name
4 Actress Gardner
5 Nom de plume
6 Pungent
7 Ear part
8 Everything
9 Passed
10 Gets up
11 Confronting one another
12 Experts
13 Relax
18 Sneer
23 Folk singer Burl ___
24 Debars
25 Perfumery substance
26 Conform (to)
27 Mendicant brother
28 Act superior to
29 Departing
30 Importuned
31 Truckler
33 Tribes
36 Slovenly
37 Identical
39 Slipped
40 Crave
42 Amigo
43 Tins
45 Move sinuously
46 Arabian gulf
47 Long live!: Italian
48 Strike with the open hand
49 Donkey's "call"
50 Showman Preminger
51 At what time?
54 Gold: Spanish
55 Eggs

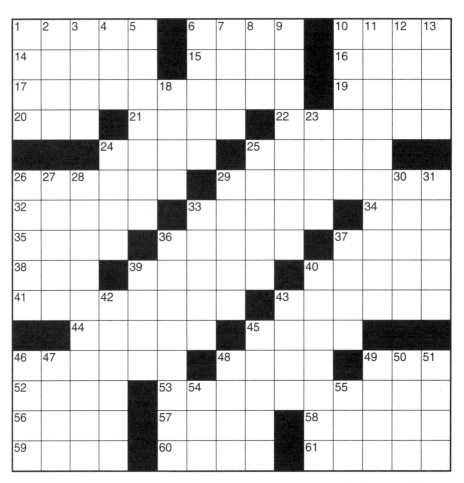

ANSWER, PAGE 269

ACROSS

1 Malt beverage
5 Bad-mannered person: Slang
9 Seasoned sailor
13 Top
14 Sea eagle
15 Mark ___ (author)
17 Foot affliction
19 Burning
20 Inn
21 Destiny
22 Enticed
23 Diving bird
25 Pertaining to birth
27 Oil-producing part of flax
31 Ignore a duty
35 One of the Great Lakes
36 Eat greedily
38 Maker of locks
39 Obtained
40 Petroleum
41 Light brown
42 Over again
44 Sharpened
46 Existed
47 Musical
49 Shiny cotton fabric
51 Nostrils
53 Wire measure
54 Gem's plane surface
57 Sleeping place
59 Signal light
63 Misuse
64 Calm
66 Exclude from
67 Tiny fly
68 Second-hand
69 Lights out signal
70 A seasoning
71 ___ Montez

DOWN

1 Great German composer
2 Sound reflection
3 Send out
4 Dismiss
5 Colloidal material
6 Verbal
7 Pungent vegetable
8 Five-sided forms
9 German prison camp
10 Unpleasantly
11 Den
12 Become weary
16 Nickname for Edward
18 Downhearted
24 Small barrel
26 Golf mound
27 Lawful
28 Satire
29 Saltpeter
30 Divining rods
32 Devoured
33 ___ Boothe Luce
34 Doctrine
37 Outfit
43 Red apple
44 Corn spike
45 Beavers' building job
46 Headstrong
48 Supplies food
50 Petty quarrel
52 Drug from cassia plants
54 Temporary fashion
55 Encourage
56 West Indies republic
58 Pull heavily
60 Too
61 Lively dance
62 Icelandic poems
65 Indian

ANSWER, PAGE 271

60

ACROSS

1 Mark of disgrace
7 Capelike vestments
12 More shabby
13 Having resemblance (to)
15 Card game
16 Fast and excitedly: Music
17 Greek letter
18 Native environment
20 Gratuity
21 Seizes suddenly
23 Ocean vessel
24 Withered
25 Sir Walter Scott heroine
27 Consumed
28 Particle
29 Oozed
31 Unity
33 Car used in coal mines
35 Soothsayer
36 Military bars
39 11th Greek letter
43 Cruel person
44 Bribe
46 Ventured
47 Pronoun
48 Member of the peerage
50 New star: Astronomy
51 Free
52 More slender
54 Jet fighter plane
55 Moslem
57 Cupidity
59 Feminine counterpart of 35-Across
60 Strips of covering
61 Tied decisions
62 Rubs out

DOWN

1 Joseph Conrad specialty
2 Capable of being defended
3 Crete's highest peak
4 Lillian and Dorothy ___ (actresses)
5 Iron
6 Where Aden is
7 Tampa product
8 Leave out
9 Peach stone
10 Click beetles
11 Works by Jonathan Swift
12 Views
13 Glossy fabrics
14 "___ in" (taken in by trickery)
19 Divided by
22 Seven-voice compositions
24 ___ Antitrust Act (1890)
26 Courage
28 "Slamming Sammy" ___
30 Patriotic organization: Abbr.
32 Fish
34 Inlaid designs
36 Journeyed by yacht
37 Track athlete
38 Standard
40 Drug used to calm
41 Contrivances
42 Proverbs
43 Actor Karloff
45 Hair ointment
48 Complete joy
49 In no case
52 Merganser
53 Genus of frogs
56 Constellation known as "The Altar"
58 U.S.S.R.: Abbr.

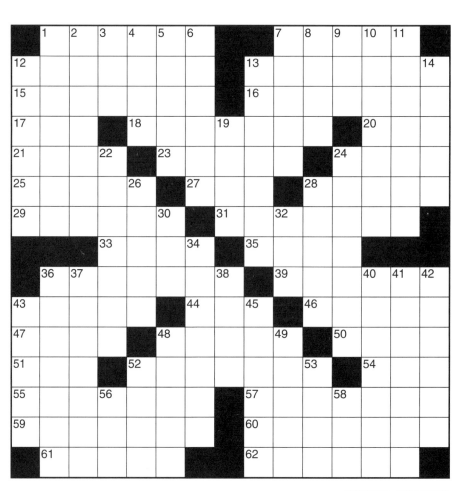

ANSWER, PAGE 273

61

ACROSS

1 The least bit
4 Word of contempt
7 Antipasto ingredient
13 Make a "boo-boo"
14 Servicemen's club: Abbr.
15 "Hamming it up"
17 Coarse cloth
19 "The Schnozz"
20 Antagonist
21 Obliterate
23 Cozy room
24 Roman poet
25 Home base
26 Coil
27 Thick roll
28 Hoisting apparatus
29 Parsonage
30 Looking like a villain
32 Dirk
33 Bound
34 Speck of dust
35 Interlocked
38 Varied
41 ___ into (take part in)
42 Repaired shoes
43 Basker's hue
45 Scorch
46 Fragrant wood
47 Abject
48 Ailurophile's pet
49 Breakfast meat
50 "The Divine Comedy" poet
51 Alive
53 Corrected, as a faulty text
55 Rubbed clean
56 Actor Mineo
57 A bard's "before"
58 Whole
59 Watch
60 Terminate

DOWN

1 Flourish anew
2 Coming
3 Furnish
4 Knot in wood
5 A King of Judah
6 One's country
7 Quiet
8 Entertain
9 Learning
10 ___ loss (confused)
11 Giving heed to
12 Strong
16 Male or female
18 Move about restlessly
22 Pealed
25 Snooped
26 Bet
28 "Newsman" of colonial days
29 Paired
31 Anesthetic
32 English seaport
34 Certain Italian
35 Pilgrimage sites
36 Augment
37 Rank
38 Extinct bird
39 S.R.O. ticket-holder
40 Oriental
42 Withdraw (from)
44 Had to have
46 Provide the bill of fare
47 Declare "verboten"
49 Italian city
50 Erase
52 Pooch: Slang
54 Is allowed to

ANSWER, PAGE 275

62

ACROSS

1 Cheat: Slang
5 Moisten while cooking, as meat
10 Stupor
14 Byway
15 Huxley's "___ Hay"
16 Singular of opera
17 He saw the act committed
19 Disguise
20 "Oh, what a tangled ___ we weave"
21 Prison: Slang
22 Restaurant equipment
24 Drizzly
26 Festive
27 Whiskey-makers
29 Meritorious mention
33 Weighty
34 Unadorned
35 Sergeant: Abbr.
36 Pillar: Architecture
37 French money
38 Josip Broz
39 Mama rabbit
40 Jeer at
41 Entrances
42 Lasting
44 Civil
45 Memo
46 Fur hood
47 Home and ___
50 French cheese
51 Pourboire
54 Impulse
55 To great distances
58 Jumping insect
59 Merge
60 Affirm
61 Sense
62 Crippled
63 Accomplishment

DOWN

1 Killed
2 Comedian Danny
3 "Loaded"
4 Novel
5 Truncheons
6 Pester
7 Short walk
8 3rd word of "America"
9 Rapturous
10 Fight against
11 Iridescent gem
12 Melpomene, for example
13 Queries
18 Uncordially
23 Famous Ladd
25 Thomas ___ Edison
26 Superhumanity
27 Tint
28 Mortise's "companion"
29 Ring loudly
30 Enterprise
31 Singing group
32 Hangman's knot
34 Dried plum
37 Steadfast
38 Chitchat
40 Horse's gait
41 Stabbed by a bull
43 Imaginary
44 Distressed
46 Prattle
47 Fit of resentment
48 Writer Gardner
49 Awry
50 Hat edge
52 "Sudden flash"
53 Saucy
56 Literary collection
57 Air Force lady

ANSWER, PAGE 277

ACROSS

1 Comedian Marx
6 Type of English pottery
11 Florida city
12 Necessary accompaniments
15 Dairy product
16 Roadster
17 Crete's highest mountain
18 Classifies
20 Numerical prefix
21 Legislative bodies
23 Plays on words
24 Stringed instrument
25 "On, Wilderness were Paradise ___"
26 Needless bustle
27 Canadian peninsula
28 Soft job
30 Edict of ___ (1598)
31 Makes known
32 Simpleton
33 Auto parts
36 Barren Midwestern region
40 Carpenter's device
41 Sensible
42 Way of walking
43 Euphemistic oath
44 Vehicle
45 French river
46 Music or poetry
47 Most gloomy
49 Actor Ayres
50 Social event
52 Doctrines
54 Outsider
55 Prevent
56 Noted golfer
57 Barnyard fowl

DOWN

1 Famous magician
2 Mythical hunter
3 Unpopular rodent
4 Entreaties
5 Paddles
6 Rejects disdainfully
7 Gasps
8 Tierra del Fuego Indians
9 Touch lightly
10 Vain person
12 Awaken
13 Continent
14 Fences' steps
15 ___ one's time (waits for a chance)
19 Urges on
22 Pulled sharply
24 Better position
26 Minks and sables
27 Impudence: Slang
29 Sky: French
30 Protuberance
32 Italian poet
33 Acts sheepish
34 Rue
35 Embodiments
36 ___-off (buttonhole-stitcher)
37 "Crackajacks": Slang
38 Place to eat
39 Budgeters' dishes
41 Seasoned
44 Latin-American dance
45 TV's ___ Allen
47 Victor Borge, for example
48 Strictly for men
51 ___ Topping (Yankee owner)
53 Born

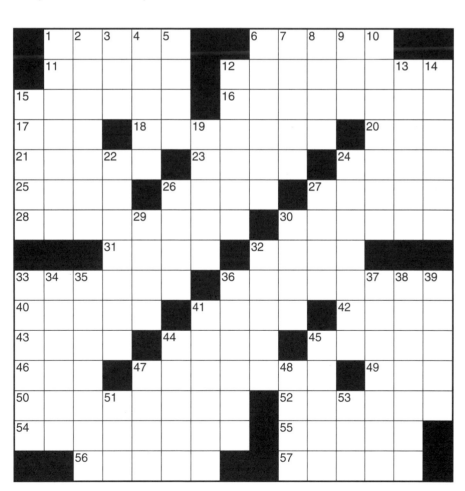

ANSWER, PAGE 278

ACROSS

1 Tins
5 Winesap or Delicious
10 Actress Freeman
14 Sign
15 Evident
16 Bard of ___
17 Malay tribesman
18 Cause to continue
20 Bully
22 Croquet stick
23 Vessel
24 Judicious
25 Sprinkles
28 Limits
32 Mournful cry
33 Pass, as time
35 Portuguese coin
36 Coral island
38 High card
39 Lavender flower
41 Witty remark
42 Painter
45 Change position
46 Teach
48 Columnist Hedda
50 Desire
51 Occupy, as a position
52 Almond-flavored syrup
55 Bitterly sarcastic
59 Home of the Cardinals
61 Costa ___
62 Graceful, rhythmic song
63 Occurrence
64 Slugger Slaughter
65 Merely
66 Seedy: Slang
67 Moist and chilly

DOWN

1 Rooster's "ornament"
2 Love: Spanish
3 He "fiddled" while Rome burned
4 Winter "battle" article
5 Pacify
6 Skirt fold
7 Actor's role
8 Mouth part
9 Foes
10 Pawed
11 Egg-shaped
12 Short letter
13 Dill
19 Fez part
21 Lad
24 Dries, as dishes
25 Hindu title of respect
26 He wrote "Too Late the Phalarope"
27 Uproars
28 Silent
29 Warship's lowest deck
30 Work on a loom
31 More pleasant
34 Door fastener
37 Cowboy's rope
40 Begged
43 Cattle thief
44 Parched
47 "Four-and-___ blackbirds ..."
49 Aged
51 Weak
52 Norway's capital
53 Shower
54 Breathing organ of fish
55 Sheep fat
56 Sister ship of the Pinta and Santa Maria
57 Image
58 Barrel for liquids
60 Eggs

ANSWER, PAGE 263

65

ACROSS

1 Settled and steady
6 ___ Alamos
9 Necessary to life
14 Author of "Mr. Pim Passes By"
15 Begone!
16 Incensed
17 Exhorter
18 With indifference to joy or pain
20 "Turn to the right!"
21 Acquit of guilt
23 Enjoy the canapés
24 Stir up sediment
26 Consultant's charge
27 Word on drug labels
28 Modulate (the voice)
30 Medieval drudge
32 Teacher's title: Abbr.
33 London foreign quarter
35 Evaluated and classified
38 Author of "Death in the Afternoon"
41 ___ Coeur Cathedral
42 October's birthstone
43 Narrow margin of victory
44 Where you are now
46 Examine officially
48 Cicatrix
50 French nobleman
52 Italian province
53 Make a "boo-boo"
54 Caprice
56 Perquisite
59 Safeguard
61 Upbraid
63 Aviary sound
64 Three: Italian
65 Cads: Slang
66 Jennets' "family circle"
67 Japanese money
68 Assault

DOWN

1 Complacent and narrow-minded
2 One for the rear compartment
3 Poet Swinburne
4 Suffix used in forming brand names
5 Run off the track
6 At a ___ (puzzled)
7 No longer in the running
8 Ecclesiastical vestment
9 Grave moral fault
10 Ida's "twin brother"
11 "A ___" (French Revolution novel)
12 Old Greek burden-bearer
13 One of the Philippine Islands
19 Currier's partner
22 Made holy
25 One who proposes to give, as aid
27 Organized system for catching criminals
28 Miss Petina, of a theater marquee
29 Silver salmon
31 Sea eagle
32 Footlike part
34 Muscat and ___ (Arabian state)
36 Sunrise direction
37 Henna, for example
39 To be: Spanish
40 Names for Frauleins
45 Age: Spanish
47 Term associated with neurotic
48 Dividing walls
49 Animals' stomachs
51 Oneness
54 Musician Waller
55 End of prayer
57 Unemployed
58 Nuisance
60 Noted Virginian
62 Setting fowl

ANSWER, PAGE 265

66

ACROSS

1 Gentle person
5 Entreaty
9 Dessert items
13 Wing-shaped
14 Flings
16 Girl's name
17 Marriage-hater
19 Replete
20 Array
21 Short rifles
23 Slur over
25 Chemist's measuring tube
26 Site for jets
29 Bank employee
32 Author John ___ Passos
33 Heroic tales
35 ___ Astaire
36 Wonder
37 Shakespeare's Kate
39 Tulsa product
40 She "wants to be alone"
43 Salty drops
45 First word of many book titles
46 Marx's confrere
48 Eludes the dragnet
50 Disease of rye
52 Piano accessory
53 Gesticulating parlor game
56 He gave no choice
59 Mrs. Rajah
60 Marie ___
62 Skill: Spanish
63 Harsh
64 Kings: French
65 Untidy state
66 Loot: Slang
67 Method: Abbr.

DOWN

1 Tibetan monk
2 Came down
3 "Top kicks"
4 Angry quarrels
5 Theseus was ___ husband
6 "___ 'n' Abner"
7 Norse explorer
8 Noted race horse of 1940s
9 Shortstop's domain
10 Famous novelist
11 Author Gardner
12 Maglie and Yvars of baseball
15 Swagger

18 Breakfast item in Dixie
22 Thorny tree
24 Pieces of ___ (pirate's loot)
26 Old saw
27 Senator Martin is one
28 Shaves off
30 Statesman Root
31 Re-lease
34 Marine mammals
38 Squirming, as in pain
41 Fruit of the holly
42 Girl's name
44 Stirring implement
47 Fountain favorites

49 Makes calm
51 Bivouac shelters
53 Stuff
54 ___ and hounds
55 State of excitement
57 Cornelia Skinner's father
58 Swarming place
61 "... a man ___ mouse"

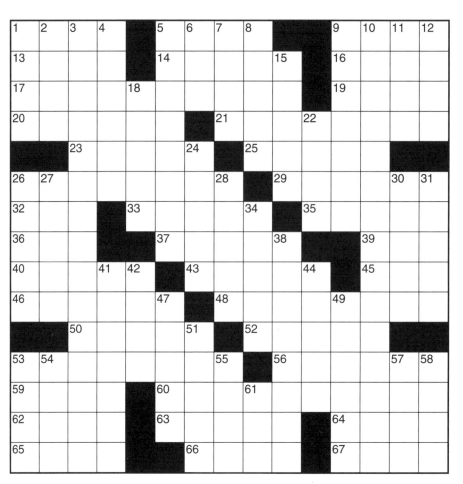

ANSWER, PAGE 267

ACROSS

1 Assaults, as a bastion
7 Serious
12 Lead an active social life
13 Charm
15 Approach gradually, as a subject
16 Picturesque Italian city
17 Frigid
18 Assail violently
20 Scoundrel
21 Like or similar
23 Hinder
24 Gentle in temper
25 Track
27 Undemure color
28 Angrily
29 Rarely
31 Quick
33 Daubs messily
35 Profuse
38 Beginning
40 Clergyman
42 Counterfeit
45 Cheering-section yell
47 Billow
48 Tarzan's "friends"
49 Bishop's headdress
51 Silent
52 Number of Commandments
53 Cloaks
55 Sesame plant
56 Street sign
58 Strives to equal
60 Site of the Comstock Lode
61 Put on new shoe bottoms
62 Great ___ (canines)
63 Simmered

DOWN

1 Don't push the "panic" button!
2 A Kennedy
3 Music work
4 Lassoed
5 Grumble
6 More portly
7 Taste
8 Portent
9 Bakery product
10 Draw forth
11 Remember
12 Obtains
14 Rough-Rider Roosevelt
15 Catalogues
19 Foot lever
22 Horribly ugly
24 Small quantity
26 Bank business
28 Busy places
30 Matron's title: Abbr.
32 Standard
34 Canarylike bird
36 Walked proudly
37 Trussed securely
39 Shreds
41 Staggers
42 ___ Rouge, Louisiana
43 Unsealed
44 Swiss city
46 Head armor
49 Yucatan Indians
50 Utilize anew
53 Fashioned
54 Deliberate
57 Pale and drawn
59 Malt beverage

ANSWER, PAGE 269

68

ACROSS

1 Pilgrimage to Mecca
5 Schweitzer's instrument
10 Seaweed extract
14 Region
15 City in Egypt
16 Gambling game
17 Falsehoods
18 Spanish roofing
19 Move swiftly
20 Hired laborer
22 Shipworm
24 Charged atoms
25 Outrigger canoe
26 Broad street
29 Time for a nest egg
33 Volcanic output
34 Singer ___ Ives
35 Store bait
36 Social insect
37 Sincere
40 By way of
41 Nobleman
43 "Cheesecake"
44 Decree
46 Perfumes
48 Rears
49 Name of a Steinbeck family
50 Rocky peaks
51 Due reward
54 Medieval wars
58 Swedish king (1550–1568)
59 Kindled again
61 Cry of acclaim
62 River deposit
63 Playing marble
64 Oast
65 Writing fluids
66 Postal areas
67 City district

DOWN

1 Semi
2 Operatic solo
3 Cervine
4 Shrub with sweet-scented flowers
5 Petroleum ingredient
6 Showers
7 Coat with gold
8 Exist
9 Nasal parts
10 Public fights
11 High wind
12 Dry
13 ___ section (newspaper part)
21 Residence
23 Long period
25 Peels
26 Open-mouthed
27 Weathercocks
28 Prominent Democrat
29 Ladder parts
30 Veteran actress
31 "___ Adams" (Tarkington novel)
32 Irish poet
34 Ilk
38 Federal prison
39 Rips
42 Repudiates
45 Disclaim
47 Conjunction
48 Itineraries
50 Stale
51 Lucy's spouse
52 "Auld sod"
53 Taffeta
54 Scotch family
55 Prima donna
56 Always
57 French writer
60 Self

ANSWER, PAGE 271

69

ACROSS

1 Astringent substance
5 Harry Truman's birthplace
10 Declare positively
14 Receptacle
15 Senseless
16 Violent anger
17 Regular
18 Mr. Barkley, for instance
20 Crusaders' enemies
22 He played Napoleon and Mark Antony in movies
23 Secret slang
24 Witnessed
25 Stratum of society
28 Made a bridge maneuver
32 Period of time
33 Sacred poem
35 Author of "La Vita Nuova"
36 Electrical unit
38 Wild animal track
40 Human being
41 "Tinker to ___ to Chance"
43 Color shades
45 "___ on a Grecian Urn"
46 Used car dealer
48 Forest clearings
50 Scorch
51 Part of a milkmaid's equipment
52 Convulsive breather
55 Wallowed
59 Restore to one's own country
61 Inca land
62 Messenger of the gods
63 Inciter
64 Recompensed
65 Dowries: Law
66 Equals
67 Mineral sources

DOWN

1 Tennis points
2 It buried Pompeii
3 Employer
4 Threaten
5 Portrait, for example
6 Concerning
7 Operates
8 It lives in a "hill"
9 "___ and Rachel" (song)
10 State with North America's only diamond mine
11 Worthless
12 Mild oath
13 Nevada city
19 Statement of faith
21 Cavil
24 ___ Legree
25 Cut off
26 Verify
27 Drags by force
28 Knock down
29 Baglike hat
30 Chopin work
31 Crosses out
34 More fitting
37 Go beyond proper limits
39 They entertain with anecdotes
42 Winter driving hazard
44 Narrow cut
47 Beat soundly
49 Syrian district and city
51 "Rob ___ to pay Paul"
52 Grating
53 Pertaining to aircraft
54 Long shoal or sandbank
55 Remuneration for a worker
56 Build
57 New York canal
58 Clothes
60 Wrath

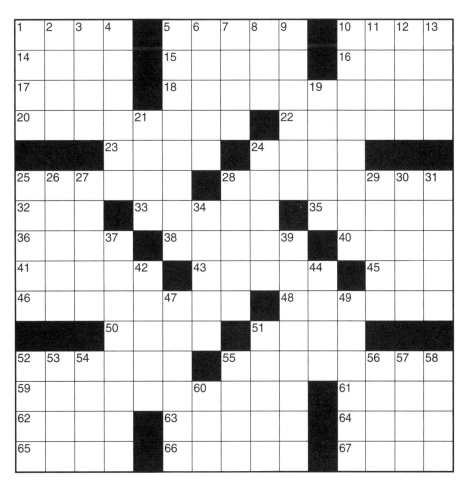

ANSWER, PAGE 273

70

ACROSS

1 "It isn't the ___, it's the upkeep"
5 ___ Flow (British naval base)
10 "Quick on the comeback"
14 Lineage
15 Filmdom's Debra
16 Track event
17 Restive area
18 Inactive
19 Again
20 Studded
22 Most skillful
24 Prayers
25 Man from Kirkcudbrightshire
26 Military groups
29 Educated
33 Aids' companion
34 Diaphanous
35 Sky's "Altar"
36 Diversify
37 Blessings
38 Box
39 Distinctive doctrine
40 Lieutenant-in-training
41 A state capital
42 Spartan king
44 George Eliot hero
45 Elevator manufacturer
46 Become limp
47 Divided; split
50 Sally Victor is one
54 Hoisted
55 Home
57 Popular piano tune
58 Seed covering
59 Open-mouthed watcher
60 Poet Thomas ___
61 Rainbows' hues
62 Delightful spots
63 ___ souci (without care)

DOWN

1 Thunder sound
2 French river
3 Quick cut
4 Boston event of 1773
5 Tower tops
6 Bamboo stems
7 Venerable
8 For each
9 Legation members
10 Cavern
11 Bathe
12 Desserts
13 Comedian Lahr
21 Nights before
23 Scanty
25 Perfume
26 Find foolish faults
27 Degrade
28 Skin: Prefix
29 Bootery items
30 Rabbit fur
31 Obliterate
32 Bold one
34 Soft drinks
37 Raillery
38 Classifications
40 Mention
41 Sphere
43 Literary works
44 Gunder Haegg and others
46 Enlarge
47 Scorch
48 Knowledge
49 Latin poet
50 Be dejected
51 Ibsen heroine
52 Spirit
53 Starfish arms
56 Corrupt

ANSWER, PAGE 275

80

ACROSS

1 Store (away): Slang
6 Wyoming mountains
12 River for Harvard boat races
14 Satires
16 Illuminating device
17 Supporting framework
18 High: Music
19 Drew idly
21 ___ blanket
22 Piece of wood
24 ___ fruit
25 Isinglass
26 Studies laboriously
28 Naval officer: Abbr.
29 Actress Davis
30 Meddles
32 Stupid
33 Jewelry
34 Descendant
35 Put into a bundle
37 Thick soup
40 Separate
41 Large snake
42 Himalayan kingdom
44 Mining products
45 Distributed
47 Mature
48 Circle on the surface of earth: Abbr.
49 Health-givers
51 Container
52 Fur animals
54 Emotionally stirred
56 Himalayan peak
57 Smiles in a silly way
58 Officials of ancient Rome
59 Gaiters

DOWN

1 Brown onion
2 Trumpet blast
3 Man's nickname
4 Santa's gift
5 Galilee ruler
6 Names
7 Made a slip
8 ___ the mark
9 Certain sides of the wicket: Cricket
10 Boobs: Slang
11 Picks out
12 Grip firmly
13 Nocturnal pests
15 Bristles
20 Says over and over
23 Buildings for worship
25 Follow a winding course
27 Hidden snoop
29 Color
31 Purpose
32 Labor union: Abbr.
34 Alpine abodes
35 Leave desolate
36 Declared
37 Tar's source
38 Descriptive expression
39 Light swords
40 French river
41 Animals
43 Gives for a time
45 Word for fogs
46 ___-Rivières (city on the St. Lawrence)
49 Cad: Slang
50 Reservoir for collecting water, oil, etc.
53 3: Prefix
55 Auditor: Abbr.

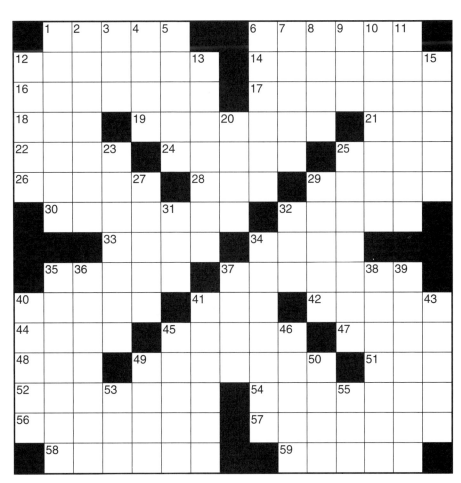

ANSWER, PAGE 277

72

ACROSS

1 Dogmatic principle
7 Rate of speed: Abbr.
10 Water barrier
13 Breathe in
14 Beguiling
16 Posture
17 Painted
18 Certain musicians
20 Congeal
21 Infuriate
22 Food regimen
23 Duck
24 Bamboolike grass
25 Oregon senator
26 "Picnic" author
27 Degree: Abbr.
28 Erase
29 Created a tumult
31 Plays on words
32 Laborer
33 London street
36 Gull-like bird
37 Magpie
40 Provokes
41 Notions
43 Split
44 Young fellows
45 Food containers
46 Shanty
47 Author Delmar
48 Going before
50 Refinement
52 Come into view
53 Took umbrage at
54 Peril
55 Periods of time: Abbr.
56 Dolt
57 Comes in

DOWN

1 Throw away
2 Chanted
3 Fees
4 Treated leather
5 Corrupting influence
6 Convene
7 Incomes: French
8 Construction workers
9 Silent
10 Water, for instance
11 Ordinary
12 Interfered
14 Want
15 Part
19 Sacred images
25 Beggars
28 Press for payment
30 Electrified particle
31 Aisle
32 "___ porridge hot"
33 Lustrous
34 Coming-attraction ad
35 Ruddiness
36 Encamped
37 Change course
38 One who exacts satisfaction
39 Wallows
42 Proms
43 Rabbit or rat
46 Marshal Dillon, for one
49 Grant
51 Literary fragments

ANSWER, PAGE 278

CHALLENGING

IQ

TESTS

INTRODUCTION

An intelligence test (IQ test) is a standardized test designed to measure human intelligence as distinct from attainments. What IQ tests do not measure, nor are they intended to measure, are ambition, personality, temperament, or compassion. IQ tests are used in educational settings to assess the individual and to improve instruction and curriculum planning, and they have become commonplace in industrial and organizational settings for selection and classification.

The tests in this book are specially compiled to provide fun and entertainment to those who take them. At the same time, the questions are designed to be similar in format to those you are likely to encounter in IQ tests. People who perform well on them are likely to do well on actual IQ tests. Because they have been specially compiled for this publication, the tests are not standardized and, therefore, an actual IQ score cannot be given. Nevertheless, we do provide an approximate guide to performance on each test for those of you who may wish to exercise your competitive instincts, and we also provide a time limit for those of you wishing to try the tests against the clock.

You will find many of the questions challenging, and deliberately so, as this is the only way to improve your mind and boost your performance. Each test consists of twenty questions and there are twenty separate tests to attempt, each of approximately the same difficulty level. If you decide to time yourself, don't spend too much time on any one question. If in doubt, skip it and return to it later using the time remaining. If options are given and you aren't sure of the answer, take an educated guess. Who knows? It may be the correct answer!

But what if you score badly on the tests? Well, you shouldn't worry! Cynics will say that the only thing having a high IQ proves is that the individual has scored well on an IQ test. The real point of this book is that you will have given your brain what we hope will prove to be an enjoyable workout, and as a result you will have increased your store of knowledge and your brainpower. It's your choice, but whichever way you choose to use the book, have fun, enjoy the questions, and happy solving!

If you've never taken an IQ test before, it's really quite easy. Answer each question with the simplest, best answer possible. You shouldn't strive for unusual interpretations of the questions or try to make them more complicated than they are. All of the questions are self-explanatory except for the analogies. These classic IQ question-types appear in the for "A : B :: C : D" and mean "A is to B as C is to D." You have to find the choice where the relationship of C to D is the same as that of A to B.

Scoring chart per test (each correct answer scores 1 point)

20	Genius level
18-19	Mastermind
16-17	Exceptional
14-15	Excellent
12-13	Very good
10-11	Good
8-9	Average

Time limit: 60 minutes per test

Answers begin on page 279.

1   Which word below is an antonym of SIGNIFICANT?

SERIOUS, TRIVIAL, ABSURD, QUIET, or SIMPLE

2   What number should logically replace the question mark?

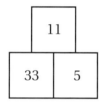 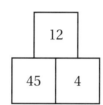 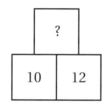

	11	
33	5	

	12	
45	4	

	?	
10	12	

3   ROTTEN LIAR is an anagram of what 10-letter word?

4   What two words that sound alike but are spelled differently mean AUDIBLY and PERMITTED?

5   At a recent small town election for mayor a total of 963 votes were cast for the four candidates, the winner exceeding his opponents by 53, 79, and 105 votes, respectively. How many votes were cast for each candidate?

6   What two nine-letter words can be formed from the six three-letter bits below?

EVE, TAG, RED, PEN, RAM, LOP

7   Change one letter in each word of FIND ANY CANDY to make a well-known phrase.

TEST   ONE

86

8   Which is the odd one out?

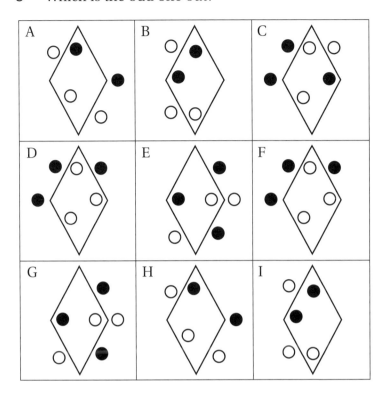

9   Fill in the blanks to make two words that are antonyms. The words spiral around the circle, one reading clockwise, the other reading counterclockwise.

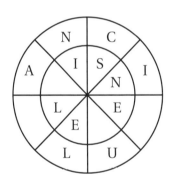

10   LIBRA : SCALES ::

A. SAGITTARIUS : FISH   B. CANCER : TWINS   C. AQUARIUS : GOAT
D. CAPRICORN : BULL   E. ARIES : RAM

11   What six-letter creature can be put in the boxes to make three-letters words reading down?

N	A	E	W	F	O
E	T	R	A	E	W

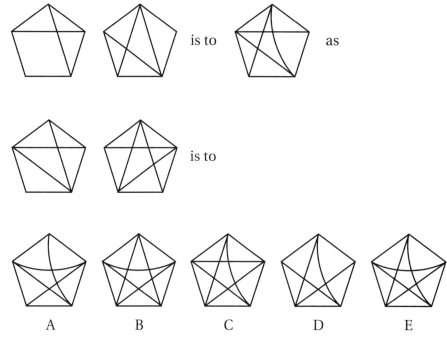

is to ... as

is to

A   B   C   D   E

13 Which two words below are closest in meaning?

GARGOYLE, WARLOCK, COCKATRICE, HARRIDAN, BASILISK, SPRITE

14 $6 + 7 \infty 8 - 9 \infty 2 = ?$

15 Which of the following is not an anagram of a type of building?

AIM DUST, RAY BIRL, AIM DRAG, OIL PATHS, or VIOLA PIN

16 What four-letter word can follow the first word and precede the second to make two new words or phrases?

SHOE, PIPE

17 What shape is a CRINOID?

A. CONE   B. TULIP   C. ARROW   D. SHIELD   E. LILY

18 What number should logically replace the question mark?

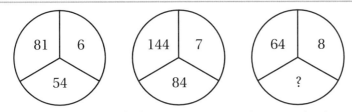

19 Which two words below are opposite in meaning?

GRANDEE, DUKE, LESSEE, SERVANT, LANDLORD, BUTLER

20 Each line and symbol that appears in the four outer circles above is transferred to the center circle according to these rules:

If the line or symbol occurs in the outer circles
one time, it is transferred,   two times, it is possibly transferred, three
times, it is transferred, and   four times, it is not transferred.

Which of the circles below should appear at the center of the diagram?

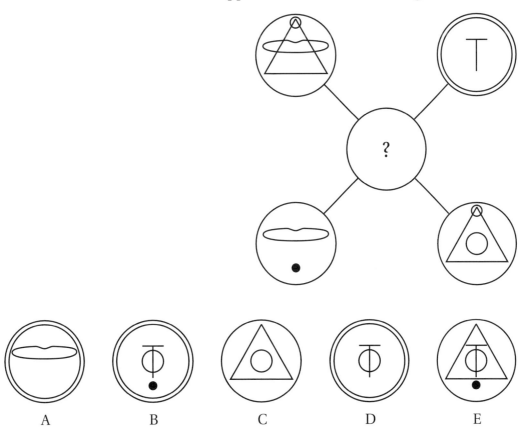

TEST 2

1   Which number is the odd one out?

    586414, 239761, 523377, 816184, 436564

2   Combine two of the three-letter bits below to make a small dog.

    BEA, COL, RES, GLE, BOX, LIC

3   Fill in the blanks to make two words that are synonyms. The words spiral around the circle, one reading clockwise, the other reading counterclockwise.

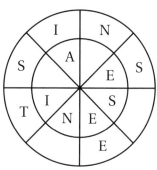

4   SILLY TREES is an anagram of what 10-letter word?

5

    What continues the above sequence?

     A   B   C   D   E

6 Which of the following is the missing segment?

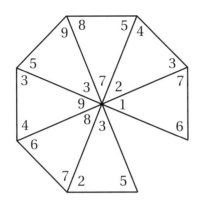 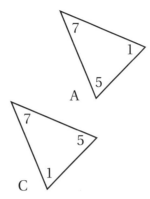 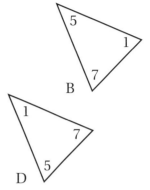

7 $76^2 - 75^2 = ?$

8 What two words that sound alike but are spelled differently mean MILITARY and ORGANIZE?

9 What shape is FASTIGIATE?

A. TAPERING TO A POINT   B. OVAL   C. HEXAGONAL   D. BOTTLE
E. HOOK

10

What continues the above sequence?

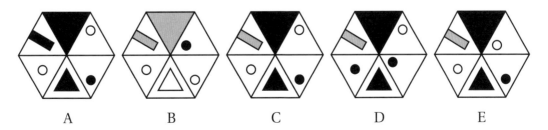

11 What phrase is represented by the following? Hint: Win some, lose some

FUNSTORE

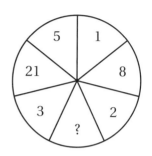

12 What number should logically replace the question mark?

13 Which is the odd one out?

OBOE, VIOLIN, TROMBONE, BASSOON, PICCOLO

14 Which two words below are opposite in meaning?

SPLENETIC, FEVERISH, HAPPY, MISGUIDED, DOMINEERING, POPULAR

15

H	S	G	H	T	Y	A	F	A
U	K	E	O	E	O	S	O	C

What nine-letter American city can be put in the boxes to make three-letters words reading down?

16 46. CONVECTION : HEAT ::

A. MAGNIFICATION : SIGHT   B. ILLUMINATION : LIGHT   C. SPECTRUM : WAVELENGTH   D. VOLUME : SOUND   E. ANOSMIA : SMELL

17 Which two words below are closest in meaning?

EGLANTINE, EGGLIKE, PATCHWORK, BRIER, HEATH, CHANGELING

18 What three-letter word can follow the first word and precede the second to make two new words or phrases?

HOG, PIN

19 586 : 46

374 : 25

Which numbers below have the same relationship to one another as the numbers above?

A. 246 : 48   B. 319 : 13   C. 642 : 20   D. 913 : 28   E. 832 : 26

20 Which circle should logically replace the question mark?

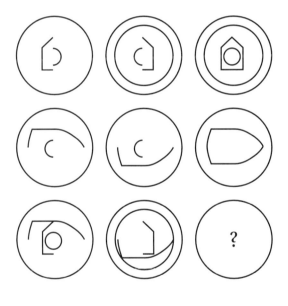

A   B   C   D   E

TEST 3

1. What number should logically replace the question mark?

   69723, 49887, 43463, 19909, ?

2. Fill in the blanks to make two words that are synonyms. The words spiral around the circle, one reading clockwise, the other reading counterclockwise.

   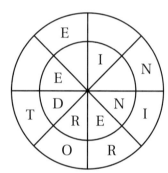

3. Rearrange the letters in the words below to spell out three colors.

   LOW ON BEANBURGER

4. What three-letter word can follow the first word and precede the second to make two new words or phrases?

   IMP, OR

5. NEAT SQUIRE is an anagram of what 10-letter word?

6. Which two words below are opposite in meaning?

   NAÏVE, HOPEFUL, SLY, BRAVE, SILLY, OPEN

7   Which of the five boxes on the right has the most in common with the box on the left?

   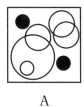   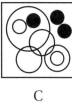   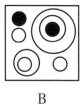

      A   B   C   D   E

8   What does LOGICAL mean?

    STRAIGHT, RATIONAL, CORRECT, PLAIN, or STRATEGIC

9   Which two words below are opposite in meaning?

    MAGICAL, DISMAL, SAGACIOUS, FOOLISH, PONDEROUS, GENEROUS

10 What two words that sound alike but are spelled differently mean CHANGE and COMMUNION TABLE?

11 Which is the odd one out?

            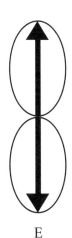

      A   B   C   D   E

12 Which of the following is not an anagram of a gem?

RIZNOC, MODNAID, NIZNAI, PIREHPSA, or THINCAJ

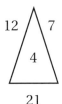 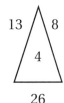 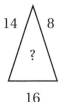

13 What number should logically replace the question mark?

14 Which word below is most likely to appear in a dictionary definition of EPOXY?

OXYGEN, GOLD, SILVER, BRONZE, or PLATINUM

15 What does HALBERD mean?

DRAGON, FISH, WEAPON, BIRD, or FLOWER

16 Which is the odd one out?

RUGBY, CRICKET, SOCCER, BASKETBALL, SWIMMING, TENNIS

17 Insert the letters below left into the blank spaces to create two words that are synonyms.

ECLLMNNRTU   _ A G _ _ _ I _   A _ _ _ _ I _ G

18 What number should logically replace the question mark?

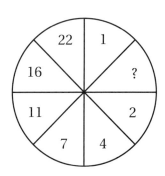

19 EMERALD : GREEN ::

A. TOPAZ : BLACK   B. JASPER : RED   C. OPAL : ORANGE

D. SAPPHIRE : BLUE   E. GARNET : YELLOW

20 Which is the odd one out?

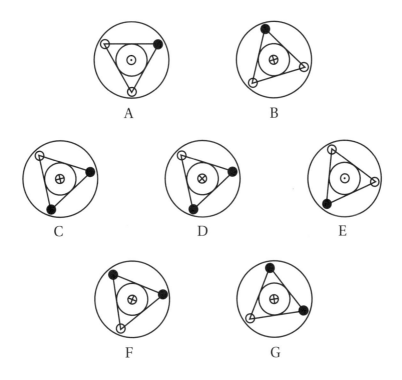

1 4839 : 5748 : 6657

Which numbers below have the same relationship to one another as the numbers above?

A. 7392 : 8273 : 9182   B. 4915 : 5824 : 6743   C. 9846 : 8827 : 7636

D. 3726 : 4635 : 5544   E. 4829 : 5738 : 7647

2 SENATE, PANAMA, DOSAGE, CURATE, BEFORE

Which word below logically belongs with the words above?

SIERRA, VOLUME, WAITER, SICKLE, or RHYTHM

3 Which two words below are closest in meaning?

PERFORM, COUNCIL, RECKON, CONCLAVE, ENDOW, MIRROR

4 Change one letter in each word of SIN ON O NUN to make a well-known phrase.

5 What letter should logically replace the question mark?

A	C	F
D	?	I
H	J	M

6 Rearrange the letters in the words below to spell out three dances.

BOWL MUG AT TARZAN

7 Fill in the blanks to make two words that are synonyms. The words spiral around the circle, one reading clockwise, the other reading counterclockwise.

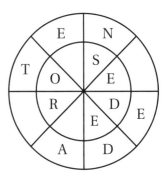

8 ENGINE : CABOOSE ::

A. BOOK : SPINE   B. MERCURY : VENUS   C. MARCH : MAY

D. ALPHA : OMEGA   E. FOLLOW : CONTINUE

9 Which is the odd one out?

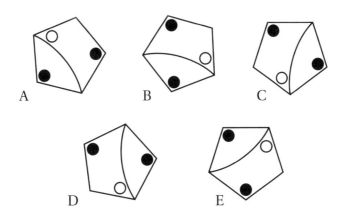

10 Which of the following is not an anagram of a cloud?

RUCSIR, STARSALTOUT, ADORNTO, LUSUMUC, or SUBMIN

11 Which is the odd one out?

PITTANCE, HEIST, FELONY, MISDEMEANOR, COUNTERFEITING

12 Which word below means a group of STUDENTS?

HARRAS, FRATERNITY, PLETHORA, or HILL

13 Which word below is most likely to appear in a dictionary definition of NEGUS?

WINE, MEDICINE, MILK, LICORICE, or AMBER

14

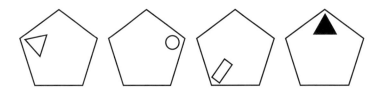

What continues the above sequence?

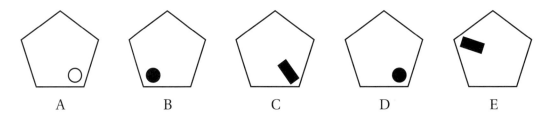

| A | B | C | D | E |

15 What does MAZARINE mean?

ORANGE, DEEP BLUE, GRAY, BROWN, or SILVERY PINK

16 What number should logically replace the question mark?

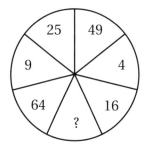

17 A farmer has 200 yards of fencing and wishes to enclose a rectangular area of the greatest possible size. How big will the area be?

A. 400 sq. yd.   B. 1000 sq. yd.   C. 2000 sq. yd.   D. 2500 sq. yd.   E. 4000 sq. yd.

18 What three-letter word can follow the first word and precede the second to make two new words or phrases?

STAND, HAND

19 Which two words below are opposite in meaning?

INFERNAL, COMMODIOUS, CRAMPED, GLORIOUS, DECOMPOSED, MAGNANIMOUS

20

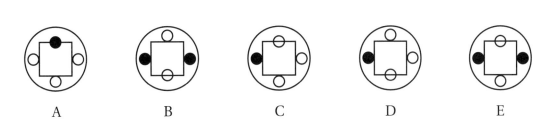

1 Fill in the blanks to make two words that are synonyms. The words spiral around the circle, one reading clockwise, the other reading counterclockwise.

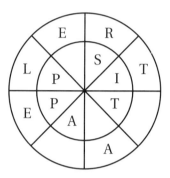

2 Insert the letters below left into the blank spaces to create two words that are antonyms.

BBEFLORSUX　　_ T _ _ B _ _ N　　_ L _ _ I _ _ E

3

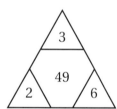 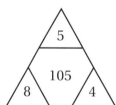 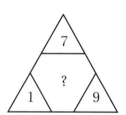

What number should logically replace the question mark?

4 Which is the odd one out?
   A. $\frac{75}{15} \infty 12$　B. $84 \infty \frac{7}{3} \infty \frac{3}{4}$　C. $78 \infty \frac{2}{4} \infty 3 - (11 \infty 25)$
   D. $(3^3 \infty 2) + 36$　E. $(80\% \infty 90) \infty 2 + 9$

5 Which two words below are opposite in meaning?

CONTEMPT, INCOMPETENT, RESTFUL, SINGULAR, INANE, ADEQUATE

6

What continues the above sequence?

A   B   C   D   E

7   Which two words below are opposite in meaning?

POSTPONE, COLLECT, ADVANCE, ADHERE, CHANGE, APPLY

8

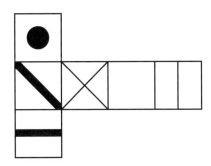

When the above is folded to form a cube, which one of the following can be produced?

A   B   C   D   E

9   SILK : GOSSAMER ::

A. LINEN : CHIFFON   B. COTTON : TAFFETA   C. JUTE : MUSLIN   D.
LATIN : ACRYLIC   E. WOOL : ANGORA

10 There are just seven letters that only appear exactly once in the grid. What U.S. geographical and biographical name can they be arranged to spell out?

L	V	C	G	T	Y	Q	J
F	I	U	P	G	A	W	F
Z	C	Y	R	K	E	H	S
H	O	J	W	Z	N	B	L
F	X	M	Q	G	P	V	U
T	B	E	K	X	R	D	C

11 What does INTAGLIO mean?

HAREM, RESTAURANT, CUT FIGURE, NARROW BOAT, or PICTURE

12 Which is the odd one out?

GRIDDLE, MICROWAVE, OVEN, REREDOS, ROTISSERIE, GRILL

13 What does EPOCH mean?

TIME FOR CELEBRATION, MEMORABLE DATE, HOLIDAY, REST, or BANQUET

14 What number should logically replace the question mark?

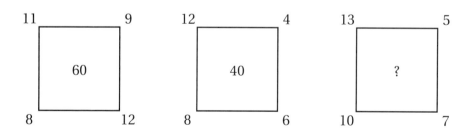

15 RIOTING OAR is an anagram of what 10-letter word?

16   What three-letter word can follow the first word and precede the second to make two new words or phrases?

SADDLE, LADY

17   3 – (7 + 5) – 2 ∞ 6 = ?

18   Combine two of the three-letter bits below to make a monster.

GIA, LOG, GON, RES, NUT, DRA

19   What two words that sound alike but are spelled differently mean THRASH and VEGETABLE?

20   Which circle should logically replace the question mark?

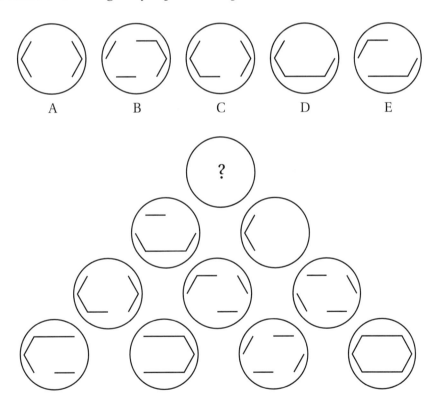

A   B   C   D   E

1   What three-letter word can precede all of the following words to make new words?
    TIES, TRY, ACHE

2   What word that means UNIVERSAL becomes a word meaning HUMOROUS when a letter is removed?

3
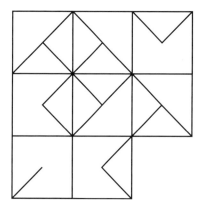

Which square below logically belongs in the lower right space above?

    A   B   C   D   E

4   Fill in the blanks to make two words that are antonyms. The words spiral around the circle, one reading clockwise, the other reading counterclockwise.

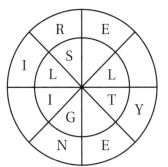

5   What number should logically replace the question mark?

7
23
71

11
36
111

17
?
169

6   RENT DEBATE is an anagram of what female given name?

7   Which two words below are closest in meaning?

DIP, SATURATE, DRAIN, DOUSE, STAIN, CLOY

8   Fill in the blanks, one letter per blank, to create a common word.

_ _ _ W A W A _

9

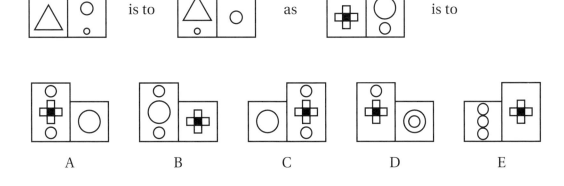

10 What six-letter word has STRAIGHTFORWARD and COMMAND as meanings?

11 What does KIBITZER mean?

MEAL, PORTRAIT, DRINK, REFUGE, or ONLOOKER

12 What two words that sound alike but are spelled differently mean MODEST and PUR-SUED?

13 Which is the odd one out?

POEM, PERSIMMON, HEPTASTICH, VERSE, QUATRAIN

14 What number should logically replace the question mark?

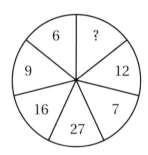

15 How many different teams of five people can be made from nine people?

16 Which two words below are opposite in meaning?

MANLY, DEXTERITY, RESPECTFUL, CLUMSINESS, INCOGNITO, WATCHFUL

17 What phrase is represented by the following? Hint: New attitude

EARTH

18 Which of the following is not an anagram of a tree?

RAPPOL, LOWLIW, LOWLIP, CHARL, or REDOAD

19 6589 : 1414 : 28

Which numbers below have the same relationship to one another as the numbers above?

A. 4839 : 2161 : 14   B. 7836 : 1590 : 69   C. 8526 : 1470 : 1011

D. 9909 : 5112 : 76   E. 3798 : 1215 : 27

20 Each line and symbol that appears in the four outer circles above is transferred to the center circle according to these rules:

If the line or symbol occurs in the outer circles

one time, it is transferred, two times, it is possibly transferred, three times, it is transferred, and four times, it is not transferred.

Which of the circles below should appear at the center of the diagram?

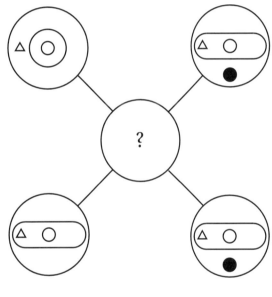

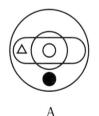 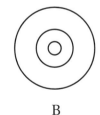 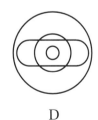 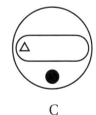 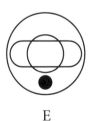

A   B   C   D   E

1

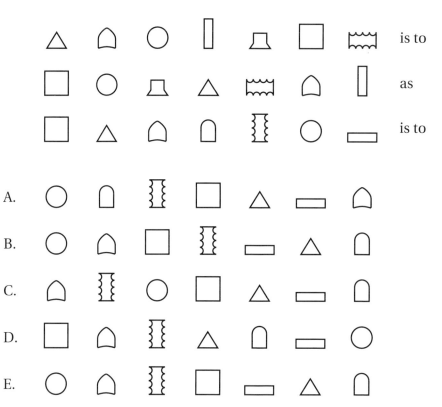

2   What two words that sound alike but are spelled differently mean
    VERGE and GROANED?

3   Which word below is most likely to appear in a dictionary definition of BUCKRAM?
    LINEN, GLASS, COPPER, LACE, or WOOL

4

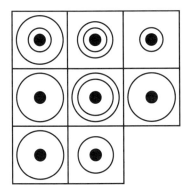

Which square below logically belongs in the lower right space above?

     A   B   C   D   E

5   What does FRANCHISE mean?

FRENCH FOOD, LICENSE TO MARKET, ABILITY, DEVOTION, or HATRED

6   What four-letter word can follow the first word and precede the second to make two new words or phrases?

PATCH, WEEK

7   BERRY, COST, KNOT, HINT

Which word below logically belongs with the words above?

FORD, DIRT, WAGE, PARTY, or SHY

8   Start at any letter and move from square to square horizontally or vertically, but not diagonally, to spell out a 12-letter word. You must provide the missing letters.

I		T
D	E	E
I		R
N	T	E

9   What number should logically replace the question mark?

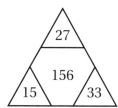 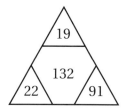 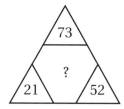

10   What letter is two to the right of the letter that is four to the left of the letter that is immediately to the right of the letter that is three to the left of the letter H?

A B C D E F G H

11   Take one letter, in order, from each of the antonyms of SEVERE given below to form another antonym.

TRACTABLE, GENIAL, EASY, MANAGEABLE, GENTLE, COMPASSIONATE, LENIENT

12   What number should logically replace the question mark?

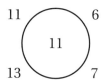 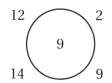 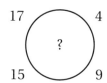

13   The letters below represent a phrase where the initial letters of each word and the spaces have been removed. What is the phrase?

POATE

14   Which two words below are opposite in meaning?

PENITENT, ASTRINGENT, SALUBRIOUS, SEPARATING, PURPOSEFUL, TRI-UMPHANT

15 What five-letter word has BANTER and HUSKS as meanings?

16 Which is the odd one out?

ICOSAHEDRON, PRISM, CYLINDER, HEXAGON, DODECAHEDRON

17 Fill in the blanks to make two words that are synonyms. The words spiral around the circle, one reading clockwise, the other reading counterclockwise.

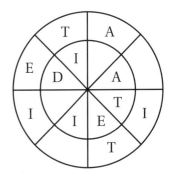

18 Combine two of the three-letter bits below to make a wrestling hold.

HEA, ARM, LOK, SON, LOC, NEL

19 Which two words below are closest in meaning?

CIRRUS, PENINSULAR, COL, SAND BAR, DEPRESSION, MISTRAL

20 Each of the nine squares in the grid marked from 1A to 3C should incorporate all of the lines and symbols that are in the squares of the same letter and number at the top and on the left. For example, 3B should incorporate all the lines and symbols that are in boxes 3 and B. Which one square is incorrect?

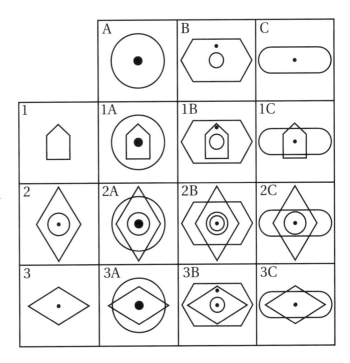

1 Fill in the blanks to make two words that are synonyms. The words spiral around the circle, one reading clockwise, the other reading counterclockwise.

2 What number should logically replace the question mark?

237 : 4280 : 582

863 : 14424 : 416

523 : ? : 826

3 Which of the following is not an anagram of a composer?

A. SCI SOAP

B. IS IRONS

C. COLD PAN

D. WE RANG

E. MR. HALE

4   Which of the five boxes on the right has the most in common with the box on the left?

   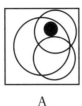 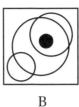  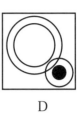 

A   B   C   D   E

5   What numbers should logically replace the question marks?

3	6	?	330
2	5	?	41

6   Insert the correct pair of words into the blank spaces in the sentence below.

The problem with the use of ___ is that they are often only ___ by the person using them.

A. COMPUTERS, ACCESSED

B. ABBREVIATIONS, UNDERSTOOD

C. ANAGRAMS, TRANSLATED

D. WORDS, SPOKEN

E. EPITAPHS, APPRECIATED

7   RUDE TAVERN is an anagram of what 10-letter word?

8   Which number is the odd one out?

67626, 84129, 36119, 25622, 32418

9   Which two words below are closest in meaning?

LIBERTINE, EPHEMERAL, BRIEF, PLACID, IMMORTAL, PRECISE

10 Which is the odd one out?

DOE, JENNY, COB, EWE, SOW

11 What two words that sound alike but are spelled differently mean SASH and COMBI-NATION OF NOTES?

12 What seven-letter word has DIVISION OF BOOK and RELIGIOUS MEETING as meanings?

13 What number should logically replace the question mark?

  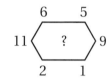

14 Which word below is most likely to appear in a dictionary definition of BISQUE?

BISCUITS, CUSTARD, PLUMS, CHICKEN, or SOUP

15 Which two words below are opposite in meaning?

POPULATED, DIMINUTIVE, DEVOTION, GARGANTUAN, DEVOID, SUCCESSFUL

16 Combine two of the three-letter bits below to make a dance.

TOT, TEZ, ANE, WAL, PAV, FOX

17 $\dfrac{3 + 6 \times 2}{3 + 2 \times 3} = ?$

18 What does KELP mean?

DRINK, SWOLLEN FEET, SEAWEED, SCAR, or MUSICAL PIECE

19 Which is the odd one out?

PEPPERONI, SAUSAGE, SAUERKRAUT, CHIPOLATA, KNOCKWURST

20 Which circle should logically replace the question mark?

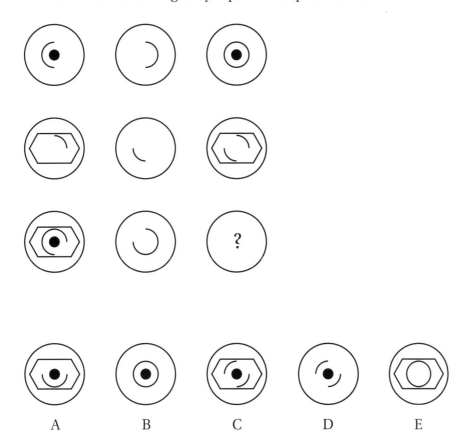

A   B   C   D   E

1 Which is the odd one out?

    A   B   C   D   E

2 TRIANGLE : HEXAGON :

A. SQUARE : PENTAGON   B. PENTAGON : HEPTAGON

C. HEXAGON : OCTAGON   D. SQUARE : OCTAGON   E. CIRCLE : PENTAGON

3 What is the result of multiplying the sum of the odd numbers in the left-hand grid by the sum of the even numbers in the right-hand grid?

28	16	5	36
22	6	2	4
9	18	3	42
17	1	6	15

4	37	10	1
3	2	15	7
14	17	19	9
5	32	23	8

4 FAME, BID, POUND, LAND, REMIT

Which word below logically continues the sequence of words above?

CREST, BOUND, GRUNT, CHARGE, or FLOAT

5

What continues the above sequence?

A   B   C   D   E

6   What number should logically replace the question mark?

6	8	12
10	2	5
15	4	?

7   ACCORD TIME is an anagram of what 10-letter word?

8   Which word below is an antonym of INTELLIGIBLE?

PROFLIGATE, LUCID, STUPID, PLAIN, or CONFUSED

9   Change one letter in each word of COME GAS LOT GUILT AN I PAY to make a well-known phrase.

10   What four-letter word has REMAINDER and REPOSE as meanings?

11 What does FRISSON mean?

CANNON, THUNDERBOLT, CREVICE, THRILL, or ESCARPMENT

12 What number should logically replace the question mark?

$26, -39, 58\frac{1}{2}, -87\frac{3}{4}, ?$

13 What six-letter word can follow the first word and precede the second to make two new words or phrases?

POST, CHEF

14 What number should logically replace the question mark?

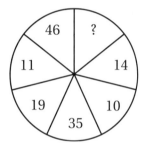

15 Which two words below are closest in meaning?

PAWNBROKER, DRAGOMAN, CHARLATAN, TRADER, ARTIST, INTERPRETER

16 What two words that sound alike but are spelled differently mean TREE and SHORE?

17 Which is the odd one out?

TANKER, CLIPPER, GALLEON, SLOOP, CARAVEL

18 What four-letter word has GOSSIP and BIRD as meanings?

19 Which of the following is not an anagram of a flower?

ADFFODLI, PULTI, LIDLAIOG, TUBERT, or NASPY

20 Which circle should logically replace the question mark?

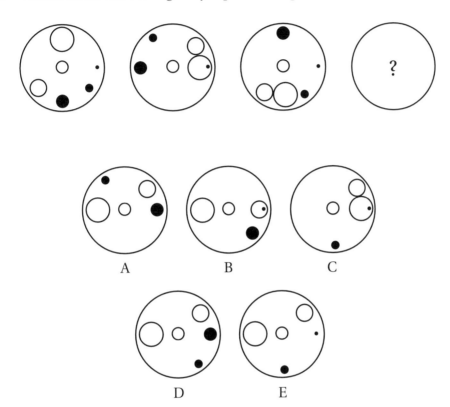

A   B   C

D   E

1 Which is the odd one out?

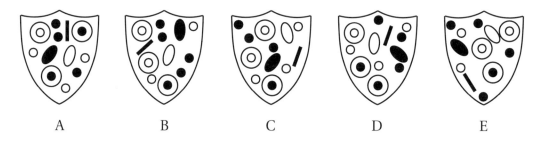

A   B   C   D   E

2 Fill in the blanks to make two words that are antonyms. The words spiral around the circle, one reading clockwise, the other reading counterclockwise.

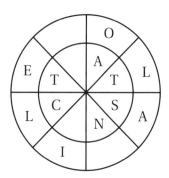

3 What number should logically replace the question mark?

14, 91, 62, 53, 64, ?

A. 78   B. 96   C. 98   D. 68   E. 44

4 GET SOUSING is an anagram of what 10-letter word?

5   Which word below is an antonym of OPTIMUM?

    GLUM, MINIMAL, MANDATORY, DISTANT, or CLOSE

6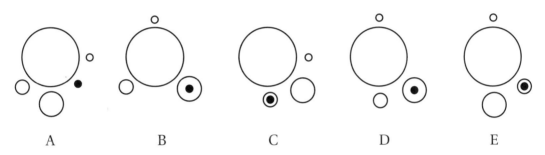

    What continues the above sequence?

    A   B   C   D   E

7   SEISMOLOGY : EARTHQUAKES

    A. CARPOLOGY : MAPS

    B. DENDROLOGY : WIND

    C. OROLOGY : MOUNTAINS

    D. DELTIOLOGY : ROCKS

    E. TOPOGRAPHY : CAVES

8   Starting at one of the corner squares, what nine-letter word
    can be formed by spiraling clockwise around the perimeter
    and finishing at the center square. (You must provide the
    missing letters.)

E	R	
		H
O	L	E

9   What letter should logically replace the question mark?

A, D, F, I, K, ?

10   What two words that sound alike but are spelled differently mean FABRICATE and INVOICED?

11   What four-letter word has STEEL INSTRUMENT and FOLDER as meanings?

12   What number should logically replace the question mark?

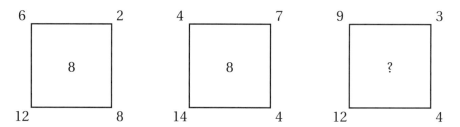

13   Which is the odd one out?

TYPHOON, FAVEOLATE, HURRICANE, MISTRAL, PAMPERO

14   Which two words below are opposite in meaning?

LANCINATE, THOUGHTFUL, DEMONIC, CONSIDERATE, MEND

15   Which of the following is not an anagram of a vegetable?

TATOOP, BAGCABE, OUTSPRS, GENORA, RORCAT

16   What eight-letter musical instrument can be put in the boxes to make three-letters words reading down?

P	F	A	L	O	H	O	M
A	L	L	A	B	E	W	A

17   Three coins are tossed in the air at the same time. What are the chances that at least two of the coins will finish heads up?

18   What does JENNY mean?

YOUNG DEER, STAMP, FEMALE DONKEY, BRIDGE SUPPORT, or STOAT

19   What four-letter word can follow the first word and precede the second to make two new words or phrases?

CAST, FILINGS

20   Which circle should logically replace the question mark?

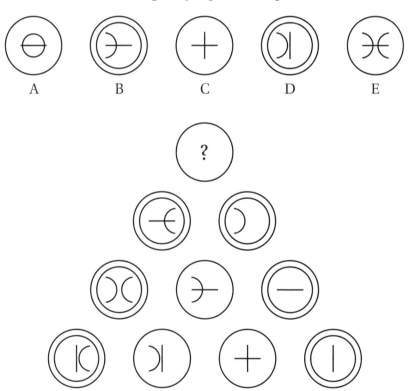

A   B   C   D   E

1 What number should logically replace the question mark?

15		17
	3	
8		12

54		74
	4	
14		39

21		89
	?	
56		18

2 What six-letter creature can be put in the boxes to make three-letters words reading down?

L	D	M	A	P	H
O	U	A	S	I	E

3 Which is the odd one out?

A   B   C   D   E

4 Which two words below are closest in meaning?

INCIDENTAL, INVASIVE, INAUGURAL, INTRINSIC, BOLD, NATIVE

5 Which is the odd one out?

APRIL, SEPTEMBER, NOVEMBER, AUGUST, JUNE

6 LARBOARD : SHIP :: VERSO :

A. POEM   B. CAR   C. TRUNK   D. PORT   E. BOOK

7 What number should logically replace the question mark?

4	5	9	4	2
8	6	2	6	4
2	3	?	2	7
7	1	2	3	5
3	8	3	6	2

8 Fill in the blanks with a part of the human body, one letter per blank, to create a common word.

C A _ _ _ E R

9

What continues the above sequence?

A   B   C   D   E

10　POLICE SECT is an anagram of what 10-letter word?

11　A man has four socks in his drawer. Each sock is either black or white. The chances of him selecting a pair at random and finding that he has a white pair is 0.5. What are his chances of the pair being black?

12　Which of the following is not an anagram of a boat?
LEVACAR, ONCAE, CHUNAL, RUTCK, or ERSCRUI

13　What does MOLLIFY mean?
TRANSFORM, CHANGE, APPEASE, ENJOIN, or SOLIDIFY

14　What four-letter word has FERMENTED LIQUOR and LEA as meanings?

15　What does KOOKABURRA mean?
KINGFISHER, NATIVE OF GUINEA, DINGHY, WATERFALL, or HUT

16　What four-letter word can precede all of the following words to make new words?
BALL, MAIDEN, SOME, CART, BILL

17　Combine two of the three-letter bits below to make another name for Japan.
PON, EAS, PAM, NIP, ISL, JAN

18　Fill in the blanks to make two words that are synonyms. The words spiral around the circle, one reading clockwise, the other reading counterclockwise.

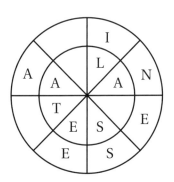

19 Which word below is most likely to appear in a dictionary definition of
    GALANTINE?

    LARD, PASTA, VINEGAR, BREAD, or MEAT

20 Each line and symbol that appears in the four outer circles above is transferred to
    the center circle according to these rules:

    If the line or symbol occurs in the outer circles
    one time, it is transferred,
    two times, it is possibly transferred,
    three times, it is transferred, and
    four times, it is not transferred.

    Which of the circles below should
    appear at the center of the diagram?

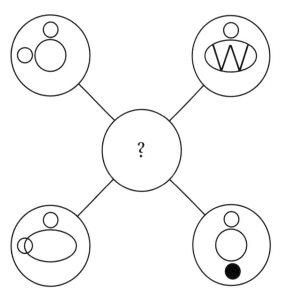

   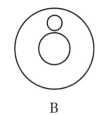   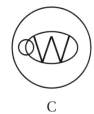   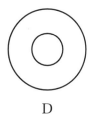   

   A   B   C   D   E

1 Which four of the five figures below can be joined together to form a perfect square?

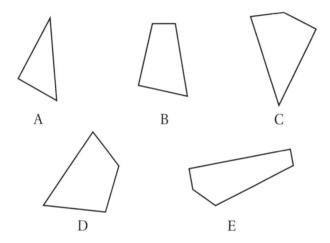

A   B   C

D   E

2 FLEW POLISH is an anagram of what 10-letter word?

3 97318462 : 86719243 :: 43967512 :

A. 13675942   B. 71364259   C. 71346295   D. 17634259   E. 71364529

4 Which of the following is not an anagram of a musical instrument?

ON CERT, AS BOSON, LIP COCO, ARTISAN, or ACID CROON

5 Which two words below are opposite in meaning?

SLANT, PLETHORA, PREDICAMENT, PLIGHT, DEARTH, AIGRETTE

6 Which is the odd one out?

      A   B   C   D   E

7 What number should logically replace the question mark?

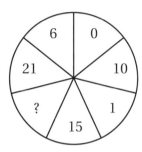

8 What does SUPPLANT mean?

PLIANT, FIX, OUST, AUGMENT, or SUSTAIN

9 Change one letter in each word of DON'S MAKE CHANGES to make a well-known phrase.

10 Fill in the blanks to make two words that are synonyms. The words spiral around the circle, one reading clockwise, the other reading counterclockwise.

11 What number should logically replace the question mark?

12, 33, 66, 132, 363, ?

12 What word is represented by the following? Hint: Pure

13 Which is the odd one out?

GASKIN, STIFLE, HOCK, FETLOCK, GIBUS

14 What does FORAY mean?

RETREAT, REBEL, SHIRK, PILLAGE, or MAGNIFY

15 Which word below is most likely to appear in a dictionary definition of PONGEE?

GABARDINE, SILK, TWEED, LACE, or LEATHER

16 What four-letter word can precede all of the following words to make new words?

FALL, MILL, WARD, SWEPT, BREAKER

17 Which of the following is not an anagram of a form of transportation?

INATR, BINMOUS, LECYC, MART, or RUGAS

18 What does CHICANERY mean?

TORTUOUS, BOASTFULNESS, OPPORTUNISM, TRICKERY, or VISION

19 What four-letter word has PARASITE and MATTRESS COVER as meanings?

20 Each line and symbol that appears in the four outer circles above is transferred to the center circle according to these rules:

If the line or symbol occurs in the outer circles
one time, it is transferred,
two times, it is possibly transferred,
three times, it is transferred, and
four times, it is not transferred.

Which of the circles below should appear at the center of the diagram?

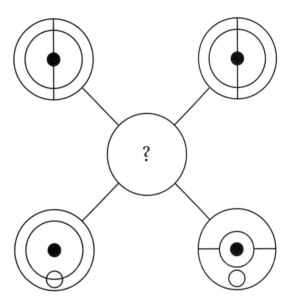

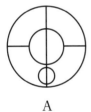

A

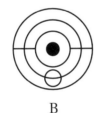

B

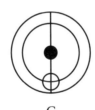

C

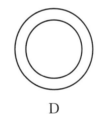

D

E

1   Fill in the blanks to make two words that are synonyms. The words spiral around the circle, one reading clockwise, the other reading counterclockwise.

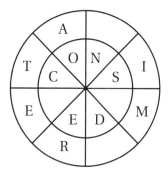

2   HOTEL NOOSE is an anagram of what well-known phrase? Hint: Fugitive

3   3469 : 3515 : 3566

Which numbers below have the same relationship to one another as the numbers above?

A. 5783 : 5861 : 5947   B. 7842 : 7914 : 8361   C. 4821 : 4842 : 4884

D. 9817 : 9899 : 9967   E. 1236 : 1248 : 1260

4   Take one letter, in order, from each of the synonyms of COMPETENT given below to form another synonym.

APPROPRIATE, CLEVER, DEXTROUS, FIT, QUALIFIED, SUFFICIENT, PRACTICED, ABLE, ENDOWED, SUITABLE

5   What four-letter word has SLIDE and UNDERWEAR as meanings?

6   Which is the odd one out?

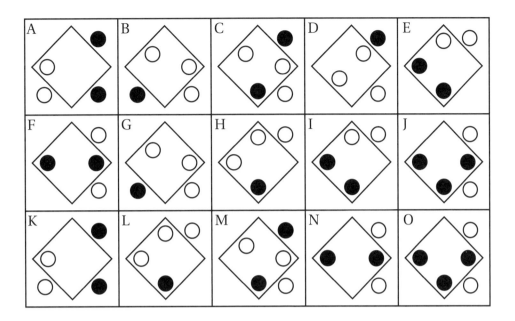

7   What four-letter word can follow the first word and precede the second to make two new words or phrases?

SO, RATE

8   What does LATENT mean?

WORTHY, VEILED, LATTERLY, FLANKING, or EVIDENT

9   Which is the odd one out?

ETHER, VACUUM, WELKIN, NEOPHYTE, SKY

10   On Digital Avenue, houses are numbered consecutively, starting at 1. There is only one house on the street that has a house number where the sum of the digits is exactly twice the product of the digits. What is that number, and what is the greatest number of houses that there could be on Digital Avenue?

11

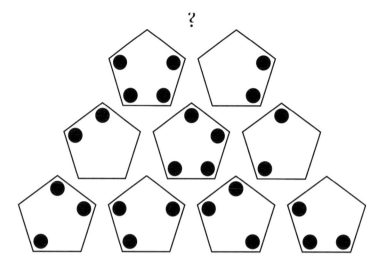

Which pentagon should logically replace the question mark?

A   B   C   D   E

12 What number should logically replace the question mark?

5	7	6	8
6	2	5	1
?	4	9	5
3	5	2	4

13 What does PALFREY mean?

BIRD, REPTILE, INSECT, FISH, or HORSE

14 Which two words below are closest in meaning?

CRISTATE, CROSSED, MORIBUND, ELEVATED, TUFTED, CRYSTALLIZED

15 What two words that sound alike but are spelled differently mean BARTER and SMALL ROOM?

16 Which of the following is not an anagram of a fish?

WALLSOW, TRUBTO, DERFOULN, CAPLIE, or DAHDCKO

17 What does CORDATE mean?

HEART-SHAPED, PEAR-SHAPED, LEMON-SHAPED, CYLINDRICAL, or DYNAMIC

18 Combine two of the three-letter bits below to make a word meaning mud.

DGE, MIR, SWA, MPE, ESE, SLU

19 What three-letter word can precede all of the following words to make new words?

DATE, DRILL, DRAKE, KIND, GO

20 Which circle should logically replace the question mark?

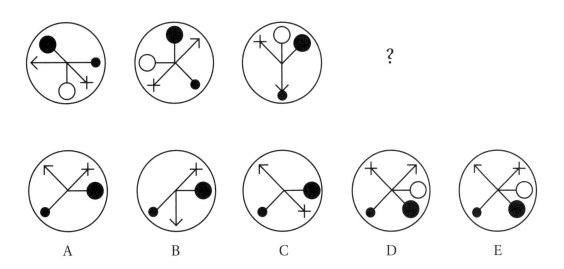

A   B   C   D   E

Math & Logic Puzzles

Black and White

Each square in the grids below will contain either a black or white circle. When filled in correctly, there will be a single connected group of white circles and a single connected group of black circles in the grid. Cells are connected horizontally and vertically, but not diagonally. Nowhere in the grid can there be a two-by-two group of squares all containing the same color circles.

ANSWERS, PAGE 288

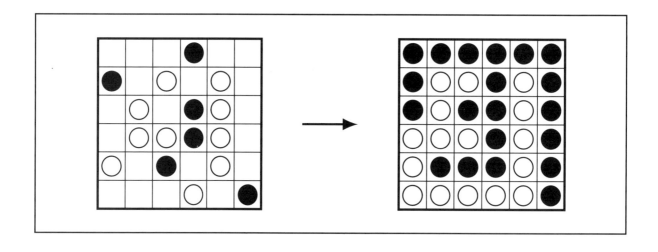

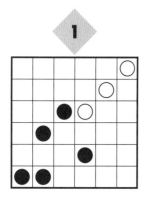

1

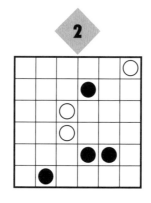

2

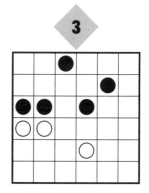

3

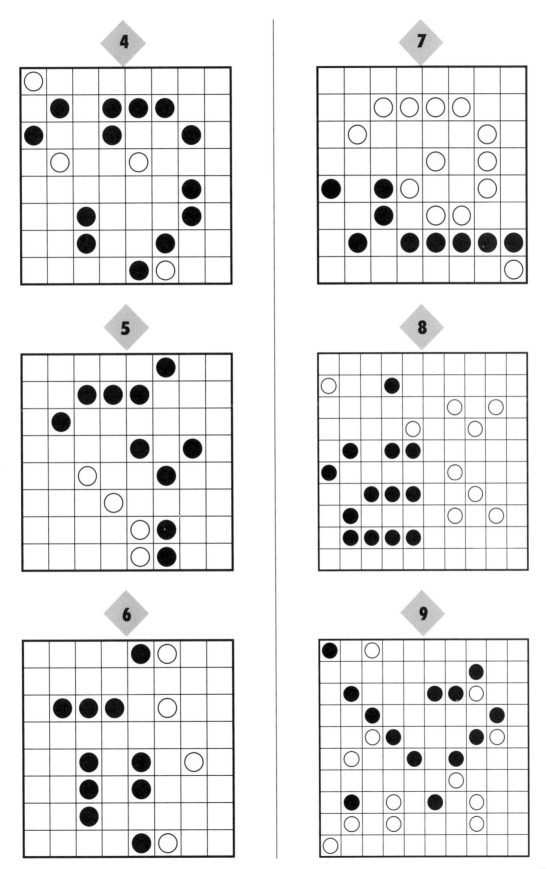

Worms

There are worms crawling about in the diagrams below. The body of the worm (from the head to the tail) travels through a chain of adjacent triangles. Your task is to find the exact path of the body. The body never crosses itself nor doubles back on itself. Triangles with numbers in them indicate the number of adjacent triangles that the worm travels through. Triangles are adjacent only if they share a side. The worm cannot pass through a numbered triangle.

ANSWERS, PAGE 288

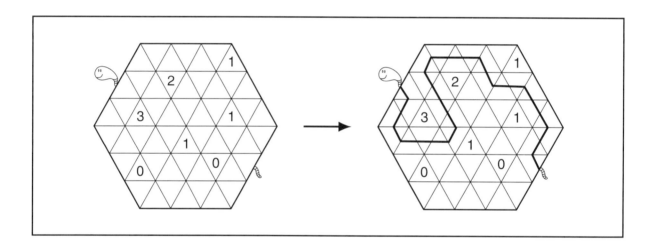

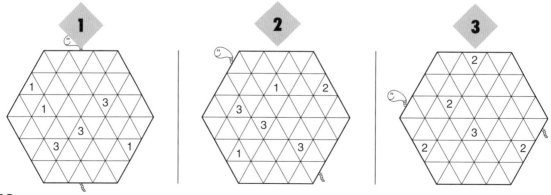

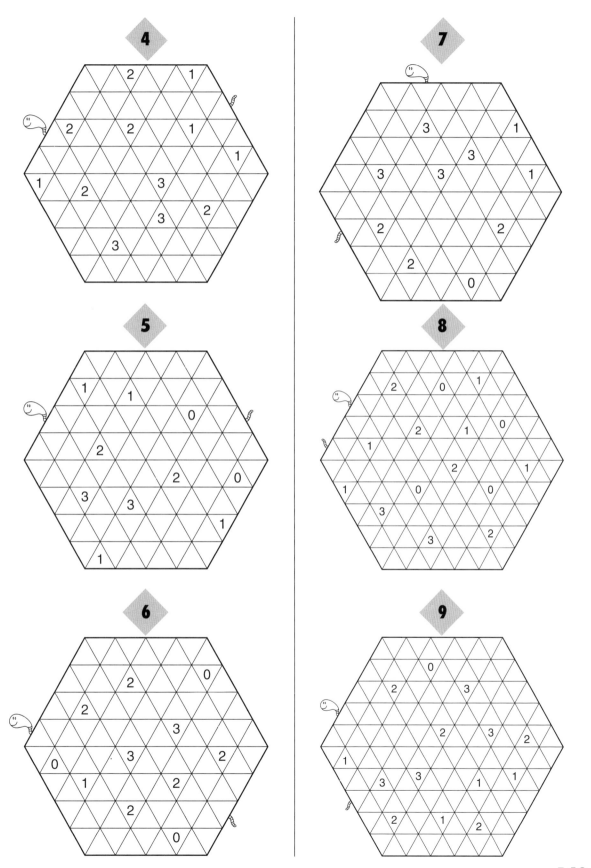

143

Minesweeper

Ten land mines, each of which occupies one grid cell, have been placed in the grids below, and it is your task to find them. The cells with numbers in them indicate the number of mines in the eight squares adjacent to that cell horizontally, vertically, and diagonally. Numbered cells cannot contain mines.

ANSWERS, PAGE 289

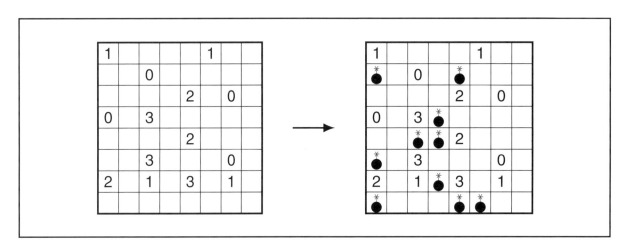

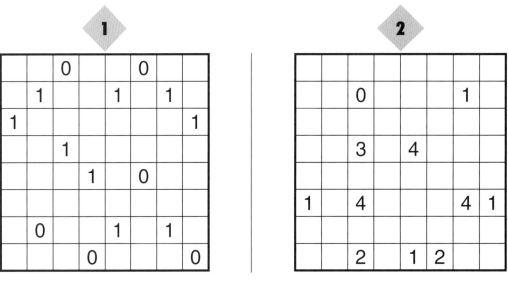

3

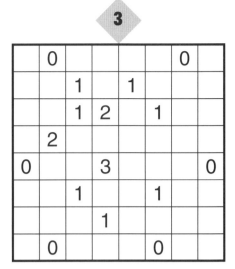

	0				0	
		1		1		
		1	2		1	
	2					
0			3			0
		1			1	
			1			
	0			0		

6

				0		
				2		
2		2				
			2	2		2
		2				
2				2		2
	2					
				2	2	

4

1		2		2			
	2					1	1
1				2			
1		2			1		
1	2	1			1		1
			2				
			1		2		

7

	2		2		2		1
		4	4		3		3
	2				2		
			2				

5

			3				
							2
		3			3		
2				2			
				3			
		2				2	

8

1					1		
	1	2		1		3	
		1					
			1	1			2
	1			1			
0					1		
	3		2		1	1	
							1

9

			2				
		2					
	2		1		2		
2							
		1			1		2
		2				2	
					2		
				2		1	

12

	2			0		2	
					0		
0		1	2		1	2	2
	2	1	2		2		2
			0		1		
1							2
	0			0			1

10

1		1					1
	1	1	1	1	1		1
1		1					1
	1			1		1	
	1			1			1
		1				1	
1							1
	1		1		1		

13

0		1		0			1
		1			1		
						1	
	3		2		1		0
					2		
		1	3				
	0					0	

11

	3	3	3				
			3		3		
		2		1		2	
				3			

14

	2						
2				2			
		2				1	
			3				
2		2					
			2			2	1
0						1	

15

		0					
	0						
		3					
	2			1		3	
		2	4				
	0					0	

16

1	1	2	3		1		
					1		
	1		3	3			
			2			0	
					1		
			1	1	2	3	

17

						1	
	2	2	2	2	2	2	
		2	2	2	2	2	
							1
			2				
				2			

18

		2		1		3	
		1		2			
	0			1			2
	1		3		1		
		2			1		
	1		3		2		

19

1		1					
	2						
			4	4			
			4	4			
	2						
	1						

20

			3	3			
			3		3		
			3		3		2
			3	3			
					3		

Lighthouses

There are ten ships hidden in each grid. Each ship occupies one of the squares in the grid. Lighthouses, which are numbered squares, have been placed in the grid. No ship can be adjacent horizontally, vertically, or diagonally to another ship or a lighthouse. The number in each lighthouse is the total number of ships seen in the row and column that the lighthouse illuminates (ships do not "block" other ships from being seen; that is, all ships in the row and column of the lighthouse are "seen.") Ships can't occupy spaces with water (wavy lines). Armed with this information, can you locate all of the ships?

ANSWERS, PAGE 290

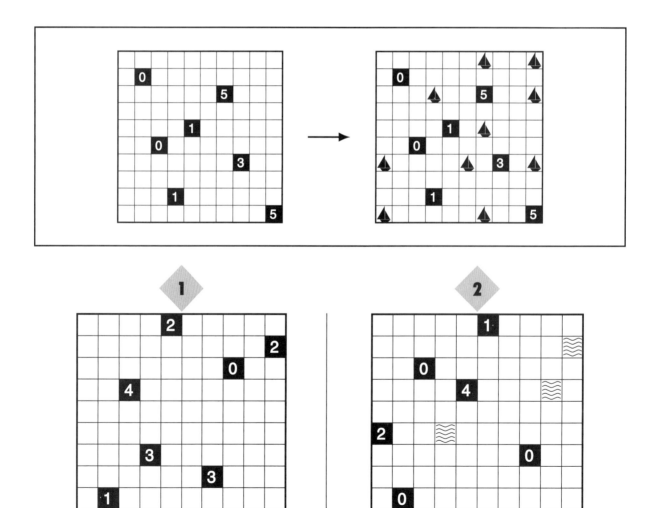

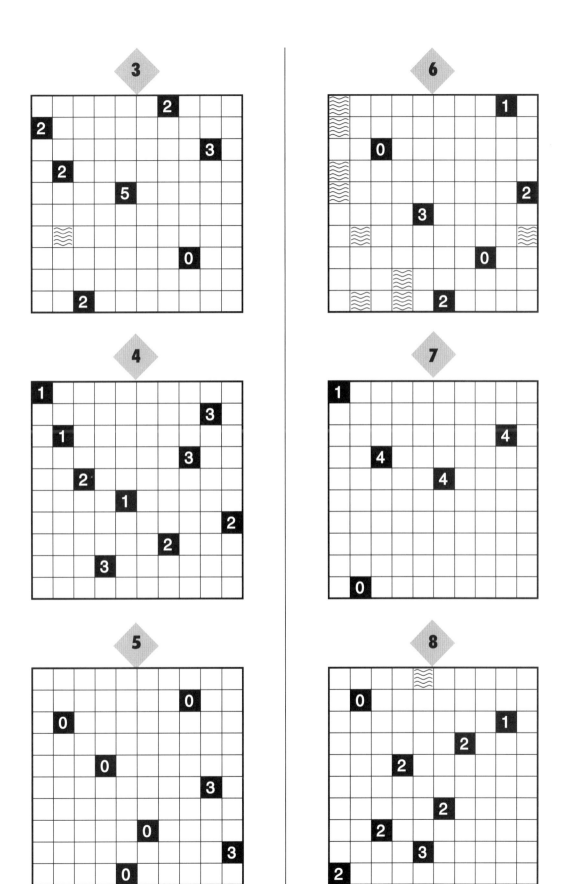

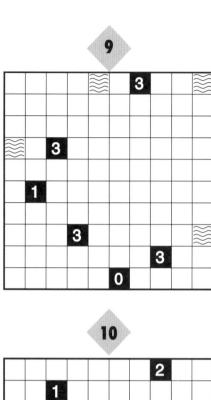

9

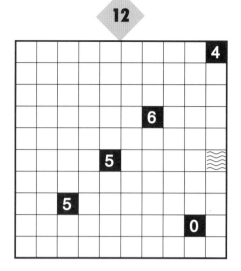

12

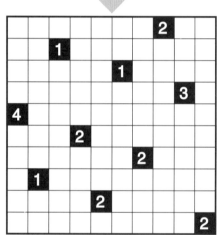

10

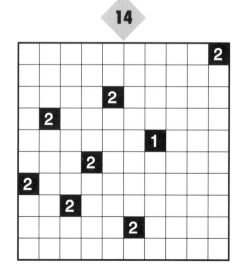

13

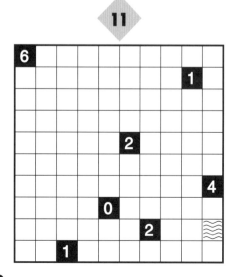

11

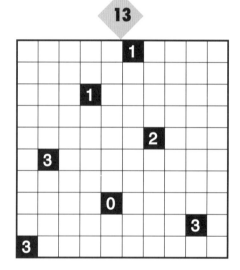

14

15

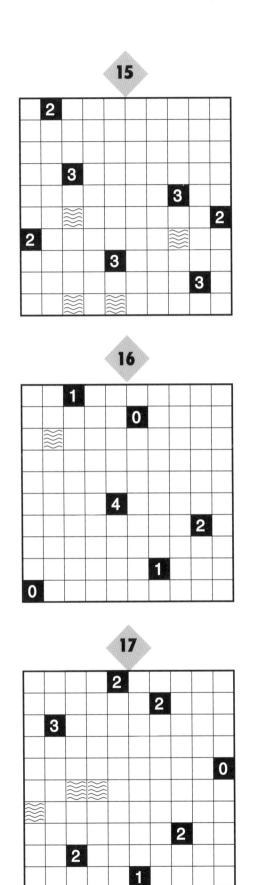

16

17

18

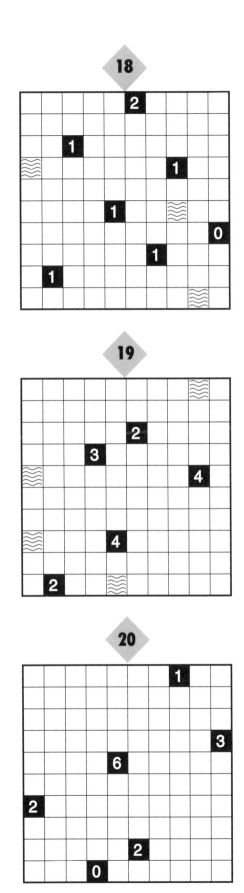

19

20

Hex Loops

Find a path that travels from hexagon to hexagon, ends where it started, and never touches or crosses itself. The path can only pass from one hexagon to another if they share a side, and the path may not make a "sharp" turn of 60°. The numbers placed in some of the hexagons indicate the number of adjacent hexagons through which the path passes. The path cannot pass through a numbered hexagon.

ANSWERS, PAGE 291

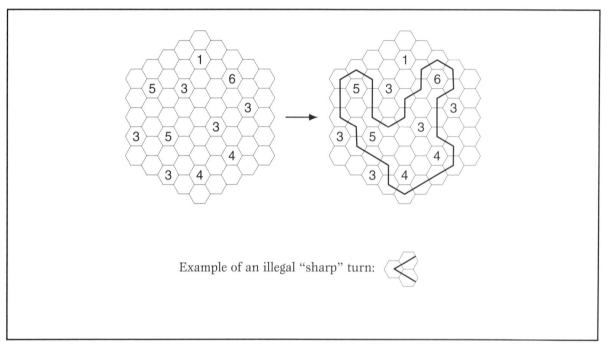

Example of an illegal "sharp" turn:

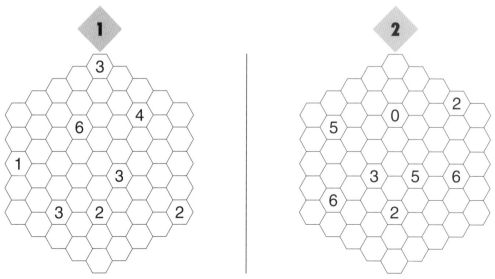

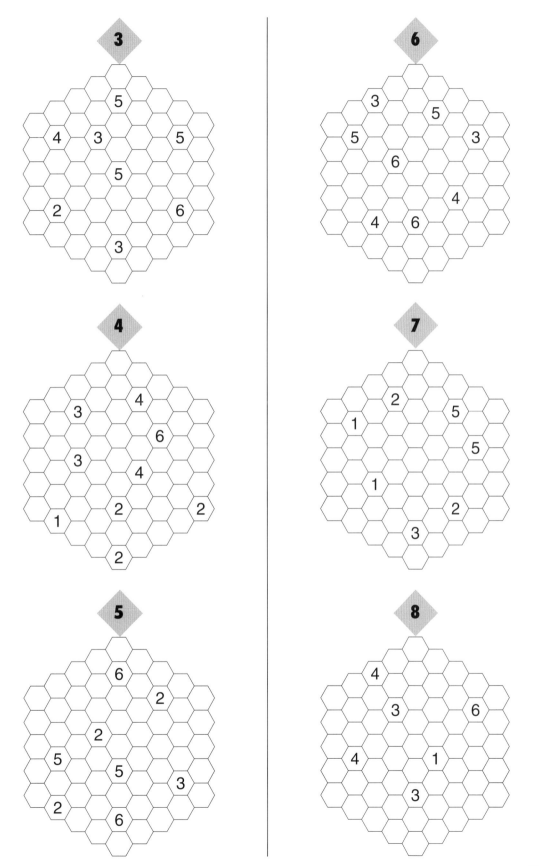

Square Routes

Each of the grids below contains a path that passes through every square exactly once, ends where it begins, and never crosses itself. The path travels horizontally and vertically but not diagonally. The path must also make a right-angled turn whenever it crosses through a light gray square, and must continue straight when it passes through a dark gray square. Can you deduce what the path is for each grid?

ANSWERS, PAGES 291-292

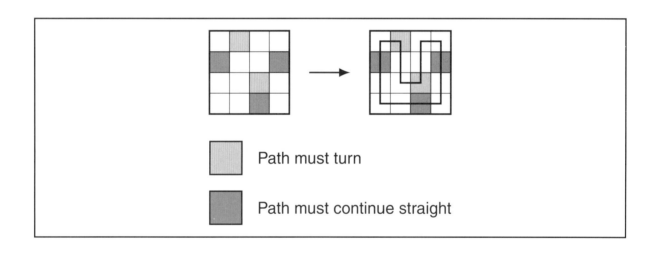

Path must turn

Path must continue straight

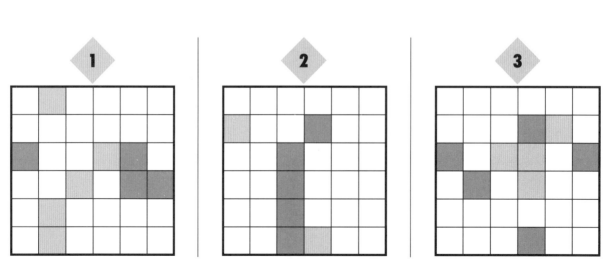

1

2

3

4

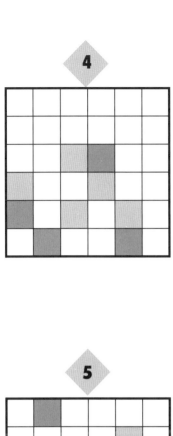

7

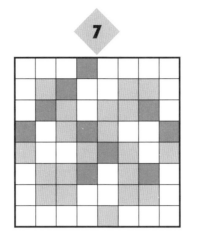

10

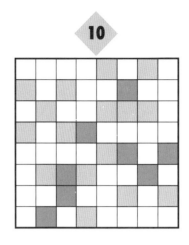

5

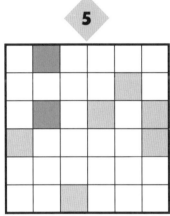

8

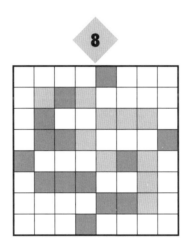

11

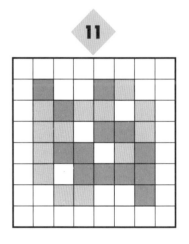

6

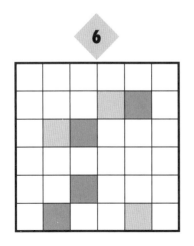

9

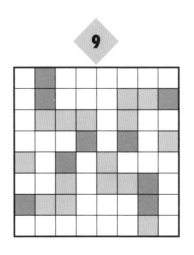

12

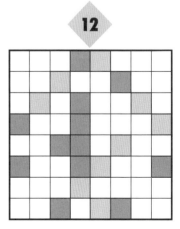

13

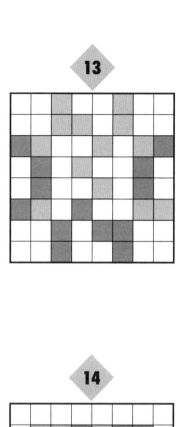

16

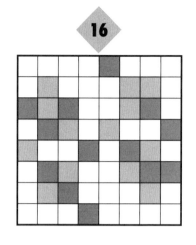

19

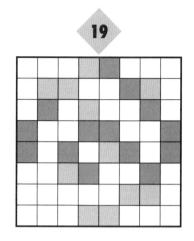

14

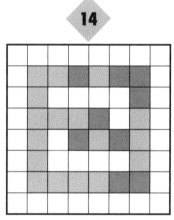

17

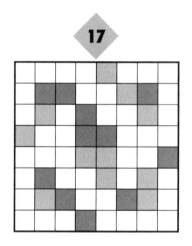

20

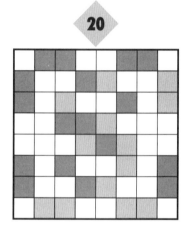

15

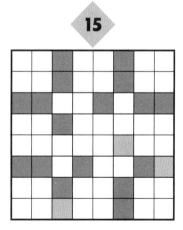

18

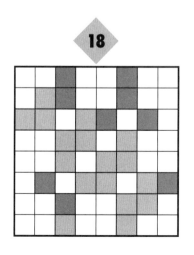

21

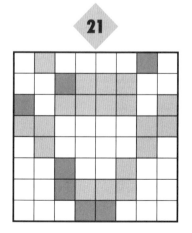

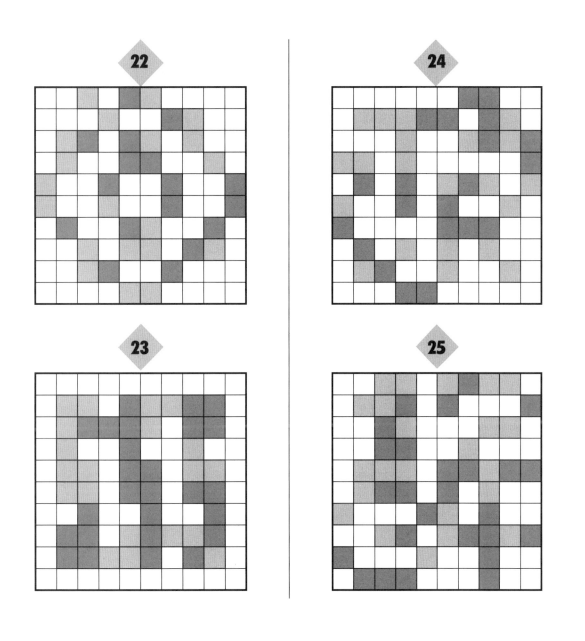

| | Path must turn |
| | Path must continue straight |

Spokes

There are spokes missing between adjacent hubs in the diagrams below. The hubs are adjacent horizontally, vertically, and diagonally. The number on each hub indicates the number of spokes that are connected to that hub. Also, no spoke is allowed to intersect another spoke.

ANSWERS, PAGES 292-294

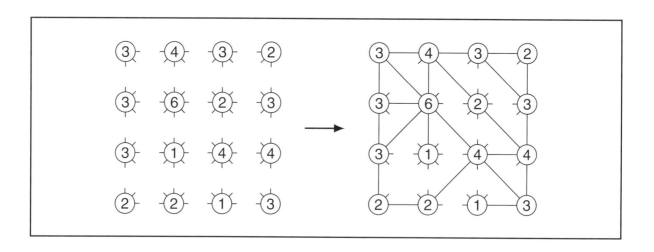

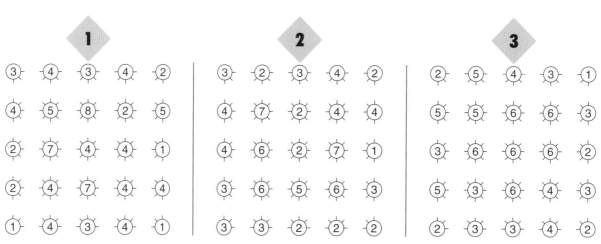

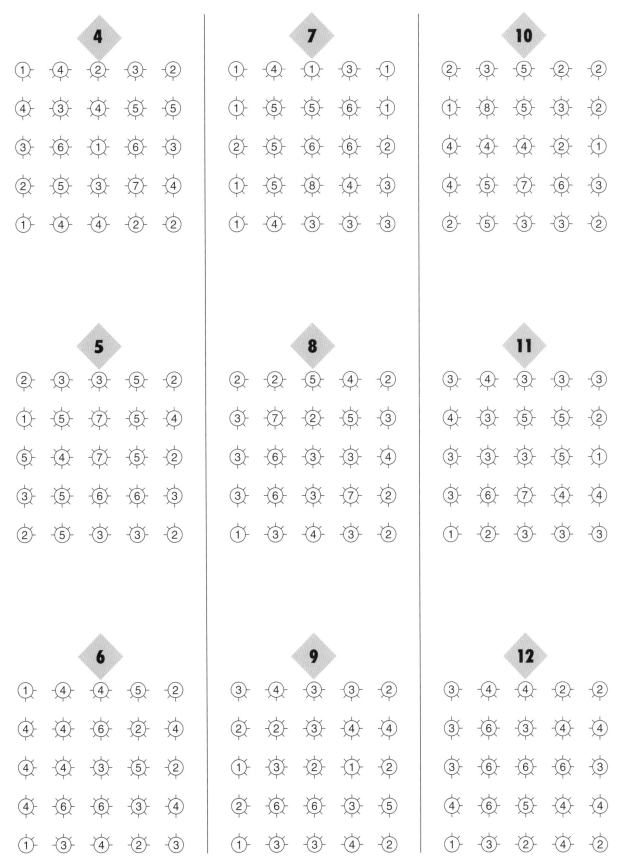

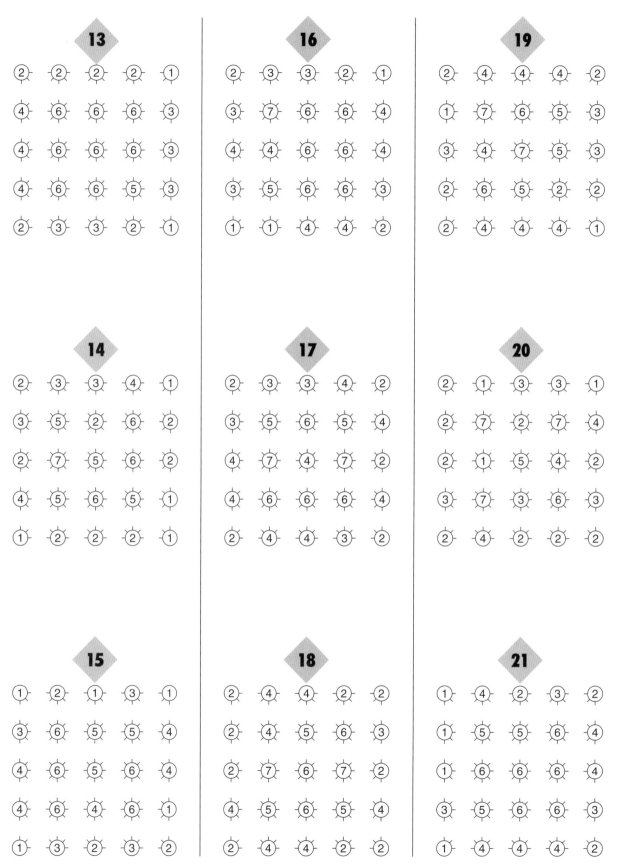

13

②	②	②	②	①
④	⑥	⑥	⑥	③
④	⑥	⑥	⑥	③
④	⑥	⑥	⑤	③
②	③	③	②	①

16

②	③	③	②	①
③	⑦	⑥	⑥	④
④	④	⑥	⑥	④
③	⑤	⑥	⑥	③
①	①	④	④	②

19

②	④	④	④	②
①	⑦	⑥	⑤	③
③	④	⑦	⑤	③
②	⑥	⑤	②	②
②	④	④	④	①

14

②	③	③	④	①
③	⑤	②	⑥	②
②	⑦	⑤	⑥	②
④	⑤	⑥	⑤	①
①	②	②	②	①

17

②	③	③	④	②
③	⑤	⑥	⑤	④
④	⑦	④	⑦	②
④	⑥	⑥	⑥	④
②	④	④	③	②

20

②	①	③	③	①
②	⑦	②	⑦	④
②	①	⑤	④	②
③	⑦	③	⑥	③
②	④	②	②	②

15

①	②	①	③	①
③	⑥	⑤	⑤	④
④	⑥	⑤	⑥	④
④	⑥	④	⑥	①
①	③	②	③	②

18

②	④	④	②	②
②	④	⑤	⑥	③
②	⑦	⑥	⑦	②
④	⑤	⑥	⑤	④
②	④	④	②	②

21

①	④	②	③	②
①	⑤	⑤	⑥	④
①	⑥	⑥	⑥	④
③	⑤	⑥	⑥	③
①	④	④	④	②

160

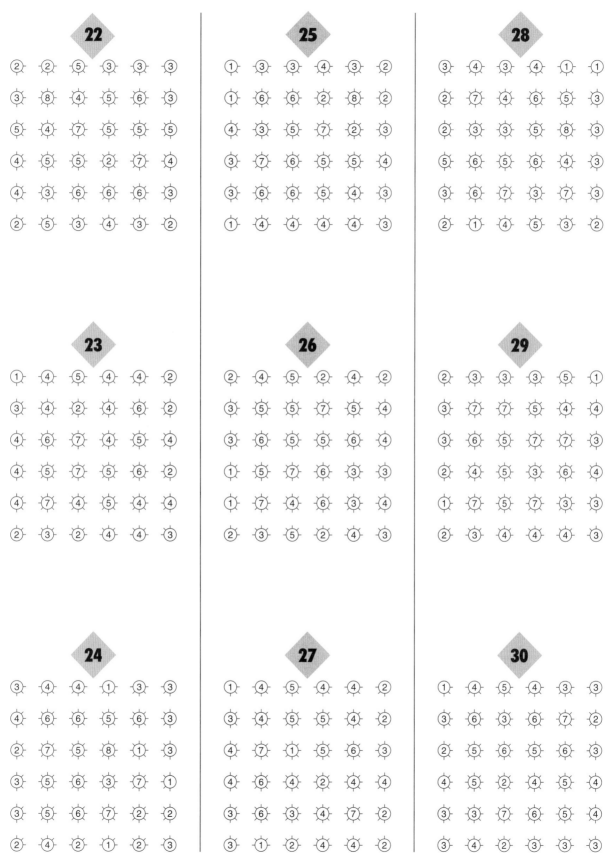

Battleships

Your job is to find the fleet of ships hidden in each of the grids below. Each fleet consists of one four-segment battleship, two three-segment cruisers, three two-segment destroyers, and four one-segment submarines. A picture of the fleet is shown in the example; note that submarines are round, the end segments of the other ships are rounded off on one end, and the center segments of the other ships are flat on all sides.

Ships are located entirely within the grid, with one grid space taken up for each ship segment. Ships are oriented horizontally or vertically and no ship touches another, even diagonally.

The numbers along the edges of the grids indicate how many ship segments are in that row or column. Missing numbers are for you to determine. A few ship segments are shown. In addition, some grid spaces are shown as water; these spaces will not contain a ship segment.

Lighthouses variant (puzzles 7 to 12): There are no guide numbers along the edges. Rather, numbers within grid spaces indicate the total number of ship segments found in the same row and the same column as that grid space. Ships cannot be adjacent to the numbered grid spaces.

Minesweeper variant (puzzles 13 to 18): There are no guide numbers along the edges. Rather, numbers within grid spaces indicate the number of ship segments adjacent to that space horizontally, vertically, and diagonally. Numbered grid spaces cannot contain ships.

ANSWERS, PAGES 294-295

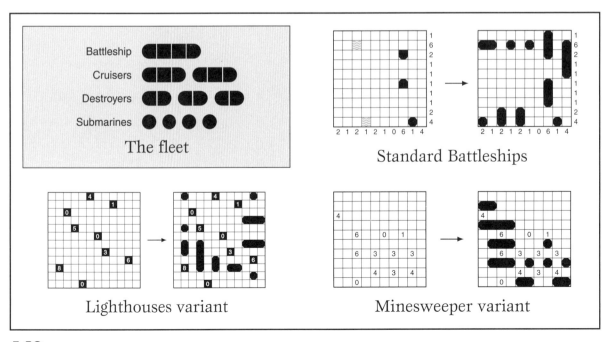

The fleet

Standard Battleships

Lighthouses variant

Minesweeper variant

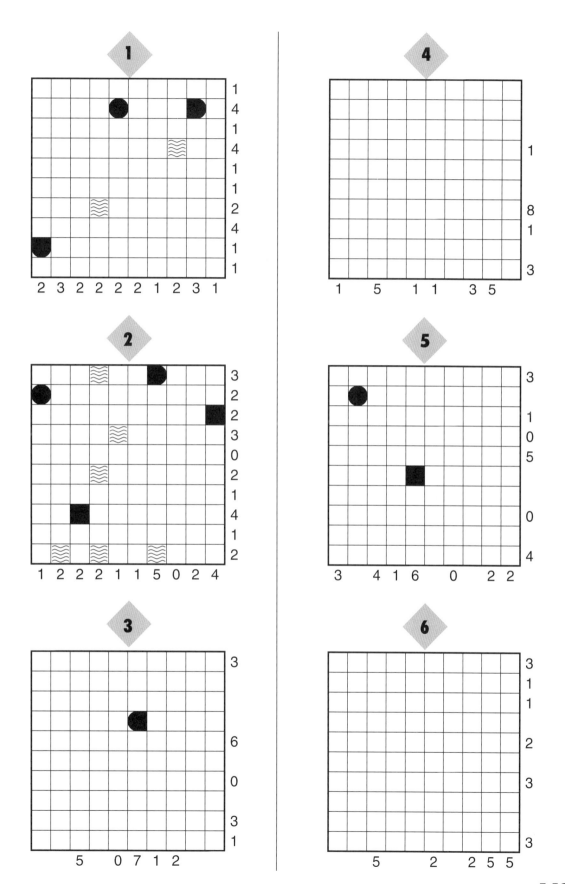

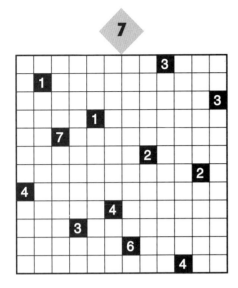

7

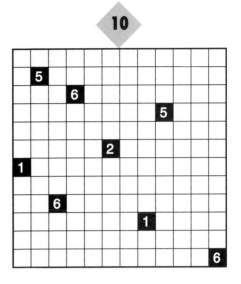

10

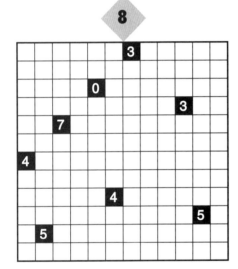

8

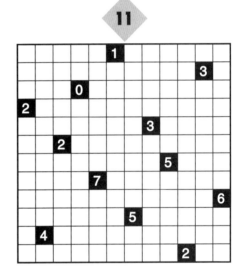

11

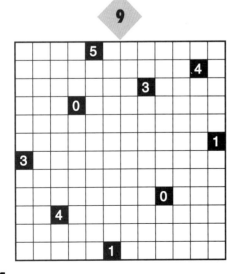

9

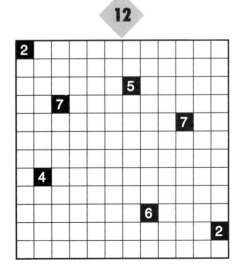

12

164

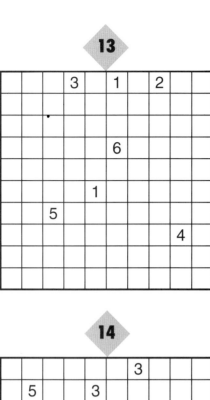

		3		1		2		
	.							
				6				
			1					
	5							
						4		

16

	2			2			
	3		4				
	3	1					3
3			1		4		
	1		3		4		
					1		

14

				3		
5			3			
					5	
	2			2		
					5	
		5				
				2		
	2		0			

17

	3	2	3		3		
				2		1	
		4					
	3		4	2			
1							
	2		4				
	2	2			0		
		1					

15

		0			1	2	2
1						0	
					1		
	2				1		
		0					
						1	
0				0			
	1		2		1		
	1					0	

18

					2		
3	3						
					3		
	3		3		2		
	2			4	2		
		2					
	4	4					
			2		1		

Number Place

In each 6 × 6 diagram, place the numbers 1 through 6 so that each row, column, and six-square subsection (there are six of them, separated by thick black lines) contains each number exactly once. Some numbers have already been placed in the diagram for you.

As the diagrams get bigger, the group of numbers to place gets bigger (1 through 7 in puzzle 3, 1 through 8 in puzzles 4 to 9, and 1 through 9 in the remaining puzzles), and the number and size of the subsections increase accordingly. Each digit will still appear exactly once in each row, column, and subsection.

ANSWERS, PAGES 295-296

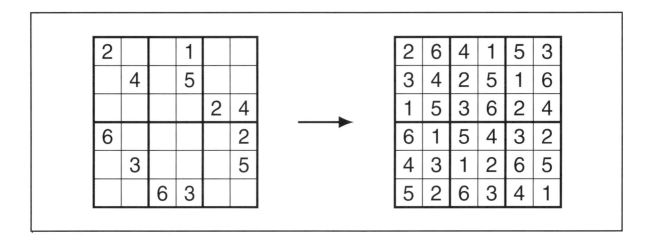

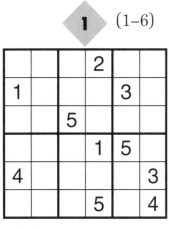

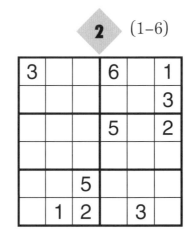

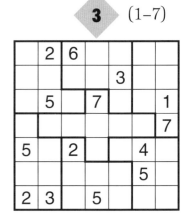

4 (1–8)

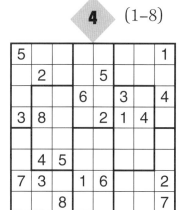

5							1
	2				5		
			6		3		4
3	8			2	1	4	
	4	5					
7	3		1	6			2
		8					7

7 (1–8)

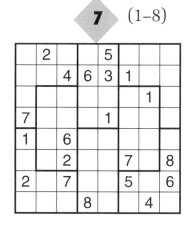

	2			5			
		4	6	3	1		
						1	
7				1			
1		6					
		2			7		8
2		7			5		6
			8			4	

10 (1–9)

		9			5	3		
	4		5		3			7
		6	7				4	
3	8		1			6	2	
9					5			
	1							9
			4					
4			6			1		8
	7	8		5				

5 (1–8)

4	8				3		
			4				
2						3	
	4			6	7		5
8	7				4		
			5				
							6
3		5					1

8 (1–8)

6							
	1					7	
8	7					5	
		4					3
	5			6	7	1	
	6						
		5					
	2		1			3	4

11 (1–9)

6	5	2					8	
8				3		1	5	
5					4	6		
	9	6		2	3			
	7							5
			6	8		3		
			1		9			
						5	2	

6 (1–8)

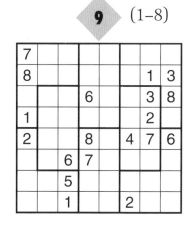

				6		2	3
	1			2			
							6
			7	3		8	4
	7	6					
4					5		2
5					8		
			5				

9 (1–8)

7							
8						1	3
			6			3	8
1						2	
2			8		4	7	6
		6	7				
		5					
		1			2		

12 (1–9)

	3		9				8	
		6	2		3	7	9	
			1					
	2		3				7	
				7			6	4
1								
	5				4	9		
	7	2						
	9			5		8	3	

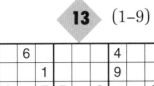

13 (1–9)

	6					4		
		1				9		
2		7	5		6			8
		4	9			6		
			1	5				9
	8	2	6					7
				7	3			
6				1			2	
					5			

16 (1–9)

9			2					
		2		1			3	4
		4		3	9	1		8
	7		3		4		5	
		6			5			3
			1					7
	2		6	5				
		7				8	1	
5								

19 (1–9)

			1	2	3		6	
8					5			
				9				
		5			9		4	
						2		6
							9	8
	3		2		1			5
1					7		8	2
	9			3				

14 (1–9)

4	9						1	
1		3		4		7		
	5							2
7			3		1		5	
	3		2				8	9
		5		9				
		6		5		1		
			6	9	2		7	

17 (1–9)

			1		2		9	
3	2						6	
6		9						
	5		6					
8	7				5			
						8		3
4							8	
		8		4	1	7	2	
2			5		7	6		

20 (1–9)

	2			1				5
7			6		9			3
1	7		4					
				8				
3			1					
	8			2		4		
		6		7				
	5	9				8		

15 (1–9)

						8		3
	7					5		9
			4	1	8			
					2		6	
1	9					4		8
2						1	7	
	3				4			
	1		3		6		5	
	8			5		9		

18 (1–9)

	4							
5			9		1	8		
			8			5		7
			2		6	3		4
	9	7						5
	8			6	2			
		3		4	9	6		1
7							9	

21 (1–9)

5		8	3					1
						9	8	
9				1				5
		5	9					6
				4				7
8					4			
	3	9		2	5	7		
						6		
	8	7	4					

22 (1–9)

			5				7	
3	5		7			8	6	1
								6
6	8	9	2			7		
							2	
		2	8			6	3	4
	6		1		9	2		
8	9				3			
					4			

25 (1–9)

	3			5	9			4
						6		8
		6				7		
	4				6			
			7				8	
2		7			4			
		8				5		
9							2	1
5				3	7			

28 (1–9)

			8	2		7		9
				1				
9	3			7			4	
6				4	9			
	8		3					
	9				2		4	
		2		7			3	
		6	5			8		7

23 (1–9)

	8				6			
3				4		5		8
					2			7
			4	5				
1		6	7					
	2	9				8		
							3	
	1							6
7	6			3	2	9	5	

26 (1–9)

				5	7		1	
	2		3		6			
								4
						7	5	
5	8							
6		2				9		
		7		8	2			6
2	7		4		1			
				4			8	

29 (1–9)

2			6		4		7	
	3	5						8
	4					2		
7		6	4					
4		9	7			5		
					1			
		2		5	3	1		
6								
	1				2	6		

24 (1–9)

	8				6		2	
						8		
9			2	3			6	
5	6				4			
2			6					
8				1		3		7
	7	3			8	1		6
	1	5			3		8	
					5		1	

27 (1–9)

2	6	5				3		1
	1			5	8			
			4		7			
	5							
				9				
	8							
			8	2				9
				4		6	3	
	4		1			5		8

30 (1–9)

						2		
4		8			7	6	1	
9	1							
			9		4	7		
		5		6				9
			6		8			1
	2				4	7		
		7	4		3			

169

Alternate Corners

Your object is to find a path that passes through every square exactly once, ends in the same square it begins, and never crosses itself. The path travels horizontally and vertically but never diagonally. Every other turn you make in the path will be in a square containing a circle, and you must make a turn in every square that contains a circle.

ANSWERS, PAGES 296-297

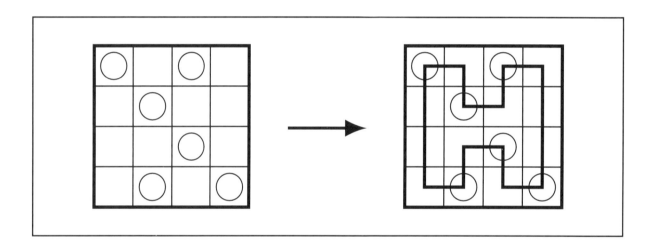

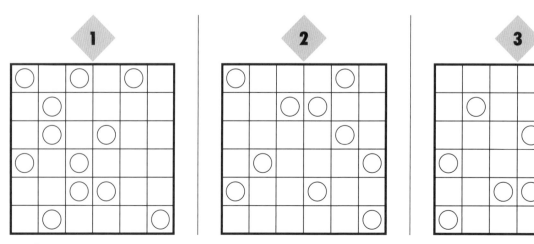

4

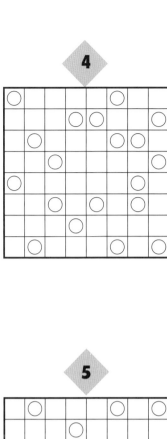

7

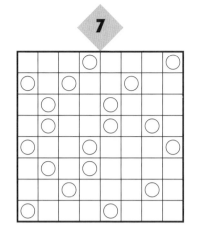

10

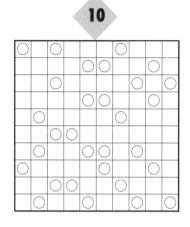

5

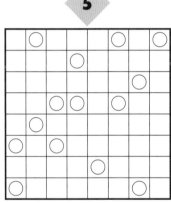

8

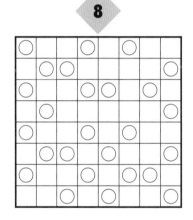

11

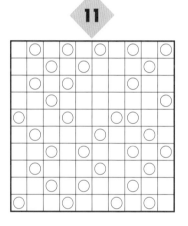

6

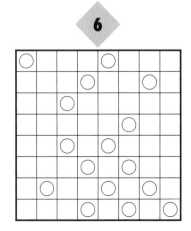

9

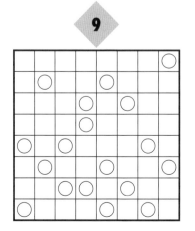

12

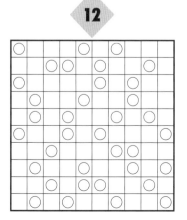

Rain Clouds

There is a storm brewing in the grids below and you need to find all of the rain clouds in each. The numbers along the edges of the diagram indicate how many squares in that row or column contain a portion of a rain cloud. All the rain clouds are shaped like rounded squares or rounded rectangles and are at least two squares wide and two squares tall. Furthermore, no rain cloud is adjacent to another horizontally, vertically, or diagonally.

There are several kinds of starting hints in the diagrams below: a rounded corner of a cloud, a non-rounded piece that can be either an edge piece or an internal piece of a cloud, or wavy lines, which are not part of any rain cloud.

ANSWERS, PAGES 297-298

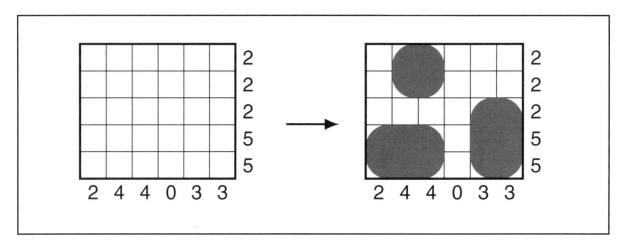

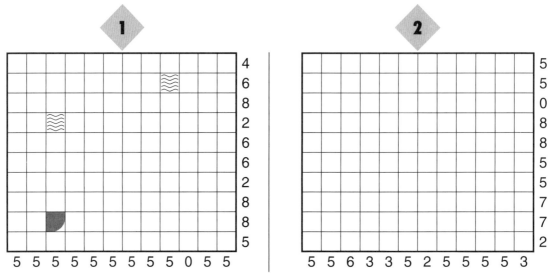

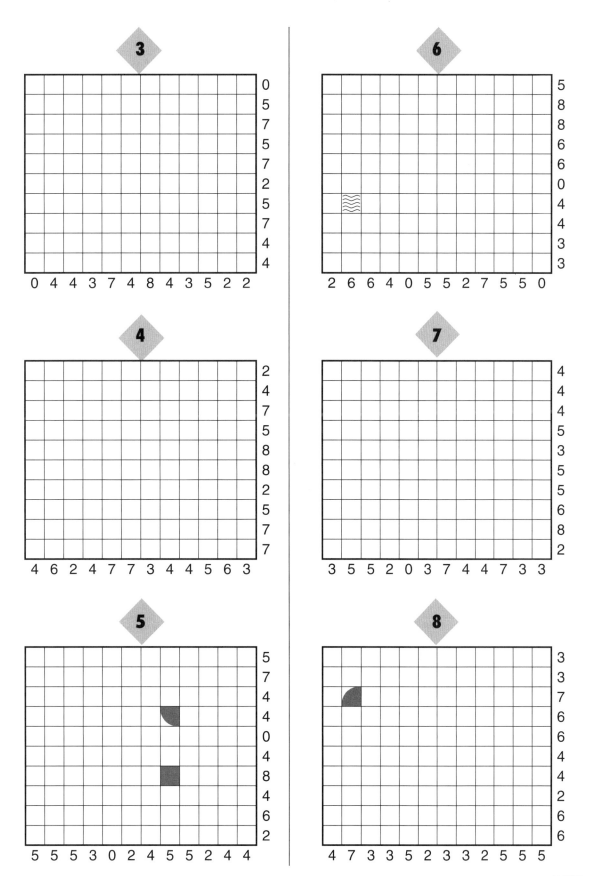

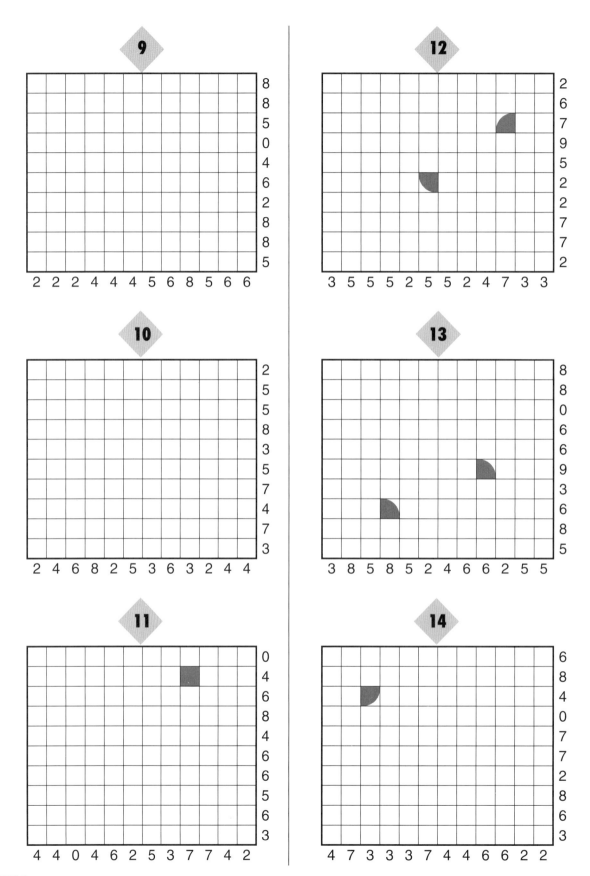

174

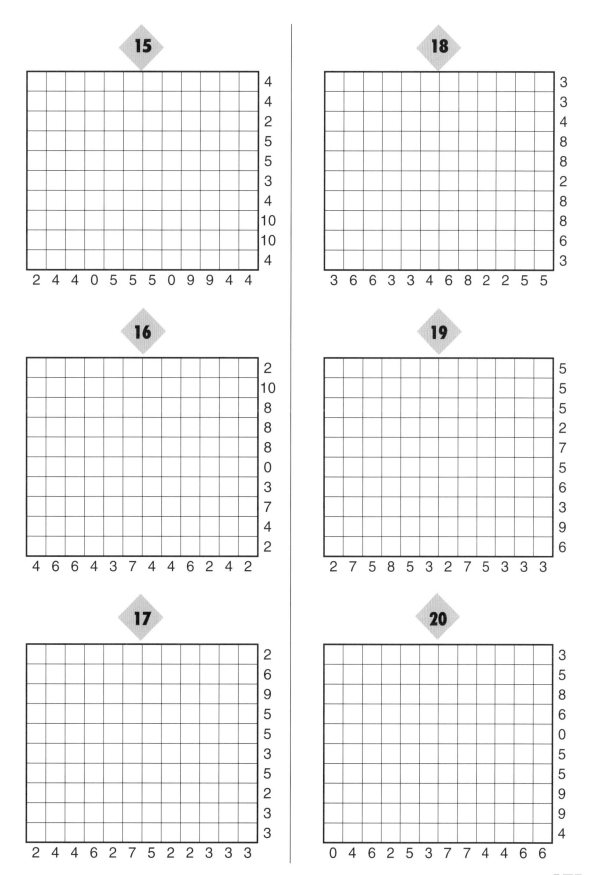

15

Right: 4, 4, 2, 5, 5, 3, 4, 10, 10, 4
Bottom: 2, 4, 4, 0, 5, 5, 5, 0, 9, 9, 4, 4

18

Right: 3, 3, 4, 8, 8, 2, 8, 8, 6, 3
Bottom: 3, 6, 6, 3, 3, 4, 6, 8, 2, 2, 5, 5

16

Right: 2, 10, 8, 8, 8, 0, 3, 7, 4, 2
Bottom: 4, 6, 6, 4, 3, 7, 4, 4, 6, 2, 4, 2

19

Right: 5, 5, 5, 2, 7, 5, 6, 3, 9, 6
Bottom: 2, 7, 5, 8, 5, 3, 2, 7, 5, 3, 3, 3

17

Right: 2, 6, 9, 5, 5, 3, 5, 2, 3, 3
Bottom: 2, 4, 4, 6, 2, 7, 5, 2, 2, 3, 3, 3

20

Right: 3, 5, 8, 6, 0, 5, 5, 9, 9, 4
Bottom: 0, 4, 6, 2, 5, 3, 7, 7, 4, 4, 6, 6

Square Numbers

There are some squares to be drawn in the grids below. All of the squares have each of their four corners in the center of a grid square and sides all parallel to the grid's sides. Exactly one corner will be in a grid square that contains a number. That number tells you how many other numbers can be found inside the square.

The squares may cross through perpendicular sides only and cannot touch anywhere else.

ANSWERS, PAGES 298-299

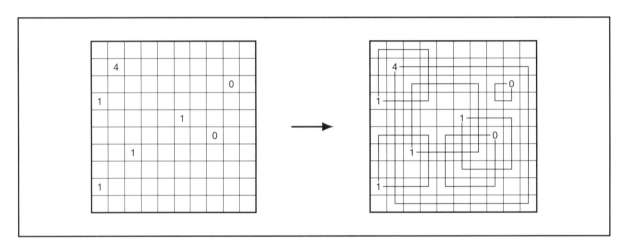

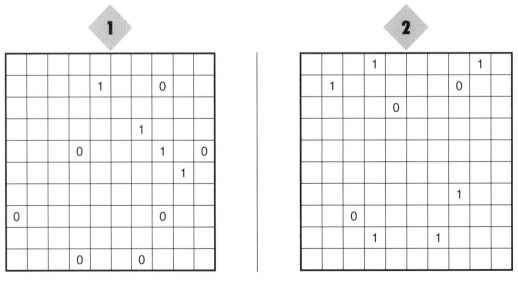

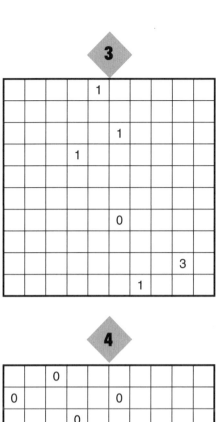

3

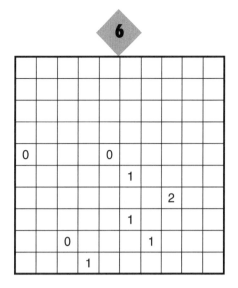

6

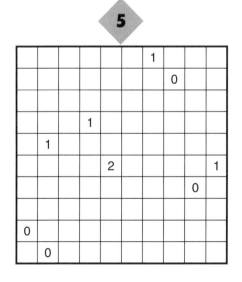

4

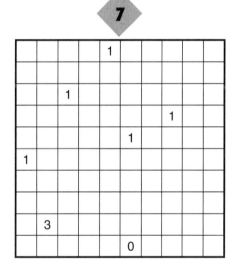

7

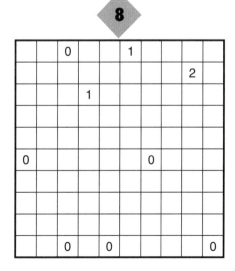

5

8

177

9

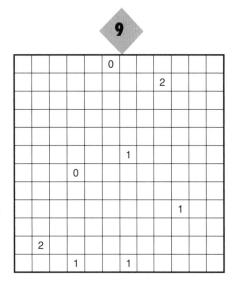

10

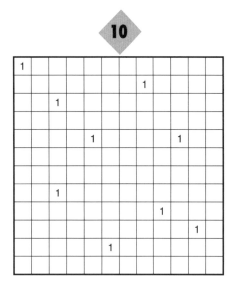

11

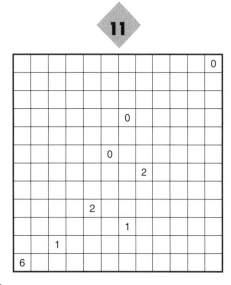

12

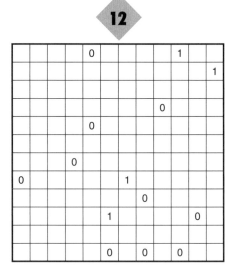

13

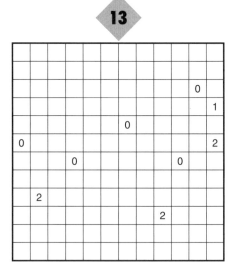

14

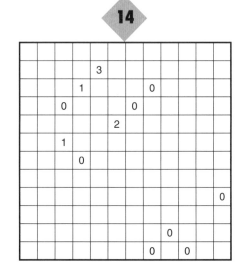

15

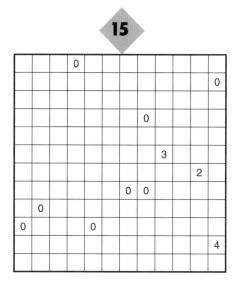

16

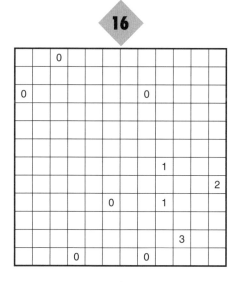

17

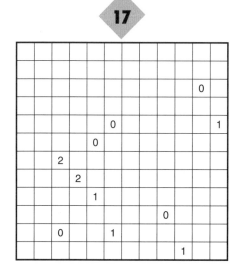

18

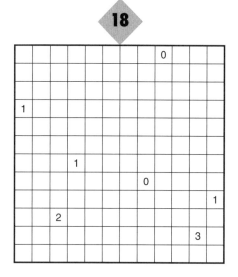

19

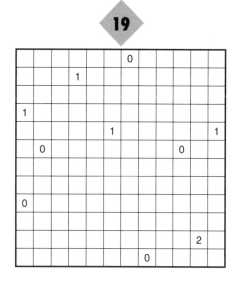

20

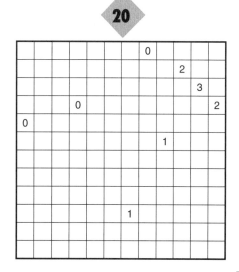

Fences

Each diagram should contain a path that travels from dot to dot, horizontally and vertically only, and ends where it began, never touching or crossing itself. The numbers that have been placed in the diagram tell you how many of the four sides of the "square" it lies in are used for the path. (The path doesn't necessarily need to touch all of the dots.) Your task is to find this path.

ANSWERS, PAGES 299-300

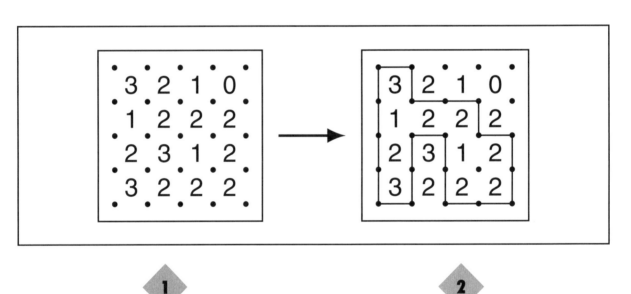

```
  1   1 2     1
1     2   1 2   2 2
2   1   2   1   1
  1   1   2 1   2 2
2 1             1
        1   1   1 2
1       1   2 1   2
  2 1   1       1
1   1     1 2 1
2     2 1   2   1 1
```

```
1   1 2   1 3   1
    1   2       0   2
  2 2 2 1           1
          0 1 2
0     3     3   0
          1
  1   0       1   0
1     1   1     0
  1   2 3   1   1 2
2 2   0       1 1
```

```
2         1   1
1   3   3   0   3
    0   1           1
    2   2   2   2   3
    3           3
          1       0
0 2 3 3
          1 1 1 3
    1   0   3
  1 3       1       3
```

```
1     3     0     3
  3   1   1     3
    3   2
3       3   0   3
  3   0   3
  0   3           3
3       1 1   3   2
  3         1
3     0   3   0   3
  3
```

```
                2
1 0   3   0 2       3
1   2 1   2   1 0
        0     1   2 2
    2         1
0   2 1 1   0 1   0
  1               2
2     0   1 3   2
    2           0   1
  0     0     1
```

```
  1 1   3     3 3
1     2     1     1
1     3     1     3
  3 1     1   1 2
3         2
          2         3
  1 2   1     3 1
2     3     2     2
2     2     1     3
  3 1     3   1 3
```

9

```
  2     1 0     2
3   2       2 1 1
1   3     0
    1       2
2   2 1   1 3       1
  2 1   3         3
1               0   0
    2 2     2 1
  3     0 2 1   1 1 3
    3           2   1
```

12

```
2         1     1   2
    2 2   1       2
1   1   3       3     2
              1 2       1
    2       1 1     1
      3     2 2       0
3       2 2
1   1       1     1   2
    3       3   2 1
2   1       1         1
```

10

```
    3   1       0
1       1 3       1
  2   0                 3
    2     2 2   0     3
1 2 1                   2
  2         2 1 1
    2         1 0       0 1
    1         2         3
        2               1
          1 3   3     1
```

11

```
          2 2 2 3     2
2 2 0     1             3
          1         1
  2         1 0 1     0
  3 3             2 2
              0           2
  1                   2 0
            1 1     0   3
2 0
    1 1       1     1 1 3
```

13

```
    1   3 2   2 1
        2   0     1
    1             2     0
0   1   0 2
              1   3   1
0     0 2       1 1     3
            0           2
          0     0   0     1
2 3   0         1   2 1
2   1         3       1
```

14

```
    3   0       1     2
1         2         .
    1 1       0       0
2 2 2
2           3         2
    0   3       1     1 1
    2 2   3 1           2
    1           1     1
2 1         1         1
    1       0         0
```

182

15

16

17

18

19

20

Snaky Tiles

The grids below have been divided up into a number of distinct tiles, and the divisions are all made along grid lines. Each tile is "snakelike" in structure: it is one square wide from end to end and never branches off. The tiles also never touch themselves, even diagonally. In addition, each tile contains within it two nonadjacent squares with the number equal to its length. Your job is to discover how the grids have been dissected.

ANSWERS, PAGES 300-301

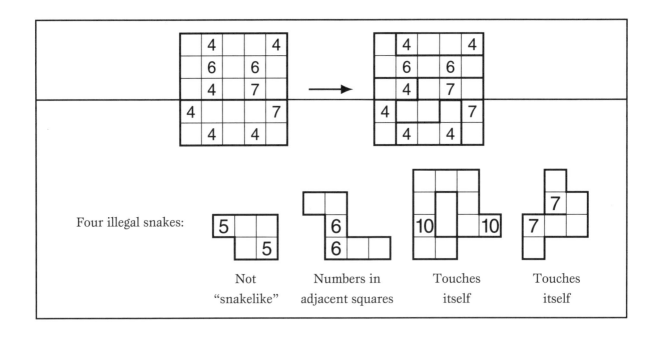

Four illegal snakes:

| Not "snakelike" | Numbers in adjacent squares | Touches itself | Touches itself |

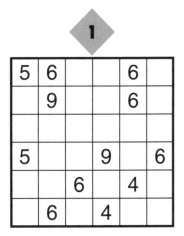

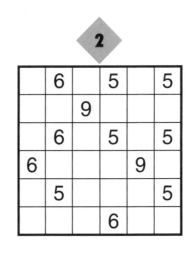

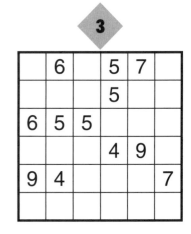

4

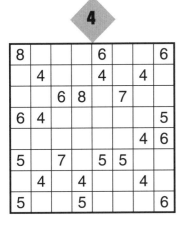

8			6				6
	4			4		4	
		6	8		7		
6	4						5
						4	6
5		7		5	5		
	4		4			4	
5			5				6

7

7							
			4			10	5
		10			4	10	
	6						5
	7	6					6
5			4				7
		4	10			6	
	5			7			

10

5	5						
	9						6
5	4				4	9	
	5		4	4		6	
	5		4	4		5	
	4				4		
	6		6	7		7	5
5							

5

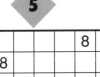

	8					8	8
		8					
		8	8	8	8	8	
8	8	8	8	8	8		8

8

		8		4		4	
7	5					8	
		5	7	6	6	6	
							6
	6						
4	5	7	6				
						6	
4		5		7			6

11

4		4				4	
							4
	4	6	4	6	6	6	
4	6		4			4	6
	4						
4	6			6		4	
				4		6	
	6	4		6		6	

6

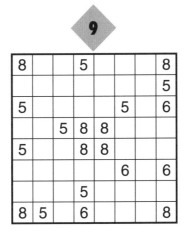

	6			7			
8			4		19	5	
		6	7	4			
	19				5		
		6					5
		4				6	
	8		4			5	

9

8			5				8
							5
5					5		6
		5	8	8			
5			8	8			
					6		6
			5				
8	5		6				8

12

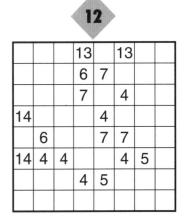

		13		13			
			6	7			
			7		4		
14				4			
	6			7	7		
14	4	4			4	5	
			4	5			

13

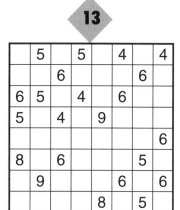

	5		5		4		4
		6				6	
6	5		4		6		
5		4		9			
							6
8		6				5	
	9				6		6
				8		5	

16

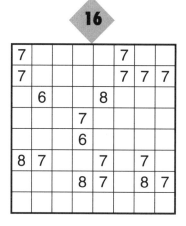

7				7			
7				7	7	7	
	6			8			
		7					
		6					
8	7			7		7	
		8	7		8	7	

19

		6	6		6	5	
6	7			6			
							5
		6		6			6
		5	5				
7	6	5			6		
			5	5		7	
	5			7			

14

		6		5		6	
		7				5	
6	5					7	
		4	5	8			6
4		5					
			7				
5			6		5	7	8
6				5			

17

	5			10			
		10				5	10
5		10	10	5			
				5			
	5				5		
	4					10	10
10			4	5			

20

	6			10			
		6					
6						10	5
	4	6	7		9	5	
		4					
4					7		
	4	6		6		9	
		7			7		

15

			6				7
6				7	5		
		4		4			
6	6	7					
		7			7	5	5
		6					
	5		6			6	5
7				5		6	

18

7				8			
	8	7		5		5	
				4			
	8		5		4	6	8
	8				5		
					6		
		8				6	
7			7				6

21

		6					
7	6	5		5	6	7	
		6		6			
		7					
5		5				6	
7		6		7			
4		7	5		6		
		4		5			

22

5	5	4			4			4
			4	14				
		5	5					
			14		4		8	
		4		8			4	
	5			4	6			
				5	14	6	4	14
4		5						
		14			5		4	
	4	14						

23

9	7			5				9
		5	7		8			
	5			7		5		
		6					8	
		4		7	5			
		9		6				
5		4		5			9	6
6	6	5		6			7	
						6		
6			7		5			5

24

	7	5		7	7			
			5		5			7
			7				5	
7	7	7		7	7	5	7	7
			7			7		
		7	5			5		5
						7		5
		7	7	5	7		5	
				5	7			

25

		6	5		5	5		5
	6	7			7			7
7								4
	4			4			7	
6			5	6			7	4
	4					4		
		4	5	5			6	4
6	7				5	6	5	
			5			7		
		7		7				6

26

			7		5			
7			8					7
					5			
5	32			5			9	
		8					7	
							6	
5	4		7	5				
					9	5		
	4			5			32	6
		7						

27

		8	6		7			
	8				6			7
8								
			5		6	6	6	7
8	5		6			7	7	
	5	4			10			
				4		7		
	4	5				7		5
4							7	
		10	5			5		5

Cross Sums

This is like a crossword puzzle, but with numbers. There will be one digit in each of the white squares instead of one letter. The clue number for a horizontal group of digits is to the left of the group and above the diagonal division, and for a vertical group of digits it is above the group and below the diagonal division.

The clue number is the sum of the digits in its corresponding group. Only the digits 1 through 9 are used, and no digit may be repeated within a group.

Variation 1 (puzzles 5 and 6): The instructions are the same as for regular Cross Sums, except each answer group *must* contain exactly one pair of matching digits.

ANSWERS, PAGE 301

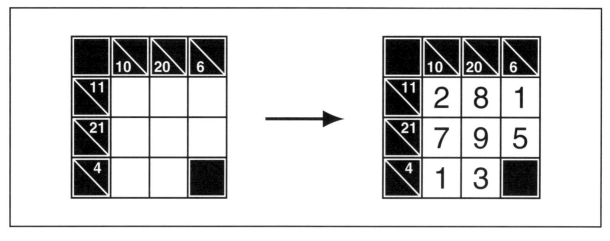

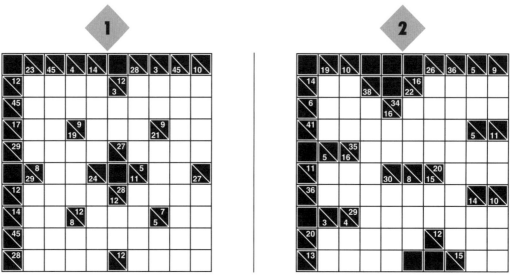

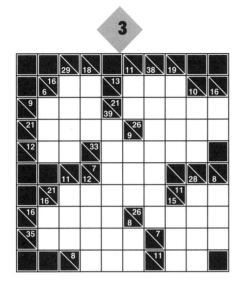

3

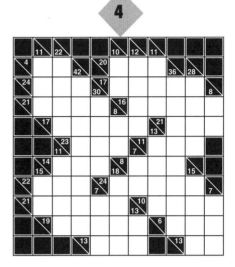

4

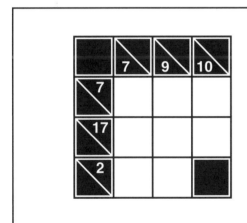

→

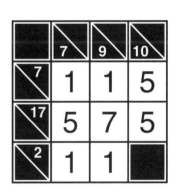

5

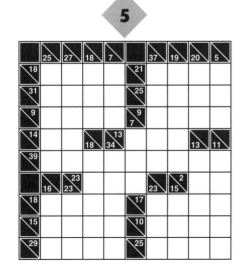

6

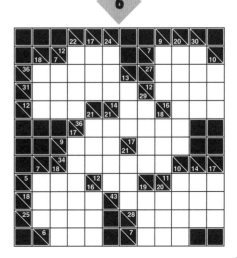

End View

Place the letters A through C into the diagram so that every letter appears exactly once in each row and column. The letters around the edge of the diagram indicate the first letter that can be found by reading the appropriate row or column, beginning at that outside letter.

In later diagrams, larger sets of letters are used (A through D in puzzles 11 to 20, A through E in puzzles 21 to 25, and A through F in puzzles 26 to 30).

ANSWERS, PAGES 301-303

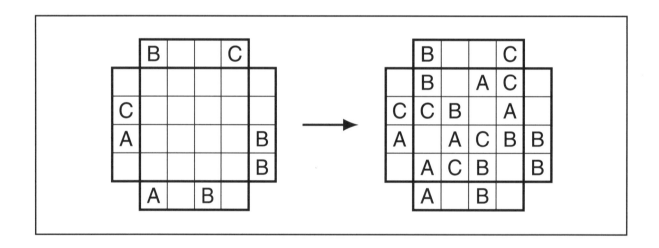

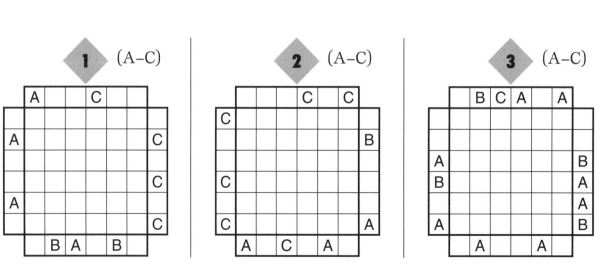

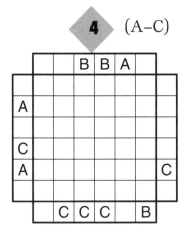

4 (A–C)

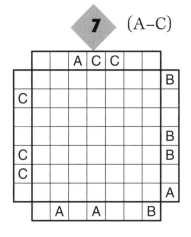

5 (A–C)

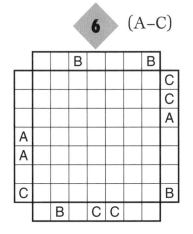

6 (A–C)

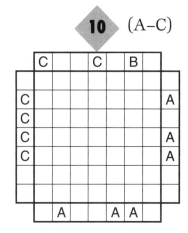

7 (A–C)

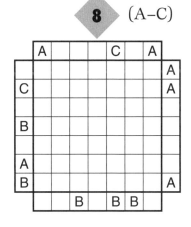

8 (A–C)

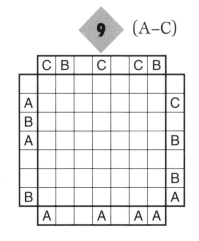

9 (A–C)

10 (A–C)

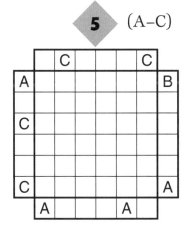

11 (A–D)

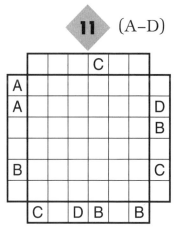

12 (A–D)

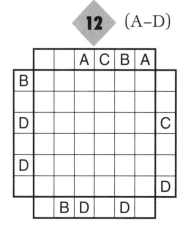

13 (A–D)

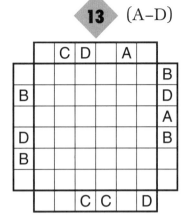

16 (A–D)

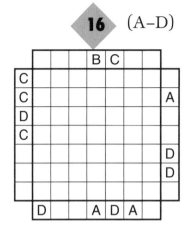

19 (A–D)

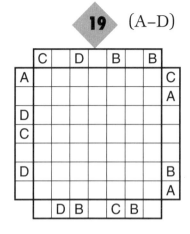

14 (A–D)

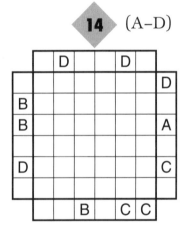

17 (A–D)

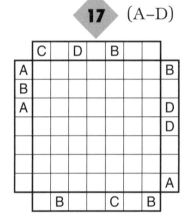

20 (A–D)

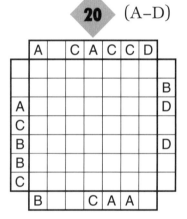

15 (A–D)

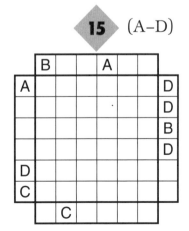

18 (A–D)

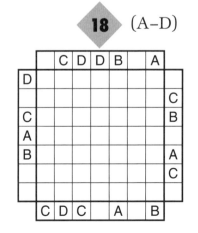

21 (A–E)

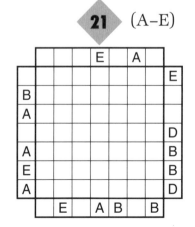

22 (A–E)

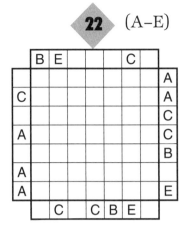

25 (A–E)

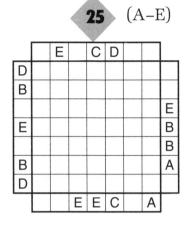

28 (A–F)

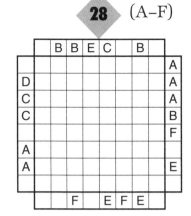

23 (A–E)

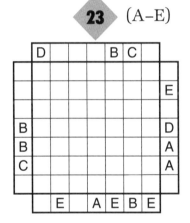

26 (A–F)

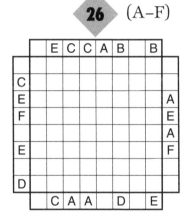

29 (A–F)

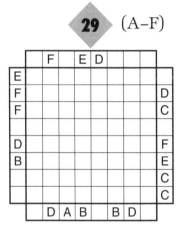

24 (A–E)

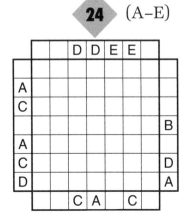

27 (A–F)

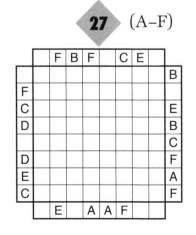

30 (A–F)

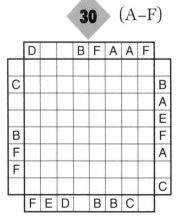

193

Skyscrapers

Each of the squares in the grids below contains a building that has anywhere from one to five stories. There will be one building of every possible height in each row and column. The numbers along the edges of the diagram indicate the number of buildings that can be seen from that point looking in. Your job is to find the height of each building. Remember, when looking into the grid, taller buildings block your view of shorter buildings.

In later diagrams, larger groups of buildings (1 through 6 stories in puzzles 3 to 6, 1 through 7 stories in puzzles 7 and 8) must be placed.

The example shows a group of buildings from one to four stories.

ANSWERS, PAGE 303

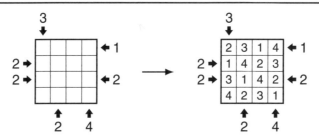

At right is a side view of a possible row in a Skyscrapers puzzle. From the left side, three buildings would be seen: 2, 4, and 6. Building 1 is hidden behind Building 2, and Buildings 3 and 5 are blocked by Building 6. From the right side, only two buildings are seen: 5 and 6. Building 3 is hidden behind Building 5, and Building 6 blocks Buildings 4, 1, and 2.

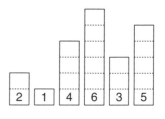

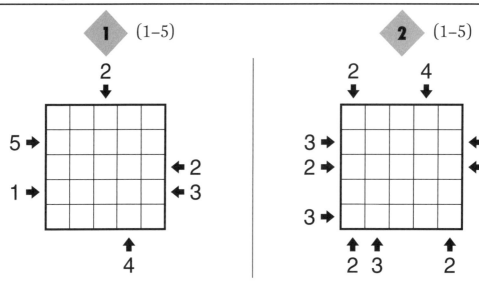

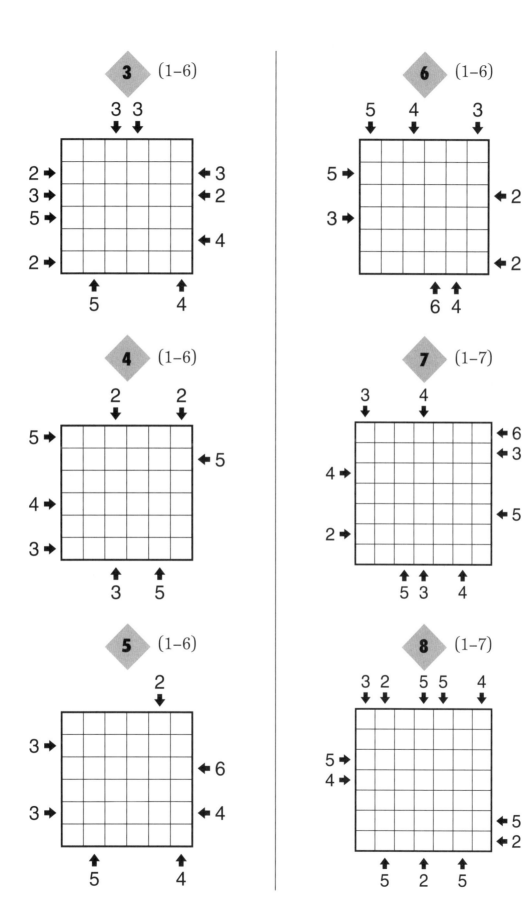

3 (1–6)

4 (1–6)

5 (1–6)

6 (1–6)

7 (1–7)

8 (1–7)

Dominoes

For the beginning puzzles, a full set of double-6 dominoes (28 total dominoes) has been laid out in each diagram, and the edges of each domino have been removed. Replace all the edges to show the location of each individual domino. Every diagram has a unique solution.

In later diagrams, full sets of double-9 dominoes (55 total) and double-12 dominoes (91 total) are used. Checkoff lists for all sets are provided.

ANSWERS, PAGES 303-304

2	5	4	0	2	4	3	1
6	0	4	4	5	4	0	1
1	2	2	3	0	5	6	0
0	3	6	1	0	6	2	5
5	3	4	4	1	5	0	4
3	1	5	1	3	5	6	2
6	1	2	6	3	3	6	2

→

2	5	4	0	2	4	3	1
6	0	4	4	5	4	0	1
1	2	2	3	0	5	6	0
0	3	6	1	0	6	2	5
5	3	4	4	1	5	0	4
3	1	5	1	3	5	6	2
6	1	2	6	3	3	6	2

1

3	5	5	0	5	4	2	1
3	4	0	1	6	0	0	0
4	2	1	3	0	6	1	6
4	0	3	4	4	4	1	6
6	6	5	5	3	2	1	4
5	2	3	5	2	1	5	3
2	2	2	3	0	6	1	6

2

1	6	6	1	2	2	2	5
5	5	3	3	2	6	0	0
1	5	0	2	1	3	4	2
1	6	4	4	5	6	3	0
1	1	2	5	4	3	3	0
0	4	1	3	6	6	4	6
0	0	4	5	3	5	2	4

Checkoff list (puzzle 1):

0 0

0 1	1 1

0 2	1 2	2 2

0 3	1 3	2 3	3 3

0 4	1 4	2 4	3 4	4 4

0 5	1 5	2 5	3 5	4 5	5 5

0 6	1 6	2 6	3 6	4 6	5 6	6 6

Checkoff list (puzzle 2):

0 0

0 1	1 1

0 2	1 2	2 2

0 3	1 3	2 3	3 3

0 4	1 4	2 4	3 4	4 4

0 5	1 5	2 5	3 5	4 5	5 5

0 6	1 6	2 6	3 6	4 6	5 6	6 6

3

6	4	5	4	1	2	5	2
4	0	5	0	3	1	3	1
3	4	6	0	3	6	2	0
3	6	2	2	5	0	3	3
2	3	5	1	5	0	4	4
0	2	4	1	6	5	5	4
1	1	6	2	1	0	6	6

```
0 0
0 1  1 1
0 2  1 2  2 2
0 3  1 3  2 3  3 3
0 4  1 4  2 4  3 4  4 4
0 5  1 5  2 5  3 5  4 5  5 5
0 6  1 6  2 6  3 6  4 6  5 6  6 6
```

5

6	5	0	6	6	5	5	0
4	4	0	4	2	1	5	5
1	5	6	6	2	0	4	4
1	3	2	2	3	0	6	2
6	2	1	2	4	4	3	2
5	3	1	3	3	3	0	5
1	4	1	3	0	1	6	0

```
0 0
0 1  1 1
0 2  1 2  2 2
0 3  1 3  2 3  3 3
0 4  1 4  2 4  3 4  4 4
0 5  1 5  2 5  3 5  4 5  5 5
0 6  1 6  2 6  3 6  4 6  5 6  6 6
```

4

4	2	6	3	3	3	2	1
3	6	1	3	4	4	1	0
5	0	5	2	5	5	1	0
6	1	2	6	3	4	6	2
5	6	5	6	4	2	4	0
5	0	4	0	0	2	2	1
1	3	1	3	0	5	4	6

```
0 0
0 1  1 1
0 2  1 2  2 2
0 3  1 3  2 3  3 3
0 4  1 4  2 4  3 4  4 4
0 5  1 5  2 5  3 5  4 5  5 5
0 6  1 6  2 6  3 6  4 6  5 6  6 6
```

6

1	2	3	6	6	2	0	3
5	2	4	4	2	4	0	1
6	6	1	4	2	5	2	5
0	0	6	1	0	0	5	5
1	3	3	1	6	2	6	3
1	3	4	5	3	3	4	5
5	2	4	1	6	0	0	4

```
0 0
0 1  1 1
0 2  1 2  2 2
0 3  1 3  2 3  3 3
0 4  1 4  2 4  3 4  4 4
0 5  1 5  2 5  3 5  4 5  5 5
0 6  1 6  2 6  3 6  4 6  5 6  6 6
```

7

5	5	0	5	2	2	4	6
0	5	2	1	0	3	3	2
0	4	1	2	3	5	0	6
3	4	1	0	5	1	4	6
1	2	6	4	1	3	3	2
1	0	6	3	4	0	6	2
1	6	4	4	6	5	5	3

```
0 0
0 1  1 1
0 2  1 2  2 2
0 3  1 3  2 3  3 3
0 4  1 4  2 4  3 4  4 4
0 5  1 5  2 5  3 5  4 5  5 5
0 6  1 6  2 6  3 6  4 6  5 6  6 6
```

9

0	2	2	4	3	0	3	6
4	4	4	6	2	2	4	3
1	3	2	5	3	1	6	2
1	5	5	1	6	6	0	0
5	5	4	1	1	0	0	6
5	2	1	3	3	4	1	0
6	4	5	0	3	5	2	6

```
0 0
0 1  1 1
0 2  1 2  2 2
0 3  1 3  2 3  3 3
0 4  1 4  2 4  3 4  4 4
0 5  1 5  2 5  3 5  4 5  5 5
0 6  1 6  2 6  3 6  4 6  5 6  6 6
```

8

0	3	1	1	2	4	4	2
5	3	1	5	6	1	6	0
5	4	4	4	3	4	6	4
0	0	2	5	5	6	1	3
5	1	6	5	0	2	3	2
5	2	0	1	3	3	6	6
1	3	6	0	0	2	2	4

```
0 0
0 1  1 1
0 2  1 2  2 2
0 3  1 3  2 3  3 3
0 4  1 4  2 4  3 4  4 4
0 5  1 5  2 5  3 5  4 5  5 5
0 6  1 6  2 6  3 6  4 6  5 6  6 6
```

10

2	6	2	3	4	4	5	5
1	3	0	0	3	3	6	6
0	5	1	5	5	2	3	4
4	6	4	2	6	0	0	6
1	6	4	3	5	1	1	3
1	2	1	4	1	3	2	4
0	0	6	2	0	5	2	5

```
0 0
0 1  1 1
0 2  1 2  2 2
0 3  1 3  2 3  3 3
0 4  1 4  2 4  3 4  4 4
0 5  1 5  2 5  3 5  4 5  5 5
0 6  1 6  2 6  3 6  4 6  5 6  6 6
```

0	1	1	2	4	3	6	1
6	6	4	4	3	0	0	6
4	5	2	5	1	2	0	4
6	6	2	0	1	3	3	1
5	2	3	1	6	6	3	2
4	2	0	5	5	2	5	1
4	0	0	5	4	3	5	3

0 0						
0 1	1 1					
0 2	1 2	2 2				
0 3	1 3	2 3	3 3			
0 4	1 4	2 4	3 4	4 4		
0 5	1 5	2 5	3 5	4 5	5 5	
0 6	1 6	2 6	3 6	4 6	5 6	6 6

1	1	0	3	0	5	4	1
0	4	2	6	1	5	5	1
6	4	3	4	3	6	0	0
1	5	3	2	3	6	1	6
2	6	6	3	2	5	5	3
0	5	0	3	4	0	2	1
2	2	2	6	4	5	4	4

0 0						
0 1	1 1					
0 2	1 2	2 2				
0 3	1 3	2 3	3 3			
0 4	1 4	2 4	3 4	4 4		
0 5	1 5	2 5	3 5	4 5	5 5	
0 6	1 6	2 6	3 6	4 6	5 6	6 6

1	6	3	0	0	0	6	1
5	6	0	1	4	4	3	0
6	5	5	3	1	4	6	2
1	2	4	5	1	3	6	2
1	3	6	2	2	1	2	5
4	5	4	2	0	5	4	0
2	3	3	3	5	6	0	4

0 0						
0 1	1 1					
0 2	1 2	2 2				
0 3	1 3	2 3	3 3			
0 4	1 4	2 4	3 4	4 4		
0 5	1 5	2 5	3 5	4 5	5 5	
0 6	1 6	2 6	3 6	4 6	5 6	6 6

4	1	5	2	2	5	0	6
4	0	2	5	1	1	0	4
3	6	2	4	6	1	5	0
5	4	3	5	6	0	3	3
6	3	4	5	5	2	4	6
0	2	4	2	1	6	6	2
1	3	1	1	0	0	3	3

0 0						
0 1	1 1					
0 2	1 2	2 2				
0 3	1 3	2 3	3 3			
0 4	1 4	2 4	3 4	4 4		
0 5	1 5	2 5	3 5	4 5	5 5	
0 6	1 6	2 6	3 6	4 6	5 6	6 6

15

6	0	2	3	1	5	3	3
6	4	4	6	1	6	2	1
5	5	5	6	2	2	0	2
6	2	5	5	1	6	3	3
0	4	3	4	3	6	0	0
4	2	5	0	1	1	0	1
4	2	0	1	3	4	5	4

0 0
0 1 | 1 1
0 2 | 1 2 | 2 2
0 3 | 1 3 | 2 3 | 3 3
0 4 | 1 4 | 2 4 | 3 4 | 4 4
0 5 | 1 5 | 2 5 | 3 5 | 4 5 | 5 5
0 6 | 1 6 | 2 6 | 3 6 | 4 6 | 5 6 | 6 6

17

1	6	4	6	6	5	6	3
1	1	2	6	2	5	5	2
5	3	3	6	0	3	2	3
4	0	3	1	5	2	2	4
3	1	3	4	0	0	5	1
0	0	4	1	0	4	4	6
4	2	2	1	5	5	6	0

0 0
0 1 | 1 1
0 2 | 1 2 | 2 2
0 3 | 1 3 | 2 3 | 3 3
0 4 | 1 4 | 2 4 | 3 4 | 4 4
0 5 | 1 5 | 2 5 | 3 5 | 4 5 | 5 5
0 6 | 1 6 | 2 6 | 3 6 | 4 6 | 5 6 | 6 6

16

6	5	4	1	3	5	0	4
0	1	5	0	0	5	2	4
1	4	6	1	5	5	3	4
1	5	2	0	2	4	3	0
6	2	1	1	2	6	5	2
4	2	3	0	4	3	3	3
6	6	6	0	6	2	1	3

0 0
0 1 | 1 1
0 2 | 1 2 | 2 2
0 3 | 1 3 | 2 3 | 3 3
0 4 | 1 4 | 2 4 | 3 4 | 4 4
0 5 | 1 5 | 2 5 | 3 5 | 4 5 | 5 5
0 6 | 1 6 | 2 6 | 3 6 | 4 6 | 5 6 | 6 6

18

3	3	1	1	4	1	3	2
5	3	1	1	2	2	2	3
6	6	4	5	2	3	0	0
2	6	4	5	0	1	0	4
5	6	4	5	0	4	6	5
4	3	0	1	6	2	6	4
2	6	0	5	5	3	1	0

0 0
0 1 | 1 1
0 2 | 1 2 | 2 2
0 3 | 1 3 | 2 3 | 3 3
0 4 | 1 4 | 2 4 | 3 4 | 4 4
0 5 | 1 5 | 2 5 | 3 5 | 4 5 | 5 5
0 6 | 1 6 | 2 6 | 3 6 | 4 6 | 5 6 | 6 6

19

6	2	0	8	2	1	5	6	9	1	5
5	6	6	3	5	8	4	6	9	1	4
7	7	7	7	9	0	8	6	4	8	3
0	8	9	3	4	7	0	6	2	1	2
0	4	4	0	4	0	1	5	4	5	0
9	1	6	1	3	3	7	7	2	7	4
5	9	4	6	8	0	1	6	1	9	3
8	9	7	9	5	6	8	3	9	9	1
8	2	2	2	0	5	7	8	2	3	3
3	2	7	3	2	5	1	8	5	4	0

0 0
0 1 | 1 1
0 2 | 1 2 | 2 2
0 3 | 1 3 | 2 3 | 3 3
0 4 | 1 4 | 2 4 | 3 4 | 4 4
0 5 | 1 5 | 2 5 | 3 5 | 4 5 | 5 5
0 6 | 1 6 | 2 6 | 3 6 | 4 6 | 5 6 | 6 6
0 7 | 1 7 | 2 7 | 3 7 | 4 7 | 5 7 | 6 7 | 7 7
0 8 | 1 8 | 2 8 | 3 8 | 4 8 | 5 8 | 6 8 | 7 8 | 8 8
0 9 | 1 9 | 2 9 | 3 9 | 4 9 | 5 9 | 6 9 | 7 9 | 8 9 | 9 9

20

2	2	4	7	8	1	2	8	4	8	5
1	2	1	6	7	3	0	5	5	6	2
7	6	4	0	2	3	5	6	6	1	9
9	4	5	3	4	4	1	3	5	5	1
2	4	0	9	8	8	4	7	7	3	1
7	5	7	5	6	1	0	2	2	9	8
9	6	6	8	0	8	3	9	3	7	7
8	2	7	5	0	4	0	6	3	5	2
8	0	0	6	9	4	0	9	1	9	1
3	1	6	4	9	9	0	7	8	3	3

0 0
0 1 | 1 1
0 2 | 1 2 | 2 2
0 3 | 1 3 | 2 3 | 3 3
0 4 | 1 4 | 2 4 | 3 4 | 4 4
0 5 | 1 5 | 2 5 | 3 5 | 4 5 | 5 5
0 6 | 1 6 | 2 6 | 3 6 | 4 6 | 5 6 | 6 6
0 7 | 1 7 | 2 7 | 3 7 | 4 7 | 5 7 | 6 7 | 7 7
0 8 | 1 8 | 2 8 | 3 8 | 4 8 | 5 8 | 6 8 | 7 8 | 8 8
0 9 | 1 9 | 2 9 | 3 9 | 4 9 | 5 9 | 6 9 | 7 9 | 8 9 | 9 9

21

6	4	1	4	12	7	8	8	1	2	0	3	5	9
4	8	7	4	0	7	0	5	9	11	0	1	0	4
10	11	5	9	12	7	2	4	9	6	9	5	2	2
10	11	12	7	7	1	6	10	7	3	1	0	0	0
7	1	8	10	8	12	6	4	4	2	1	2	8	6
2	9	3	5	12	7	6	9	0	9	11	5	8	3
10	8	7	5	10	0	1	9	4	11	9	7	6	3
4	1	9	3	4	6	1	2	3	11	11	12	11	2
12	12	10	12	8	11	2	6	1	6	4	6	10	10
10	8	5	5	11	1	3	3	4	8	11	5	8	3
3	7	0	1	10	11	6	2	4	7	0	7	3	5
9	0	8	8	10	5	6	10	6	11	0	12	12	12
9	12	2	13	3	5	1	10	11	3	2	9	5	2

0 0 | 1 1 | 2 3 | 3 6 | 4 10 | 6 8 | 8 10
0 1 | 1 2 | 2 4 | 3 7 | 4 11 | 6 9 | 8 11
0 2 | 1 3 | 2 5 | 3 8 | 4 12 | 6 10 | 8 12
0 3 | 1 4 | 2 6 | 3 9 | 5 5 | 6 11 | 9 9
0 4 | 1 5 | 2 7 | 3 10 | 5 6 | 6 12 | 9 10
0 5 | 1 6 | 2 8 | 3 11 | 5 7 | 7 7 | 9 11
0 6 | 1 7 | 2 9 | 3 12 | 5 8 | 7 8 | 9 12
0 7 | 1 8 | 2 10 | 4 4 | 5 9 | 7 9 | 10 10
0 8 | 1 9 | 2 11 | 4 5 | 5 10 | 7 10 | 10 11
0 9 | 1 10 | 2 12 | 4 6 | 5 11 | 7 11 | 10 12
0 10 | 1 11 | 3 3 | 4 7 | 5 12 | 7 12 | 11 11
0 11 | 1 12 | 3 4 | 4 8 | 6 6 | 8 8 | 11 12
0 12 | 2 2 | 3 5 | 4 9 | 6 7 | 8 9 | 12 12

Critical
Thinking
Puzzles

Critical Thinking Puzzles

When we think critically we are engaging in intellectual strategies to probe the basic nature of a problem, situation, or puzzle. By these strategies, we mean making observations, predictions, generalizations, reasonings by assumptions, comparisons and contrasts, uncovering relationships between the parts to the whole, and looking for sequences. It sounds like a lot, but everyone has these skills and the puzzles in this book are designed to challenge, exercise, and stretch the way you interpret the world.

Some of the puzzles here are old favorites that have entertained people for years. Several of them are presented in their time-tested way. Most of the standards, however, have a new twist or updated story added. Other puzzles require some inventive solutions, so don't be afraid to be creative. Most of them can be done with pencil or pen.

Some require inexpensive material that can probably be found around the house: a pair of scissors, markers, tape, toothpicks, and a yardstick. Even though some puzzles can be solved using algebra, they were selected for their ability to be visualized and figured out this way. Therefore, in addition to being fun to do, they offer an arena to practice thinking skills.

Statements such as "I want you to memorize this list!" or "That's a good answer, but it wasn't the one I expected" help to extinguish critical thought. Although you'll never have to measure an ant's path or alter a flag, the process of creating and evaluating a reasonable answer is a worthwhile experience. By the time you finish this book, those powerful skills will be back on track, probing your everyday experiences for a more thorough and deeper understanding. Ready to start? Great, because the fun is about to begin.

Puzzle Paths

Sam Loyd was one of the most published and brilliant puzzle creators of all time. Born in 1841, Sam was an accomplished chess player by his early teens. He created puzzles based upon the moves of chess pieces. Loyd also produced thousands of other puzzles, many of which still appear today with contemporary twists and slight modifications. The maze below is based upon one of his earliest puzzle ideas. Can you complete the challenge?

The Amusing Amusement Park has three rides. It also has three gates with signs that identify the ride to which they lead. The only problem is that the architect forgot the layout of the connecting paths. Can you help? Draw three paths that connect the rides to their gates. The paths can't meet or cross.

Answer on page 312.

Turn, Turn, Turn

Ever heard of a multiaxial stimulator? Years ago, it appeared as a training device for astronauts and pilots. Nowadays, it's often found at beaches, amusement parks, and fairs. The MAS consists of three loops, each inside of the other. Each loop is free to rotate in only one dimension. The "pilot" is fastened to the middle of the innermost loop. In this position, a person gets to experience all three turning motions at the same time.

Let's strap the number "4" in this simulator. Suppose each of the loops made one half rotation. How would the "4" appear after it was flipped, turned, and spun halfway in all three dimensions? You can select from the choices below.

Answer on page 315.

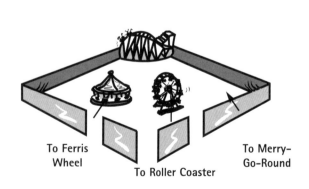

To Ferris Wheel

To Roller Coaster

To Merry-Go-Round

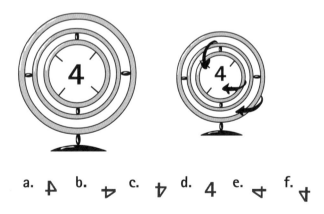

a. b. c. d. e. f.

Mind Bend

According to Einstein, in some places the shortest distance between two points is not a straight line! Consider this: In space, the gravitational field of huge objects is strong enough to warp space. In these curved dimensions, the concept represented by a straight line bends to fit the framework of the distorted space. Mind bending, huh?

Here's another type of mind bender. The shape below is made from a single index card. No section of the card has been removed or taped back in place. Can you duplicate its appearance using several snips of a scissors? Have fun!

Answer on page 310-311.

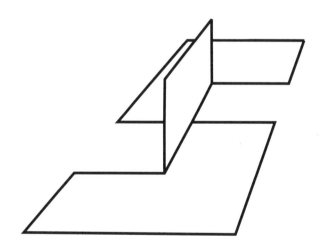

Whale of a Problem

In spite of their name, killer whales don't hunt and kill people. In fact, these dolphin-like animals prefer to eat smaller marine animals, such as seals and penguins. Biologists believe that rare attacks on humans occur because of misidentification. Obscured by daylight or icebergs, the image of a person may be mistaken for that of a penguin from below.

Now here's the problem. Acting alone, it takes two killer whales 2 minutes to catch two seals. Based upon this rate, how long will it take a pod of ten killer whales to catch ten seals?

Answer on page 315.

Main Attraction

Like all magnets, a bar magnet has a North and South Pole. At each of these poles, the magnetic force is the strongest. It is powerful enough to attract and repel iron objects. Near the middle of the magnet, however, the force is hardly detectable.

Suppose you have two identical iron bars. Only one of the bars has been magnetized. Suppose you can only pick up and manipulate one bar of these two bars. How can you tell if it is the magnetized or unmagnetized bar?

Answer on page 310.

Runaway Runway

"Good afternoon. This is your captain speaking. We're fourth in line for departure. As soon as these four albatross birds take off, we'll begin our flight. Thank you for your patience."

Strange, but true. Pilots must sometimes compete with birds for runway usage. The same physical principles that lift an aircraft into the sky are at work in our feathered friends. Runways that are constructed to offer better lifting conditions for aircrafts inadvertently produce great takeoff locations for birds.

Speaking of runways, here's our puzzle. If an airport has three separate runways, there can be a maximum of three intersections. Suppose there are four runways. What is the maximum number of possible intersections?

Answer on page 312.

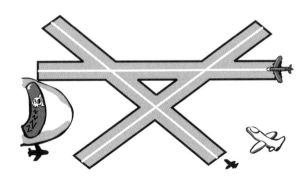

Raises and Cuts

Like many modern-day products, paper toweling arose from a factory mistake. A mill-sized roll of paper that should have been cut and packaged into soft bathroom tissue was manufactured thick and wrinkled. Instead of junking the roll, the workers perforated the unattractive paper into towel-sized sheets. And so, the paper towel was born.

Several years ago, Moe and Bo began work at a paper towel factory. At the end of the first week, the owner evaluated both workers. Pleased with Moe, she increased his weekly wage by 10%. Disappointed with Bo, she cut her salary by 10%. The following week, the owner decided to make their salaries more equal. To do so, she cut Moe's new salary by 10%. At the same time, she increased Bo's salary by 10%. Now, which worker earned more?

Answer on page 312.

The Race Is On

The material we call rubber is another product of a mishap in the kitchen! Prior to the mid-1800s, rubber was a troublesome material. In the summer heat, it became soft and sticky. In the winter cold, it became hard and brittle. In searching for a way to improve the properties of rubber, Charles Goodyear accidentally spilled a spoonful of a rubber and sulfur mixture onto his stove. When he later examined the solidified spill, he uncovered a flexible material that could withstand heat and cold.

Take a look at the two solid rubber wheels below. Both have been modified by retired ice skaters. On the first wheel, 4 pounds of lead are positioned in one central lump. On the second wheel, the same amount of lead is spread out into four 1-pound lumps so that they are positioned closer to the wheel's rim.

Suppose these wheels are released down identical inclines. If we don't consider air resistance, will these wheels accelerate at the same rate?

Answer on page 313.

Screwy Stuff

Take a close look at the two screws below. Suppose they were both turned in a counterclockwise rotation. What will happen to each screw?

Answer on page 313.

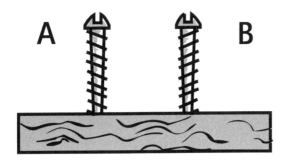

Screws in the Head

The pitch made by a vibrating string is dependent upon several factors, including the tension in the string. The more tightly pulled (greater tension), the higher the pitch. Likewise, if the string is relaxed (less tension), it produces a note of lower pitch. Many guitars have a screw-like arrangement that varies the tension in the individual strings. As the tuner head is turned, this movement is transferred to a post. The turn of the post changes the tension in its wrapped string to produce a note of different pitch.

Take a look at the tuning heads below. What happens to the pitch of the sound when the head is rotated in a clockwise manner?

Answer on page 313.

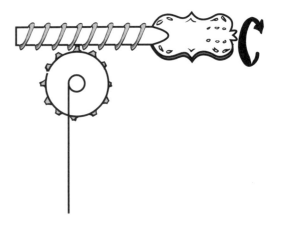

Change of Pace

Here are several puzzles that use a handful of change.

Consider this: I have ten coins in my pocket. The value of these coins is 50 cents. How many coins of each denomination are there?

Okay, so that one wasn't too difficult. How about finding the identity of thirty coins whose value is $1.00?

Answer on page 3078.

Spiral²

While exploring the ruins of an ancient city, an archaeologist uncovers an odd structure. The structure is made of stone walls that form a square spiral. The sides of the outside spiral measure 100 feet X 100 feet. The path throughout the entire structure is 2 feet wide.

If the archeologist walks along the exact center of the path, how far will he travel from the entrance to the end of the spiral?

Answer on page 313.

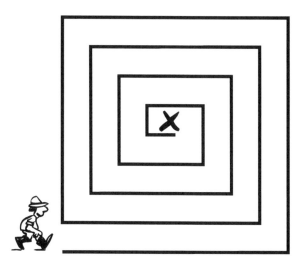

Take 'em Away

This arrangement of toothpicks forms fourteen different squares of various sizes. Can you remove six toothpicks and leave only three squares behind?

Answer on page 314.

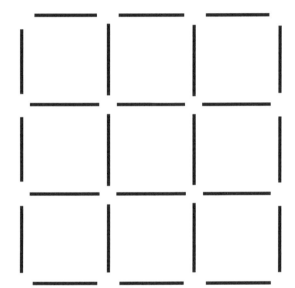

Get Set. Go!

Two cyclists race along a straight course. The faster of the pair maintains an average speed of 30 mph. The slower cyclist averages 25 miles per hour. When the race ends, the judges announce that the faster cyclist crossed the finish line one hour before the slower racer. How many miles long was the racing course?

Answer on pages 308.

Don't Stop Now

Now that you are familiar with the pattern, let's try one more removal problem. Starting with the same twenty-four toothpick grid, remove eight toothpicks and leave exactly three squares behind.

Answer on page 308.

Coin Roll

Run your fingernail around the rim of a dime or quarter and you'll feel a series of small ridges. These ridges appeared on coins hundreds of years ago. At that time, many coins were made out of silver and other valuable metals. To prevent people from "shaving" the metal from the edge of the coin (and selling the metal shavings), telltale ridges were added to the coin's rim. If a coin's edge was cut away, the telltale ridges would be lost.

In this problem, we'll use those ridges to prevent the coins from slipping. Consider two dimes within a track formed by parallel chopsticks. Although the coins can move, their snug fit makes both coins move at the same time. Therefore, if we were to rotate one of the dimes, the other would spin at the same speed but in the opposite direction. This results in both dimes moving along the track and maintaining their

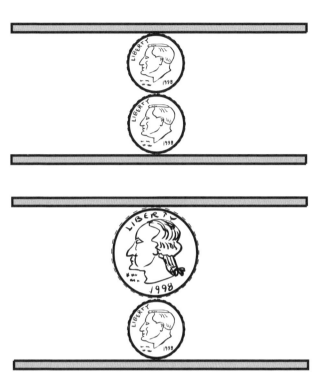

relative head-to-head position. Suppose, however, we change our setup and replace one of the dimes with a quarter. If the quarter is rotated along the track, how would its head-to-head position with the smaller dime change?

Answer on page 307.

More Coinage

The four coins are positioned at the corners of a square. The side length of this square (measured from the center of each coin) is 8 inches. Here's the challenge. Can you change the positions of only two coins so that so that the new square formed by the coin arrangement has a side length slightly more than $5\frac{1}{2}$ inches?

Answer on page 311.

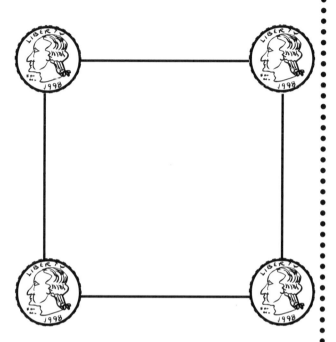

Some Things Never Change

People have written down puzzles for nearly 5000 years. One of the first puzzle collections was recorded about 1650 b.c. on a scroll called the Rhind papyrus. The word Rhind comes from the name Henry Rhind, a Scottish archaeologist who explored Egypt. Papyrus is a paper-like material that was used as a writing tablet by the ancient Egyptians.

The Rhind papyrus is a scroll that is over 18 feet long and about a foot wide. It was written on both sides by a person named Ahmes. Roughly translated (and somewhat updated), one of the puzzles from the scroll is presented below.

There are seven houses, each containing seven cats. Each cat kills seven mice, and each mouse would have eaten seven ears of corn. Each ear of corn would have produced seven sacks of grain. What is the total number of all of these items?

Answer on page 313.

Doing Wheelies

The outer rim of each "double wheel" is twice the diameter of the wheel's inner rim. Suppose the top wheel rotates at ten revolutions per second. At what speed will wheel A and wheel B spin?

Answer on page 308.

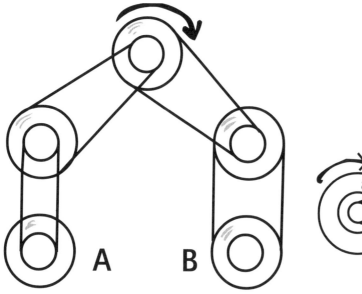

More Wheelies

The outermost rim of these wheels is twice the diameter of the middle rim. The middle rim is twice the diameter of the innermost rim. Suppose wheel A rotates at sixteen revolutions per second. How many revolutions will wheel C complete in a minute?

Answer on page 311.

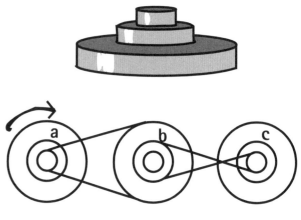

Good Guess

In order to win a free visit to the dentist, students had to guess the exact number of gumballs in a fish bowl. The students guessed 45, 41, 55, 50, and 43, but no one won. The guesses were off by 3, 7, 5, 7, and 2 (in no given order). From this information, determine the number of gumballs in the bowl.

Answer on page 309.

Check It Out

The six sections below are parts of a 5 x 5 checkerboard grid. Can you piece them back together to form the original pattern?

Answer on page 307.

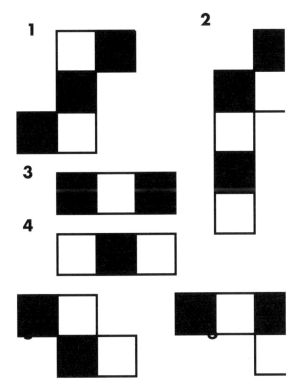

Oops, I Wasn't Concentrating

A pitcher is filled to the brim with grape juice. While raiding the refrigerator, Anthony accidentally knocks the pitcher over so that half of the contents spill out. Hoping no one will notice, Anthony adds tap water to the half-filled pitcher, bringing the volume of the diluted juice to the top. He then pours himself a glass of the watered down juice, leaving the pitcher three-fourths full.

"Yuck! This needs more flavor!" he exclaims and then adds more grape flavor by filling the pitcher to the brim with double-strength grape juice.

How does the concentration of this final solution compare with the original grape drink?

Answer on page 312.

217

Bridge, Anyone?

Ever heard of Galloping Girdie? If not, perhaps you've seen an old science fiction movie that showed a clip of a large suspension bridge twisting apart and falling into the river below it. That was Galloping Girdie.

It spanned a large river in the state of Washington. Soon after it was constructed, people noticed that winds would cause the bridge to sway and shake. During one incident of heavy winds, the bridge shook so violently that it fell apart into the river below. Bye-bye, Girdie.

Now, it's your turn to design a bridge. To build it, you'll need three ice cream sticks. If you don't have these sticks, you can use three pieces of stiff cardboard. The cardboard sections should be $4\frac{1}{2}$ inches long and $\frac{1}{2}$ inch wide.

Position three cups in a triangular pattern. The cups should be placed so that the edge-to-edge distance between any two of the cups is 5 inches.

Hmm... 5-inch canyons, but only $4\frac{1}{2}$-inch bridges. Your job is to construct a bridge using these three pieces and span the gaps connecting all three cups.

Answer on page 307.

Face Lift

Take a look at the shape below. Although it is made up of four identical cubes, you can only see three of them. The fourth cube is hidden in the bottom back-corner. Imagine picking the shape up and examining it from all angles. How many different cube faces can you count?

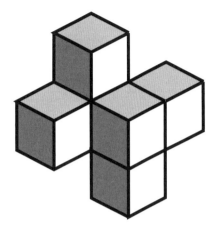

Okay, okay, okay. Here's one more. This one consists of only five cubes. Actually it

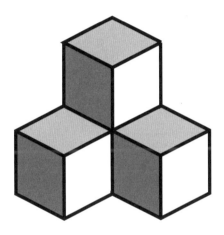

Okay, so it wasn't that hard. Try this one. The "double L" shape is made up of six cubes. The sixth cube is hidden in the back of the middle layer. If you could examine the stack from all angles, how many faces would you see?

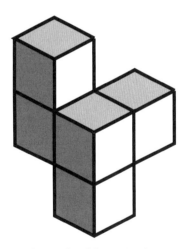

resembles the "double L" shape, except that one of the cubes is removed.

Answer on page 308.

Trying Times

The triangle below is divided into four equal parts. Suppose you can paint one or more of these four smaller parts black. How many different and distinguishable patterns (including the pattern which has no painted triangles) can you form?

Remember, each pattern must be unique and not be duplicated by simply rotating the large figure.

Answer on page 314.

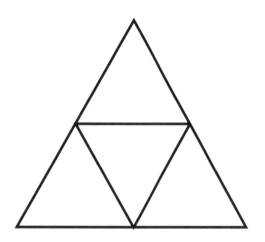

Weighty Problem

Did you know that during periods of weightlessness, astronauts lose bone mass? To prevent any serious loss, people in space must exercise. Stressing and stretching body parts help keep bone material from being reabsorbed into the body.

For a moment, let's imagine our weightless astronaut returning to Earth. She steps onto a scale and weighs herself. When the lab assistant asks her for her weight, she offers an obscure (but challenging) answer.

"According to this scale, I weigh 60 pounds plus half my weight."

Can you figure out how much this puzzling space traveler weighs?

Answer on pages 315.

Number Blocks

Take a look at the three stacks of numbered blocks below. Can you rearrange the blocks by exchanging one (and only one) from each of the three stacks so that the sum of the numbers in each stack is equal to the sum of numbers in either other stack?

Answer on page 311.

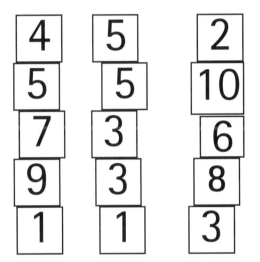

Separation Anxiety

Using three straight lines, separate the apples from the oranges.

Answer on page 313.

Give Me Five

How many 5's are in the number 5555?

Answer on page 308.

Breaking Up Is Hard to Do... Sometimes

Take a look at the square and triangle below. Both figures are divided into four equal and identical parts so that each part

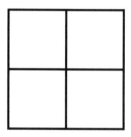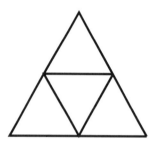

has the same shape of the original figure (only smaller).

So far, so good. Now try to divide the figure below into four equal and identical parts, each with the same shape as the original figure.

Answer on page 306.

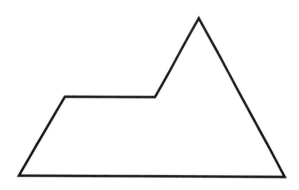

Mind Slice

Close your eyes and imagine a perfect sphere. Now, imagine a cleaver placed at a point anywhere on the surface of the sphere. How does changing the angle of the cleaver slice affect the shape of the exposed faces?

Answer on page 311.

Satellite Surveyor

Satellites that orbit the Earth can see all sorts of things. Spy satellites, for example, have lenses that are powerful enough to "read" license plate numbers on cars. Other types of satellites can "look beneath" the Earth's surface. Some of these images have been used to uncover lost civilizations that have been buried for thousands of years under shifting desert sands.

In this problem, we'll use our satellite to help survey a plot of land.

The basic plot is a square that measures 20 miles on a side. Suppose the midpoint of each side is used as a marker to divide the entire plot into nine plots of various sizes and shapes. Without performing any higher math magic (just stick to plain ol' logic, with a little geometry), what is the area of the shaded central square?

NOTE: Before you bask in premature glory, it is not equal to 100 square miles!

Answer on page 312.

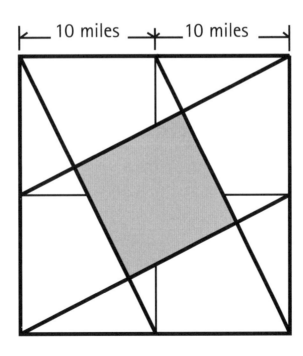

Say Cheese

The total surface area of any cube is equal to the sum of the surface areas of each of the six sides. For example, the cheese cube below measures 2 inches on each side. Therefore, the surface area of each side equals 2 inches x 2 inches, or 4 square inches. Since there are six sides, the total surface area of this cube is 24 square inches.

Now, the challenge. Using as many cuts as needed, divide this cube into pieces whose surface area sum is twice the surface area of this 2 x 2 cube.

Answer on page 312.

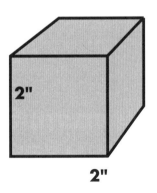

2"

2"

Magic Star

For those of you who are tired of magic squares and magic triangles, may we present The Magic Star? In this puzzle, you'll have to use the numbers one through twelve. Only one number can be placed in a circle, and all the numbers must be used. When placed correctly, the sum of all rows of four must be the same.

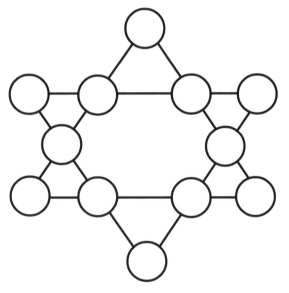

HINT: All of the side sums equal twenty-six.

Answer on page 310.

Keep on Tickin'

Divide the face of a watch into three sections. The sum of the numbers included on each section must equal the sum of the numbers on either of the other two sections. Let's not waste any time—the clock is ticking.

Answer on pages 309.

Going Batty

Click, click, click, click. Like submarines, bats have a sonar system called echolocation. They use their echolocation to find objects. The clicking sounds made by bats move outward like the beam of a lighthouse. When the sounds strike an object (such as an insect meal), they are reflected back to the bat's large ears. With incredible speed, the bat's brain analyzes the echo return time and uses it to accurately locate the target's position.

Now, let's put that echolocation to work. Over a five-night period, a bat targets and captures a total of a hundred beetles. During each night, the bat captured six more beetles than on the previous night. How many beetles did the bat catch on each night?

Answer on page 308.

Cards, Anyone?

Use a pair of scissors to carefully cut out two unequal corners of an index card as shown below. Can you now use the scissors to cut this modified card into two identical halves?

NOTE: The identical halves must be formed without flipping either piece over.

Let's keep up the cutting challenge. Copy the pattern below onto an index card. Use your scissors to trim off the excess card stock. Now, here's the challenge. Divide this shape into four equal and identical parts that can fit back together to form a perfect square.

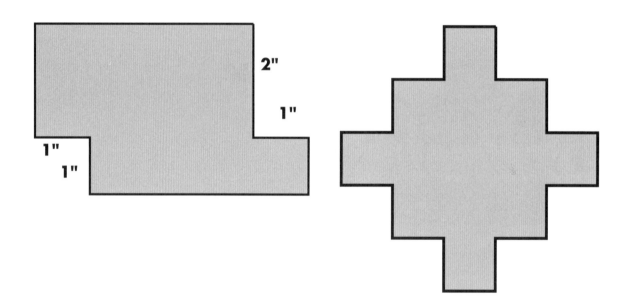

Answers on page 307.

Sequence Grid

A sequence grid is formed by items that are related by their order. Here are two examples. As you can see, the placement of the numbers and letters reflects a sequence.

   The first square is filled in an order based on dividing a number in half. The second square illustrates a sequence of letters that is separated by single (but not recorded) middle letters.

512	256	128
64	32	16
8	4	2

A	C	E
G	I	K
M	O	Q

Now that you know what a sequence grid is, here's one to sharpen your puzzling skills on.

Answer on page 313.

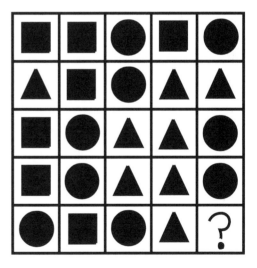

Breaking the Rules

A ruler is placed on two pieces of chalk as shown below. As the ruler is pushed, it moves 4 inches ahead. How far did either one of the chalk pieces roll?

Answer on page 306.

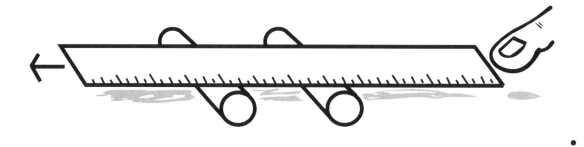

Balance

Suppose you have a balance and a 2-gram and 5-gram mass. How can the balance be used only three times to separate 80 grams of fat into piles of 13 grams and 67 grams?

Answer on page 306.

Togetherness

A computer and its monitor weigh a total of 48 pounds. If the monitor weighs twice as much as the computer, how much does each piece of hardware weigh?

Answer on page 314.

Big Magic

The figure below is called a magic square. Do you see why it's called magic? The sum of any three-box side (and the two three-box diagonals) is equal to the sum of any other side (or diagonal). In this case, they are all equal to fifteen.

The sections belong to a four-by-four magic square. Your job is to assemble these sections into a complete sixteen-box magic square. To do so, you'll first have to uncover the sum of the side for this figure.

8	3	4
1	5	9
6	7	2

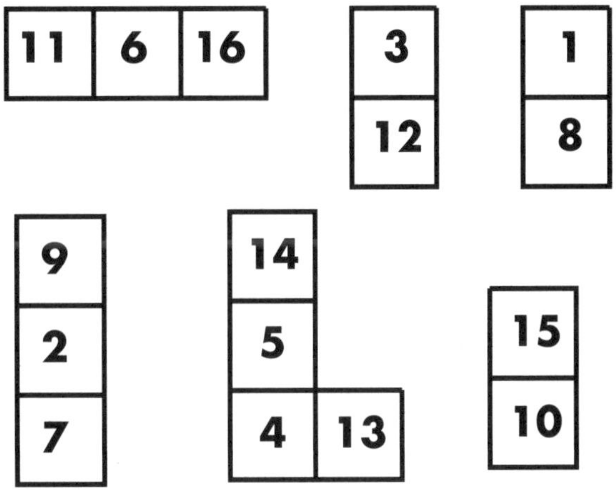

Answer on page 306.

Look Over Here

Note the direction in which each eye looks. Can you uncover the pattern? Good. Now find the empty eye. In which direction should this eye be looking?

Answer on page 310.

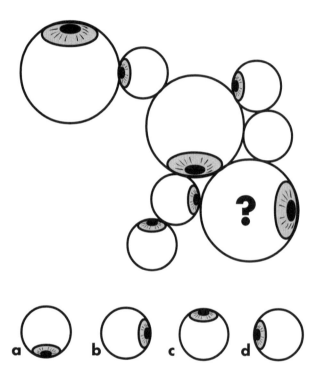

Time on Your Hands

Examine the series of three clock-faces shown below. When you uncover the pattern of the hand movement, select from the choice of times that will be closest to what the fourth clock should read.

Answer on page 314.

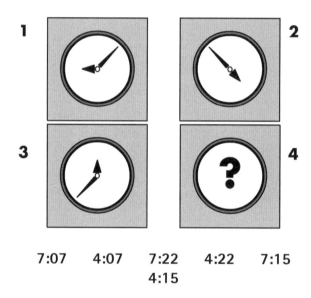

7:07   4:07   7:22   4:22   7:15
4:15

. . . .

Take Your Pick

Arrange eight toothpicks (on a flat surface) so that they form two squares and four triangles.

Answer on page 314.

. . . .

One Way Only

Can you trace the following figure using only one continuous line? Place your pencil anywhere on the figure. Then, draw the rest of the figure without lifting your pencil from the page.

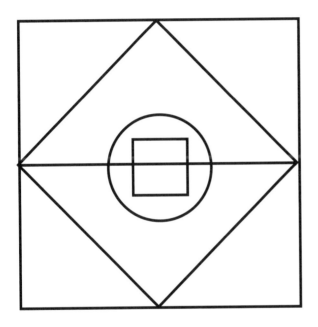

NOTE: This line cannot cross over itself nor retrace any part of its path.

Answer on page 311.

Lasagna Cut

A square pan filled with piping-hot lasagna is set aside to cool. When the hungry chefs return, they discover that a quarter of the lasagna has mysteriously disappeared (as shown below). Frustrated, they decide to divide the remaining piece into four equal portions before any more is eaten. All cuts must be normal—no slicing through the plane of the surface allowed.

What is the cutting pattern that will meet the needs of these chefs?

HINT: The simplest solution requires cutting this meal into eight pieces and supplying each person with two smaller pieces.

Answer on pages 309-310.

Iron Horse Race

Two trains race against each other on parallel tracks. The Casey Jones Special is a coal-fed steam engine that travels at a respectable speed. The newer, oil-burning Metropolitan Diesel travels $1\frac{1}{2}$ times the speed of The Casey Jones Special. To make the race a closer competition, The Casey Jones Special begins the race $1\frac{1}{2}$ hours before its opponent. How long will it take the Metropolitan Diesel to catch up to the slower steam engine?

Answer on page 309.

Thick as a Brick

If the chimney below is complete on all four sides, how many bricks does the whole structure contain?

Answer on page 314.

Here, Art, Art, Art

How quickly can you uncover the perfect five-pointed star hidden in the design below?

Answer on page 309.

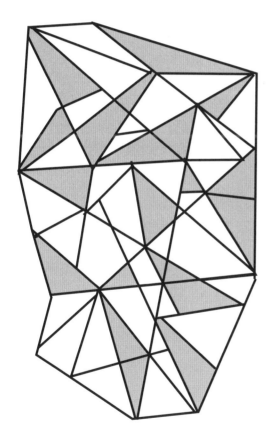

Surrounded By Squares

How many squares can you uncover in the pattern below? Don't forget to count the outer border as one of your answers!

Answer on page 314.

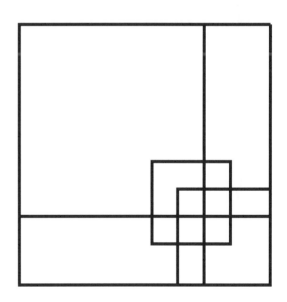

More Cheese

A grocer has a large cube of cheese that she wishes to divide into twenty-seven smaller and equal-sized cubes. To cut out the twenty-seven blocks, she uses two cuts to divide the cube into three slices. She stacks these slices atop of each other and makes two more cuts. Finally, she rotates the cube a quarter-turn and makes the final cut. The result is twenty-seven identical cubes made with six cuts. Is it possible to get the twenty-seven cubes with fewer cuts? If so, how?

Answer on page 311.

Break It Up!

If you look carefully, you'll be able to uncover thirty squares in the toothpick pattern below. Your challenge is to find the fewest number of toothpicks that, when removed, leaves no complete square pattern intact.

Answer on page 306.

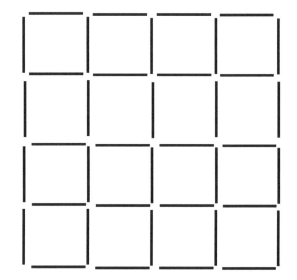

Exactly... Well, Almost

Which of the designs below is unlike the other five?

Answer on page 308.

Parts of a Whole

Copy the five shapes shown below onto a separate sheet of paper. Use a pair of scissors to carefully cut out the shapes. Here's the challenge. Arrange them to form a triangle whose three sides are of equal length.

Answer on page 312.

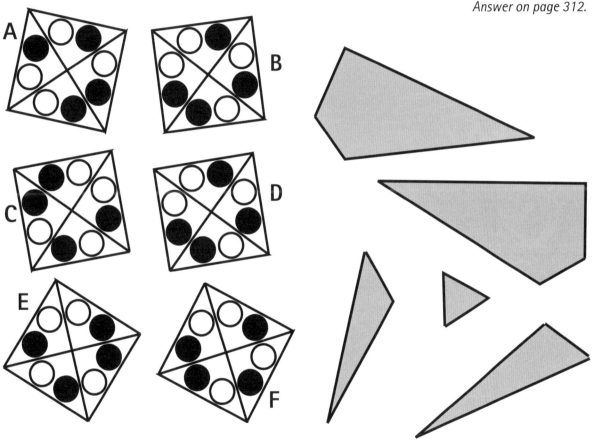

A Game for Losers

The object of this modified game of tic-tac-toe is to lose! In order to win, you must force your opponent to complete three squares in a row. Let's enter a game that has already been started. You are "O" and it is your turn. In which box or boxes should you place your "O" marker to ensure that you win by losing (no matter where your opponent goes)?

Answer on page 308.

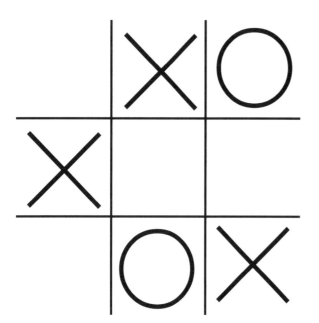

Roller Coaster, Roll!

Ed and his identical twin brother Ed build roller coaster tracks. They've just completed two hills that are both 40 feet high. As you can see, the slopes of the two hills are somewhat different. Ed (the older twin) rides a car that will travel along on a straight slope. Ed (the younger twin) rides a car that will travel along a curved slope. If both cars are released at the exact same time, which Ed will arrive at the bottom of this slope first?

Answer on page 312.

Another Ant Walk

A queen ant finds herself climbing onto the metal framework of a bridge at the spot marked by the arrow.

Can you trace the path she'd need to follow in order to walk across every piece of frame only once and end up at the top of the bridge (marked by an X)?

Her path must be a continuous line.

Answer on page 314.

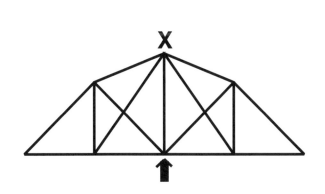

A Class Act

There are thirty students in a class. Five of these students do not play any sort of musical instrument. Among the others, eighteen students play guitar. Six of these guitar players also play keyboards. How many of students in the class play only keyboards?

Answer on page 307.

Cool Cut

Shut your eyes and try to imagine a perfect ice cube. If you're good at visualizing, you may be able to "see" the edges and faces that are positioned on the far side of the cube. Good. Now, here's the challenge. With one cut, how can you divide this cube so that a perfect triangular face is exposed? Don't forget, a regular triangle has all three sides of equal length.

Answer on page 307.

Melt Down

Unlike most liquids, water freezes into a solid that is less dense than its former liquid state. Since it is less dense, ice floats in water. At the surface, the ice acts as an insulator to help trap heat within the water below. This layer of frozen insulation actually insulates lakes, rivers, ponds, and oceans from freezing into a complete solid.

Now let's bring this information back to the kitchen. An ice cube floats freely in a glass filled to the brim with water. Will the water level rise or sink as the ice cube melts?

Answer on page 310.

What's the Angle?

An equilateral triangle has three sides that are all of equal length. This familiar shape can be constructed from three identical pieces. Examine the shapes below. Which of these shapes illustrates this building block? Once you've selected the shape, make three copies of it on a separate sheet of paper. Cut out and arrange these pieces so that they form an equilateral triangle.

Answer on page 315.

Here, Spot, Spot, Spot

Without lifting your pencil from the paper, draw six straight lines that connect all sixteen of the dots below. To make things more of a challenge, the line pattern that you create must begin at the "x".

Answer on page 309.

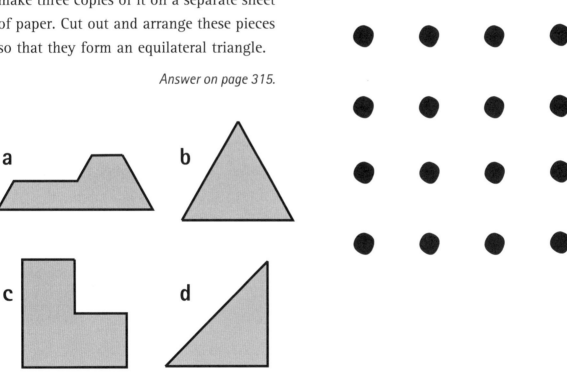

Keeping Time

The strike of a lightning bolt can create a tremendous surge of electricity. If this electric flow reaches the delicate circuits of a computer, it can "burn out" the sensitive components. To prevent against this damage, computers are plugged into surge protectors, which stop the electric flow if a damaging level of electricity is detected.

In this problem, there are no surge protectors. Two electronic clocks are plugged directly into the wall socket. A surge of electricity flows through both clocks and affects their time-keeping circuits. One clock is now 5 minutes per hour fast. The other clock is now 5 minutes per hour slow. In how many hours will the clocks be exactly one hour apart?

Answer on page 309.

Wrap It Up

You are about to engage your intellect in quite an interesting challenge.

Did you know that fortune cookies didn't originate in China? They were created in the U.S. by the owner of an Asian restaurant who wished to amuse his customers while they waited for their meals to be cooked. Over time, fortune cookies evolved into a treat that is now offered at the end of the meal. That's a wrap. And speaking of wraps...

Take a look at the steps in which the cookie wrapper below was folded. In the final step, two holes were punched through the layers of the folds.

Now unroll this wrapper. Which of the patterns would it resemble?

Answer on page 315.

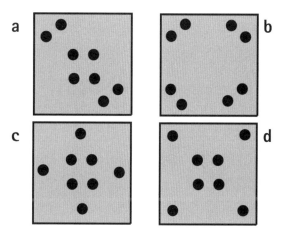

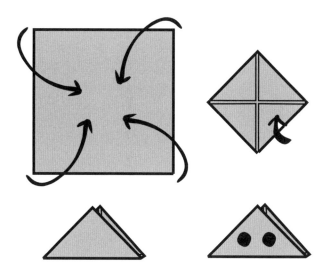

And a Cut Below

Have you ever heard of the cheesemobile? It's a giant refrigerated truck that was built to carry a piece of Cheddar cheese. Why, then, all the fuss? Simple. The cheese weighed over 40,000 pounds!

Take a look at the smaller barrel of cheese below. If you make these three complete and straight cuts, how many pieces of cheese will you have?

Answer on page 315.

Egg Exactly

Suppose you have only two egg timers, a 5-minute and a 3-minute. Can you use these two measuring devices to time an egg that must be boiled for exactly 2 minutes?

Answer on page 315.

242

Losing Marbles?

Marbles have been around for a long time. In fact, archaeologists have discovered marbles buried alongside an Egyptian child who died over 4000 years ago! The word "marble," however, comes from the Greek word marmaros, which is a white polished stone made from the mineral agate.

Now it's your turn to play with them. Place a marble in a cup and carry it to the opposite side of the room. Too easy, huh? To make this more challenging, the cup must be turned upside down. This may take a little bit of creative problem solving, but it can be done.

Answer on page 315.

JUST A LITTLE LONGER. I KNOW I CAN FIGURE IT OUT

A Puzzle of Portions

Did you know that 3 ounces plus 3 ounces doesn't always equal 6 ounces? As illogical as this may sound, its true because of the behavior of the small particles (and spaces) that make up liquids. When different liquids are mixed, the particles tend to fill in some of the open spaces. As a result, the liquid becomes more compact and occupies less volume. It's only a small difference, but it is measurable.

Let's try mixing something whose volume does not change. Your challenge is to split some apple juice into three equal portions. The juice comes in a 24-ounce container. You have only three other containers, each holding 5, 11, and 13 ounces. How can you divide the juice into three equal portions?

HINT: At the very least, it will take four steps.

Answer on page 316.

Mixed Up?

Root beer, not cola, is the oldest-marketed soft drink in America. Before it was sold in the United States, root beer was brewed in many colonial homes. It contained many ingredients including molasses, licorice, vanilla, and the bark from birch trees. It was going to be called root tea but was later changed to root beer to attract the tavern crowd.

Here is one 8-ounce cup filled with root beer and another 8-ounce cup filled with cola. Take 1 tablespoon of root beer and add it to the cola. Stir the mixture. Now take 1 tablespoon of the mixture and add it to the root beer. Is there more root beer in the cola or cola in the root beer?

Answer on page 316.

Toothpick Teasers

For the puzzles in this group, you can also use pieces of straws or small sticks if you don't have toothpicks.

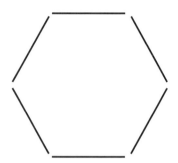

These six toothpicks are arranged in a hexagon. Starting with this arrangement, can you form two identical diamonds by moving only two toothpicks and adding just one more?

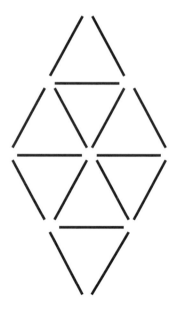

These sixteen toothpicks form eight identical triangles. Can you remove four toothpicks so that four of these triangles are left? All of the toothpicks that remain must be a side of the triangles with no loose ends sticking out.

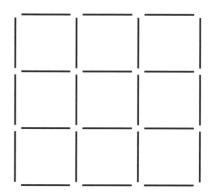

Form four (and only four) identical squares by removing eight toothpicks.

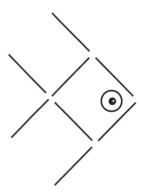

Move only three of the toothpicks (and the eye) to make the fish swim in the opposite direction.

Answers on pages 316.

Going to the Movies

Let's take a break from these puzzles and go to the movies. The map below shows an assortment of routes from your home (H) to the movie theater (M).

If you can only to travel in a north, east, or northeast direction, how many possible routes are there from your home to the theater?

Answer on page 316.

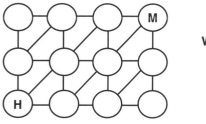

Weighing In...

The movie playing in the theater is about a scientist who changes into a fly. Before she transforms herself, she carefully weighs a jar of sleeping flies. Then, she shakes the jar to wake them up. While they are flying, the scientist weighs the jar again. Does the jar full of flies weigh less when the insects are flying?

Answer on page 316.

I COULD HAVE SWORN WE STARTED OUT WITH MORE FLIES

Monkey Business

The theater shows a double feature. The second movie is about Tarzan going into the moving business.

For his first job, Tarzan must raise a 35-pound crate into his neighbor's tree house. To do this, he first attaches a pulley to a tree branch. He then passes a rope through the pulley and ties it to the crate. Just as he is about to lift the crate, he is called away to help a nearby elephant.

A passing chimp observes the situation and decides to help. The chimp also weighs 35 pounds. As the chimp pulls down on the rope what happens to the crate?

Answer on page 316.

The Strangest Eyes

The scientist has transformed herself into a fly. One of her eyes is made up of one loop coiled into a spiral-like design. The other eye is made up of two separate loops shaped into a similar design. Can you tell which eye is the single loop and which one is the double without tracing the lines with a pencil?

Answer on page 316.

▼◀▲▼◀▲▼◀▲▼◀▲▼◀

Now Seating?

Suppose two boys and three girls go to the movie theater and they all sit in the same row. If the row has only five seats:

1. How many different ways can the two boys and three girls be seated in this row?
2. What are the chances that the two children at the ends of the row are both boys?
3. What are the chances that the two children at the ends of the row are both girls?

Answer on page 316.

▼◀▲▼◀▲▼◀▲▼◀▲▼◀

Möbius Strip

Here is one the strangest loops you'll ever see. It's called a Möbius strip in honor of the German mathematician who first investigated its properties.

To build a Möbius strip, you need a strip of paper about 1 inch wide and 10 inches long. Coil the paper into a simple loop. Then put a single twist in the loop before securing the ends together with a piece of tape. Use a marker to color one side of the strip red and the other side blue. You'll soon discover that this loop has only one side!

Möbius strips are used in manufacturing. Many machines have belts that are used to connect different spinning parts. By using a belt sewn into a Möbius strip, the belt wears evenly on both sides.

Suppose you divide right down the middle of the Möbius strip. What shape would you get? Make a guess; then use a pair of scissors to carefully divide the strip.

Answer on page 317.

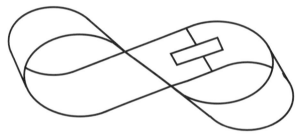

Head Count

In the final scene, a pet store owner is counting the birds and lizards that Tarzan has delivered to her store. For some odd reason, she decides to tally only the heads and scaly legs of these animals. When she has finished, she has counted thirty heads and seventy legs. How many birds and how many lizards are there?

Answer on page 316.

THINK ABOUT IT!

If we place two ants side by side on a Möbius strip and start them off in opposite directions, they will never pass each other! One ant will be walking on the top side of the strip, while the other will be on the bottom side.

Squaring Off

Make a copy of these four rectangles. Cut out the shapes and then arrange them to form a perfect square.

Answer on page 317.

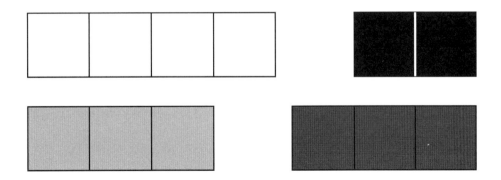

Ant Walk

Let's pick up an ant from the strip and place it on one corner of a sugar cube. This cube has sides all measuring 1 centimeter. If the ant can only walk along the edges of the cube, what is the total distance it can travel without retracing any part of its path?

Answer on page 317.

Cubic Quandaries

A wooden cube is painted red. Suppose it is divided with four equal cuts into the smaller cubes as shown.

1. How many smaller cubes are there?

2. How many of these smaller cubes
a. have only one side that is painted red?

b. have two sides that are painted red?

c. have three sides that are painted red?

d. have no sides that are red?

Answers on page 317.

Saving Face

How good are you at visualizing things? These next few puzzles test your ability to rotate and construct objects in your mind.

These blocks below represent the same block. What figure is missing on the upper face of the last block?

Finally, if you fold up this flat sheet along the inner lines, which figure represents the result?

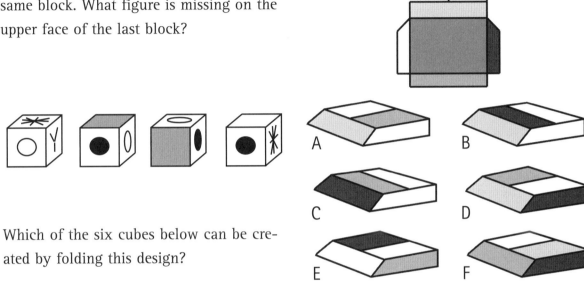

Which of the six cubes below can be created by folding this design?

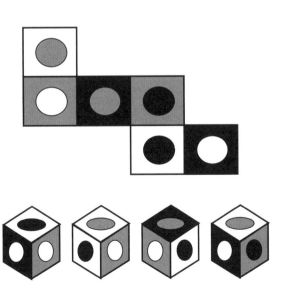

Answers on page 317.

Cut the Cards

Have you ever played cards and wished you had a different hand? Suppose you need a heart instead of a spade. Well, here's your chance to change one suit into another.

Photocopy the spade below. Then use a pair of scissors to cut it into three pieces so that the pieces can be fitted together to form a heart. Can you do it?

Answer on page 317.

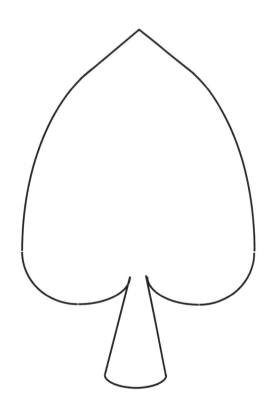

Stripped Stripe

There is a legend about a king who had six brothers and six sisters. His country's flag reflected this family structure with twelve bold stripes. When two of his brothers moved out of the kingdom, the king had two of the stripes removed.

Can you figure out how to cut the flag into as few pieces as possible so that the pieces can be put back together to make the same type of flag, but with two less stripes? No part of the flag can be discarded.

Answer on page 317.

Missing Square

Count the number of blocks that make up this pattern. If you don't want to count each block, you can multiply the number of rows by the number of columns to get a total of sixty-four blocks.

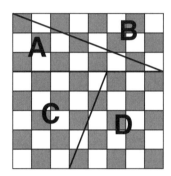

Now photocopy the pattern. Using a pair of scissors, separate the checkerboard along the inner lines. Reassemble the pieces as shown below.

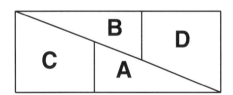

Now count the blocks, or, if you'd rather, just multiply again. The new figure is thirteen blocks long and five blocks high. That gives us sixty-five blocks. Where did the extra block come from?

Answer on page 318.

Tipping the Scales

What whole animal(s) must be added to balance the fourth scale?

Answer on page 318.

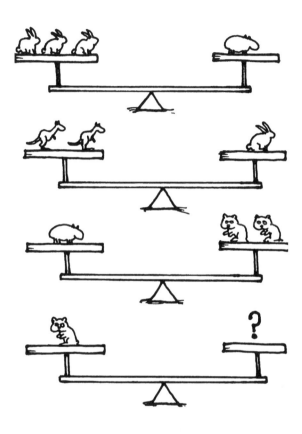

Snake Spread

These hungry snakes are swallowing each other. Since they began this odd dining experience, the circle they formed has gotten smaller. If they continue to swallow each other, what will eventually happen to the circle of snakes?

Answer on page 318.

Falcon Flight

Two bicyclists are situated 60 miles apart. One has a falcon on his shoulder. The bicyclists start riding toward each other at the same time, both maintaining a constant speed of 30 mph. The moment they begin, the falcon flies off the first cyclist's shoulder and towards the other. The falcon flies at a constant ground speed of 45 mph. When the falcon meets the other rider, he reverses direction and flies back to the first cyclist (who is now considerably closer). The falcon continues this back and forth pattern until the riders finally meet. How far did the falcon fly?

Answer on page 318.

A Question of Balance

Place two fingers at the ends of a yardstick. Slowly move the fingers toward each other. As you'll discover, your fingers always meet in the middle of the yardstick. Now place both fingers in the middle of the stick. Slowly try moving the two of them out to the opposite ends. This time you'll find that one finger remains in the middle while the other moves to the end. Can you explain this behavior?

Answer on page 318.

Well-Balanced Plate

Here's a game that you are guaranteed to win as long as you let your opponent go first. Start with a plate on the exact center of a table. Your opponent must place another plate on the table. Then, it's your turn. During each turn, both of you must continue placing plates until no more plates will fit, but, don't worry, you'll win. Can you figure out the secret?

Answer on page 318.

Robot Walkers

Have you ever seen a robot walker? It is designed to move over various types of terrain so that scientists can use it to explore nearby planets. Our robot walkers are positioned at the corners of a square plot of land. Each robot is programmed to follow the robot directly ahead of it. If all the robots move at the same speed, what will happen to the square pattern? Will the robots ever meet?

Answer on page 318.

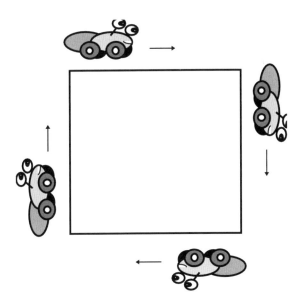

Chain Links

Suppose you own four pieces of chain. One chain has 5 links, two chains have 4 links, and one chain has 3 links.

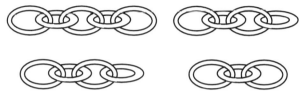

You go to the jeweler and ask her to make a bracelet using all of these chains. She says it would cost $.50 to break a link and $1.00 to weld a link together. You calculate that it would cost $6.00 to build the bracelet. The jeweler, however, says that it would only cost $4.50. Can figure out how she can assemble your bracelet for less?

Answer on page 318.

Money Magic

Look at the picture to your right. Can you guess what will happen when the bill is pulled from both ends?

After you've made your prediction, use a dollar bill and two paper clips to assemble this puzzle. Make sure that each paper clip grips only two of the three side-by-side sections. Slowly pull the bill apart. What happens to the clips? How is it possible?

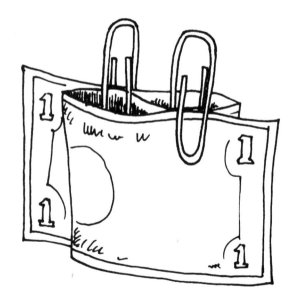

Answer on page 319.

Revolutionary Thoughts

Different things orbit the earth at various speeds and distances. For example, satellites and space instruments released by the space shuttle are only several hundred miles away from the earth, while communication satellites circle at a distance of about 22,300 miles!

In this puzzle, Satellite X-1 orbits our planet once every 9 hours, Satellite Beta once every $4^{1}/_{2}$ hours, and Satellite Parking once every 3 hours.

At time zero, the satellites are positioned in a straight line. How long will it take for all three objects to position themselves again in a straight line?

Answer on page 319.

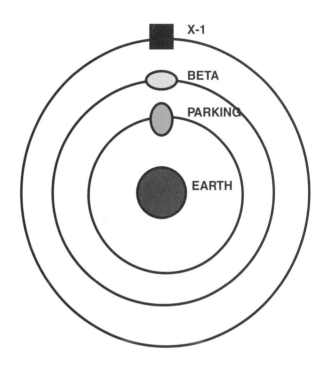

Rope Ruse

There is an old legend about an ancient magician who could tie a rope into a knot while holding on to each end of the rope. Can you?

Answer on page 319.

Baffling Holes

Black holes are celestial objects created by collapsed stars. These holes have tremendous concentration of matter and produce such a strong gravitational field that even light can't escape from it. If a black hole was placed on the surface of the earth, our entire planet would be sucked into it!

The hole in this puzzle is not as large as a black hole, but finding its solution can be a big challenge. Do you think a quarter can pass through a hole that is the size of a nickel? You can't tear, cut, or rip the hole. Impossible, you say? Trace the outline of a nickel onto an index card. Carefully cut out this outline.

HINT: Bends and twists can open up a whole new geometry.

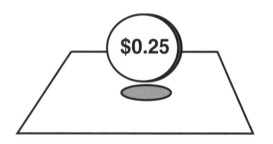

Answers on page 319.

A Giant Step

Passing a quarter through a nickel-sized hole is nothing when you can step through an index card. Carefully use a pair of scissors or a modeling knife to cut out the pattern of slots shown here. When you are finished, the hole will open in an accordion-like style and allow you to step through it!

A Fair Solution

Two teenagers are deciding how to share the last piece of pizza. One of them must divide the slice. Both are afraid that the other will cut the slice unfairly and take the larger piece. Can this conflict be resolved by these teenagers so that both will be satisfied by the other one's cut?

After finishing their pizza, the happy teenagers bring out a box of toothpicks and arrange the toothpicks as follows:

Can you remove four toothpicks and leave ten on the table?

Answers on pages 319.

Nuts!

When you rotate a bolt clockwise, it travels into the threads of a nut. When that same bolt is rotated counterclockwise, the nut and bolt will separate.

Suppose you have two bolts aligned within each other's threads. If both bolts are rotated clockwise, will they move together, separate, or remain the same distance apart?

Here's something else to think about. In many large cities, the light bulbs used in places such as subway stations are unique. Instead of screwing into the socket with a clockwise motion, they require counterclockwise turns. What sense does it make to have these different from most other bulbs?

Answers on page 319.

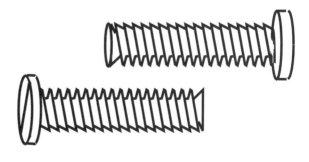

Puzzle
ANSWERS

Crosswords to Exercise Your Mind Puzzle Answers

1

```
A L A S   M A C O N   S I T E
C O S T   E R O D E   T R A Y
T R I O   T R A D E   R O L E
S N A P S H O T   D R I N K S
      P L O W   G L A D
S P R E A D   P R E C E D E S
H E A R T   T E A S E   R A W
E A T S   S H E D S   W A G E
A C E   S W I P E   C H I L E
R E S C U E R S   P L A N E T
      L E A D   M O A T
R E P O R T   S U S P E N S E
A X I S   E R A S E   V E I L
M I L E   R O V E R   E R R S
S T E T   S E E D S   R O S E
```

10

```
C L A M   L A Y E R   S P A N
L I M E   A G A V E   H O N E
U S E S   T A P E S   I O T A
B A N Q U E T   S T A R L E T
      U P S E T   O F T
L A R I A T   H A R A S S E S
E D I T S   M I S E R   H A W
A I D E   S A C K S   B A S E
D E E   B A R K S   C A R E D
S U S P E N S E   C A C K L E
      L A D   T H A N K
M O R O N I C   A R T L E S S
A R O W   E A G L E   O B O E
P A L E   G L O V E   G O R E
S L E D   O L D E R   S N A P
```

19

```
V A M P   P O I S E   M A W
I B A R   A D D I S A B A B A
E L S E   D E E R S L A Y E R
D E S S E R T S   I T A L Y
      T I E S   S A G E
T A P I R S   S T E N D H A L
R O U G E   C H A R S   A L I
U R G E   P L U T O   S L I T
E T E   D R O N E   D E L V E
S A T I R I S T   C E N S E R
      T I M E   M A L T
L E V E E   A I R L I N E S
A D A M S A P P L E   N O L A
C O N S T R A I N S   E V I L
E M S   A P S E S   L A S T
```

28

```
C A S T   A R M S   A B A S H
O U T A N D O U T   T O Q U E
P R O X I M I T Y   T R U E R
Y A P   P I L E   H A R A S S
      S P R Y   C O C O
P E E W E E   B O O K W O R M
A C R I D   M O C K S   Z O O
C L O G   H U S K Y   D O U R
T A D   F U S S Y   L I N G O
S T E A L T H Y   C A R E E N
      L A C Y   D O T E
S H E A T H   H U G E   D U B
W O R S T   S I D E S W I P E
A L I K E   I D E N T I C A L
P E C A N   P E S T   T E S T
```

2

```
C A P E   R E A D   I R I S
A W O L   E T T U   M O D E S
B A W L   P H O N E B O O T H
L I D   K E E P   M I S L A Y
E T E R N A L   D E B T
    R O O T   F I R E S I D E
D E P O T   P A N G S   M I X
A L U M   R A N G E   S P C A
R A F   B A G G Y   H A R E M
E N F O R C E S   C O V E
    R A I D   H O N E S T Y
R E M A I N   S O M E   S U E
O P E N S E S A M E   N I N A
B I N G E   A G E D   I V E S
    C U E S   W A R Y   P E S T
```

11

```
D E B U T   B L A B   S A F E
A M U S E   A U R A   P I E S
T O Y E R   D R E S S E D U P
E T A   R A G E   S P E E D Y
D E N T I N E   C H I C
    D E F T   C L O T H I N G
S I S S Y   C H O R E   N O R
P O E T   F R O W N   T A P E
A W L   T I E I N   S I N E W
T A L K O V E R   S U E Y
    N O E L   F O R R E N T
S H O O T S   F I L M   V O W
N O R T H P O L E   I R E N E
A B E T   O R A L   S I N C E
P O L Y   T E N D   E A T E N
```

20

```
B O L D   P A P E R   S H A M
A L O E   A B O V E   T U N E
S E A L   Y O K E L   U L N A
S O M E B O D Y   I S R A E L
    G A L E   S A I D
C A N A D A   H A N D Y M A N
A G A T E   D A N C E   E R A
B A K E   P R I D E   G R I T
L I E   D A I L Y   F I L E T
E N D O R S E S   L O V E L Y
    P U S S   V O L E
S H R I M P   B A N D A N N A
L O O N   O V U L E   W O O L
A B L E   R I G E L   A T O M
W O E S   T E S T Y   Y E N S
```

29

```
C L E F   T U F T   C E D A R
H E A R   A S I A   O V E T A
I N S I S T E N T   P A N T S
P A Y E E   D I T T Y   S A P
    G N A T   S L I C K E R S
H O O D L U M   E L A N
E L I   S C O O T   T O T A L
L E N S   K N E A D   B A L I
M A G I C   O R L O N   N E E
    G A S P   E N A C T E D
M U S H R O O M   S O R A
A L L   A T L A S   M A L L S
R E A R M   I N T U I T I O N
I M B U E   Z E A L   E Z R A
E A S E L   E D G E   D E E P
```

37

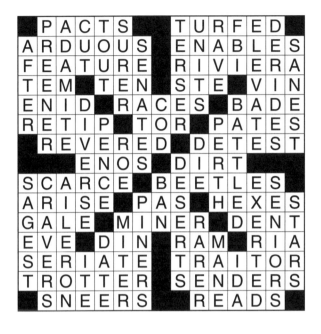

```
  P A C T S     T U R F E D  
A R D U O U S   E N A B L E S
F E A T U R E   R I V I E R A
T E M   T E N   S T E   V I N
E N I D   R A C E S   B A D E
R E T I P   T O R   P A T E S
  R E V E R E D   D E T E S T
      E N O S   D I R T      
S C A R C E   B E E T L E S  
A R I S E   P A S   H E X E S
G A L E   M I N E R   D E N T
E V E   D I N   R A M   R I A
S E R I A T E   T R A I T O R
T R O T T E R   S E N D E R S
  S N E E R S     R E A D S  
```

46

```
H E R O   S H I M     R O M P
A V O W   L O L A   R O M E O
H I L L B I L L Y   A G E N T
A L L   O D D S A N D E N D S
      T O E S     A I R      
S P O O K S   C O T S   G O P
C A R T S   P E N T H O U S E
A L G A   S U R L Y   V A I N
R E A L M C C O Y   H A V E N
F A N   O A K S   R O T A R Y
      O U R     M I R E      
D O U B L E C R O S S   P F C
A S S E T   R A C K E T E E R
B L E S S   A C H E   I N T O
S O R E   B E A D   S T E W  
```

55

```
B E S T O W     T R A P P E D
I N T O N E   H E R O I N E  
S H A P E L Y   R A M P A G E
C A R   S T A T E L Y   N I P
U N D O   C R A M   D I N E  
I C O N   C H A T   M I S E R
T E M E R I T Y   B E S T    
      R A T S   H E A T      
    C O P Y   C O N N I V E S
S C O U T   B O L D   L I S P
C A N S   F I N D   L O S E  
A D S   C O N S U L T   L E E
L E O P A R D   P O R T E N D
E N L A R G E   F I A N C E  
S T E N T O R   T O T T E R  
```

64

```
C A N S   A P P L E   M O N A
O M E N   P L A I N   A V O N
M O R O   P E R P E T U A T E
B R O W B E A T   M A L L E T
    B O A T   W I S E        
S P R A Y S   T I E S D O W N
W A I L   E L A P S E   R E I
A T O L L   A C E   L I L A C
M O T   A R T I S T   M O V E
I N S T R U C T   H O P P E R
    W I S H   F I L L        
O R G E A T   S A R D O N I C
S A I N T L O U I S   R I C A
L I L T   E V E N T   E N O S
O N L Y   R A T T Y   D A N K
```

3

12

21

30

38

HASP CLAMP MANS
IGOR AIMER EPEE
NUDE NAOMI NEAT
TEAMWORK SCARPS
IRES STAG
TEPEES CHIMERAS
ACORN PLANE HIE
POLE CHILE TORT
ELL GROPE MANET
SESSIONS TOLEDO
ERSE RUNE
BERETS SARASOTA
OVID BEAST MIEN
METE ANGEL ASEA
BRED READE NEST

47

TIGHT SWAP MESA
ALLOY PICA EVIL
BLUEPRINTS TERM
USE HACK SCENES
SOME SPORT
TIPTOP CHOPSUEY
ASHEN GLORY ARA
SLOW TAUNT GLOW
KEN BRINE PULSE
STEALING BRAYED
BLUES TEEM
ABOARD SEAM IRE
LOOM OPENMINDED
ALTO URGE SALAD
ETHS TOOT EMERY

56

BLASE WHALER
PREPARE HAVENOT
LEOTARD ELEANOR
ASP ROGUES DOME
CLAM REND BIN
EARED SILOS LED
RUDDER TEMPTERS
ICED SALE
STACKERS RIPRAP
URN SKITS TIARA
ROT LOKI DIGS
GOOS PLAINT SIT
EPICURE RESTIVE
SENATOR TRAINED
RENEWS TRESS

65

STAID LOS VITAL
MILNE OUT IRATE
URGER STOICALLY
GEE ABSOLVE EAT
ROIL FEE DOSE
INFLECT SERF
PROF SOHO RATED
ERNESTHEMINGWAY
SACRE OPAL NOSE
HERE INSPECT
SCAR DUC ASTI
ERR FANTASY TIP
PALLADIUM CHIDE
TWEET TRE HEELS
ASSES YEN ONSET

4

C	H	U	M	■	D	A	T	U	M	■	S	P	A	N
R	I	P	E	■	E	R	A	S	E	■	H	O	N	E
O	D	O	R	■	B	E	R	E	T	■	A	U	T	O
P	E	N	C	H	A	N	T	■	H	A	S	T	E	N
■	■	■	I	O	T	A	■	V	O	L	T	■	■	■
S	T	I	F	L	E	■	S	I	D	E	A	R	M	■
A	R	G	U	E	■	M	A	G	I	C	■	E	A	R
L	O	L	L	■	H	A	V	O	C	■	C	L	U	E
T	O	O	■	M	O	T	O	R	■	S	L	A	V	E
■	P	O	P	O	V	E	R	■	F	L	E	X	E	D
■	■	■	A	D	E	S	■	D	O	U	R	■	■	■
S	E	T	T	E	R	■	F	O	R	G	I	V	E	N
A	L	I	T	■	■	I	M	A	G	E	■	C	A	V	E
I	S	L	E	■	N	A	Z	I	S	■	A	S	E	A
L	E	E	R	■	G	R	E	E	T	■	L	E	N	T

13

B	O	S	S	■	V	E	R	S	E	■	A	S	T	A
L	A	T	H	■	A	V	A	I	L	■	B	L	I	P
O	H	I	O	■	L	I	M	P	S	■	S	A	T	E
C	U	R	E	A	L	L	S	■	I	C	E	B	O	X
■	■	■	H	I	E	S	■	A	N	O	N	■	■	■
P	A	R	O	D	Y	■	S	P	O	T	T	E	R	■
A	D	O	R	E	■	S	T	A	R	E	■	L	I	P
S	I	G	N	■	S	C	O	R	E	■	S	I	L	O
S	E	E	■	S	P	O	R	T	■	F	A	Z	E	D
■	U	R	A	N	I	U	M	■	D	E	C	A	Y	S
■	■	■	W	A	N	T	■	S	U	N	K	■	■	■
S	C	R	A	P	S	■	H	A	R	D	R	O	L	L
H	O	O	K	■	T	A	U	P	E	■	A	R	E	A
A	C	M	E	■	E	L	L	I	S	■	C	A	S	T
M	A	P	S	■	R	E	A	D	S	■	E	L	S	E

22

W	H	I	P	■	I	M	P	E	L	■	R	A	C	K
H	I	L	O	■	N	E	R	V	E	■	O	B	O	E
I	D	L	E	■	H	A	Y	E	S	■	C	L	O	Y
Z	E	S	T	F	U	L	■	N	I	C	K	E	L	S
■	■	■	R	U	M	■	S	T	O	L	E	■	■	■
P	L	A	Y	M	A	T	E	■	N	E	T	T	I	E
R	I	G	■	E	N	O	C	H	■	F	E	R	N	S
I	V	A	N	■	E	R	R	E	D	■	D	A	D	S
M	E	T	E	S	■	S	E	D	A	N	■	D	I	E
P	R	E	E	N	S	■	T	Y	R	O	L	E	A	N
■	■	■	D	I	E	T	S	■	L	E	O	■	■	■
S	C	A	L	P	E	R	■	D	I	S	C	U	S	S
H	O	L	E	■	S	I	M	O	N	■	K	N	E	E
O	D	E	S	■	A	P	I	N	G	■	E	D	N	A
D	Y	E	S	■	W	E	L	T	S	■	T	O	T	S

31

S	L	A	M	■	S	L	E	E	K	■	D	O	S	S
A	U	T	O	■	N	I	X	O	N	■	E	D	N	A
I	C	O	N	■	A	L	I	N	E	■	L	O	A	F
D	E	M	O	C	R	A	T	■	E	M	E	R	G	E
■	■	■	T	A	L	C	■	S	P	A	T	■	■	■
A	C	R	O	S	S	■	S	P	A	R	E	R	I	B
S	A	I	N	T	■	S	P	A	D	E	■	O	N	E
P	U	N	Y	■	T	W	I	N	S	■	H	U	L	A
E	S	S	■	C	H	I	N	K	■	P	A	T	E	N
N	E	E	D	L	E	S	S	■	C	A	R	E	T	S
■	■	■	R	U	S	H	■	H	A	I	R	■	■	■
B	O	P	E	E	P	■	P	A	T	R	I	C	I	A
O	L	L	A	■	I	R	A	T	E	■	M	O	O	T
L	I	A	R	■	A	U	G	E	R	■	A	L	T	O
T	O	N	Y	■	N	E	E	D	S	■	N	E	A	P

39

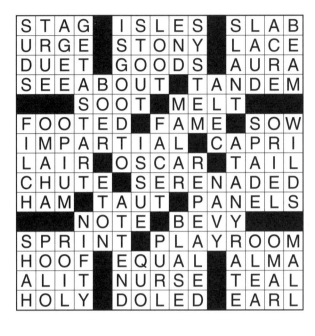

```
S T A G   I S L E S   S L A B
U R G E   S T O N Y   L A C E
D U E T   G O O D S   A U R A
S E E A B O U T   T A N D E M
      S O O T   M E L T
F O O T E D   F A M E   S O W
I M P A R T I A L   C A P R I
L A I R   O S C A R   T A I L
C H U T E   S E R E N A D E D
H A M   T A U T   P A N E L S
      N O T E   B E V Y
S P R I N T   P L A Y R O O M
H O O F   E Q U A L   A L M A
A L I T   N U R S E   T E A L
H O L Y   D O L E D   E A R L
```

48

```
B A R S   S L E E K   S M O G
R O O T   K O R A N   H O M O
A N T I C I P A T E   A R E A
D E A L E R S   L E V A N T
      T N T   P E L L E T
C A P E T   B E L   D R O S S
U S E D   D E N U D E   R U T
S I R   P A R A D E R   I C E
P A P   A G A T E S   C U R E
S N E A D   T E D   H O M E R
      T R U C E S   S O N
P A R I A H   P L O D D E D
U P A S   E S C R I T O I R E
M E T E   S H O O T   R A G E
A R E S   S E N D S   S L O P
```

57

```
B L O B   D O F F   G Y P S
O A H U   I V I E S   R E A L
G R I N   N A S T Y   I G L U
  D O G I N T H E M A N G E R
    A L E E   P I G
S T A L E R   B E T R O T H S
P H L O X   M O R O S   R A H
A R O W   B U X O M   M I L E
N E O   M E T E S   S I E V E
K E F A U V E R   S O D D E N
    U S E   S T U N
T A T T E R D E M A L I O N
U T A H   L A P I N   G L O W
B O B O   Y I E L D   H E R O
S P U R   S E E S   T O M E
```

66

```
L A M B   P L E A   I C E S
A L A R   H U R L S   N O R A
M I S O G A M I S T   F U L L
A T T I R E   C A R B I N E S
    E L I D E   B U R E T
A I R S T R I P   T E L L E R
D O S   S A G A S   A D E L E
A W E   S H R E W   O I L
G A R B O   T E A R S   T H E
E N G E L S   S L I P S O U T
    E R G O T   S T O O L
C H A R A D E S   H O B S O N
R A N I   A N T O I N E T T E
A R T E   S T E R N   R O I S
M E S S   S W A G   S Y S T
```

5

B	O	D	E		S	P	A	S	M		M	E	S	S
A	K	I	N		T	A	B	O	O		A	X	L	E
L	I	S	P		I	N	U	N	D	A	T	I	O	N
D	E	C	L	I	N	E	S		E	L	A	T	E	D
		J	A	N	G	L	E		R	E	D			
	B	O	N	N	Y		L	A	C	O	N	I	C	
F	A	C	E	S		T	W	I	T		R	I	C	H
A	S	K		S	H	A	V	E		P	O	I		
D	I	E	S		W	I	N	E		S	C	A	N	T
S	C	Y	T	H	E	S			F	E	R	N	S	
			R	U	E		S	P	I	C	E	D		
D	E	P	A	R	T		C	A	N	T	A	T	A	S
I	L	L	I	T	E	R	A	T	E		S	U	C	H
S	L	O	T		S	O	R	E	R		E	C	H	O
H	A	T	S		T	E	E	N	Y		S	K	E	W

14

S	H	O	P		C	A	R	V	E		G	L	O	W
P	O	U	R		A	L	I	E	N		L	A	V	A
A	L	T	O		S	O	F	T	S	P	O	K	E	N
N	E	O		S	H	U	T		C	O	V	E	R	T
		F	L	U	I	D		M	O	R	E			
C	A	R	E	E	N		L	O	N	G	S	H	O	T
I	D	E	A	S		S	A	U	C	Y		I	V	Y
G	O	A	D		F	O	R	T	E		S	T	E	P
A	R	C		C	O	U	G	H		N	A	C	R	E
R	E	H	E	A	R	S	E		F	I	G	H	T	S
			T	R	E	E		D	I	N	A	H		
F	R	A	C	A	S		D	O	N	E		I	D	A
L	I	G	H	T	H	O	U	S	E		A	K	I	N
A	C	R	E		O	L	D	E	R		S	E	N	D
T	E	A	S		W	E	E	D	Y		P	R	E	Y

23

C	H	I	P		S	T	E	E	P		C	E	L	L
L	O	R	E		C	R	A	V	E		A	R	E	A
U	P	O	N		R	A	V	E	N		R	I	S	K
B	E	N	E	F	I	C	E		C	H	E	E	S	E
			L	O	P	E		B	I	A	S			
S	A	V	O	R		R	E	A	L	I	S	T	I	C
T	R	O	P	E		P	I	E	R		U	N	A	
R	I	T	E		S	C	O	L	D		F	L	A	P
A	S	E		B	E	A	D			S	E	I	N	E
P	E	R	F	O	R	M	E	R		P	A	P	E	R
			R	A	G	E		O	B	I	T			
S	P	R	I	T	E		F	O	R	T	U	N	E	S
A	L	A	S		A	L	I	K	E		R	O	V	E
T	U	S	K		N	O	R	I	A		E	D	E	N
E	S	P	Y		T	W	E	E	D		D	E	N	T

32

	M	A	R	S	H		M	O	U	N	T			
C	A	L	I	C	O		M	A	R	R	O	W	S	
A	L	L	O	U	T		I	N	A	G	R	O	U	P
V	A	T		D	E	F	L	A	T	E		S	I	R
E	G	I	S		L	E	D	G	E		V	O	T	E
D	A	M	E	S		L	E	E		M	E	M	O	S
	S	E	N	A	T	O	R		M	I	T	E	R	S
			T	W	I	N		T	A	R	E			
S	H	A	F	T	S		C	E	N	T	R	A	L	
T	A	B	O	O		J	A	M		H	A	L	E	S
O	V	E	R		C	O	R	P	S		N	A	V	E
N	E	T		T	A	K	E	O	U	T		M	E	W
E	N	T	W	I	N	E	S		R	E	S	O	L	E
	S	E	E	D	E	R	S		G	R	A	D	E	D
	D	E	E	D	S		E	N	D	E	D			

40

```
M I S H A P ▢ ▢ S T A T E S
I N H U M A N ▢ A M E R I C A
S T A T U R E ▢ B E R S E R K
T O M ▢ L O W ▢ C A R ▢ D U E
▢ ▢ H E L M S ▢ R A P ▢ ▢ ▢
A M B I T ▢ E T C ▢ P U R S E
M A R T ▢ E X O R B I T A N T
A N I ▢ O P I N I O N ▢ B A H
S I M P L I C I T Y ▢ H I K E
S A S S Y ▢ O N E ▢ Y O D E L
▢ ▢ I M P ▢ G R E A T ▢ ▢ ▢
P E P ▢ P A W ▢ I N K ▢ F I B
A V A R I C E ▢ O R I F I C E
R E D U C E D ▢ N O M I N E E
A S S E S S ▢ ▢ L A T E S T
```

49

```
S W A Y ▢ P U R L S ▢ N E B R
P I L E ▢ O N I O N ▢ A X L E
A S I A ▢ T A N G O ▢ S P A N
R E C R U I T S ▢ R E S E N T
E R E ▢ N O T E ▢ T R E N D S
▢ ▢ N I N E ▢ P E A R S ▢ ▢
S T O U T ▢ N E A R S ▢ I C E
P O U T ▢ O D O R S ▢ I V A N
Y E T ▢ E V E N T ▢ B L E N D
▢ ▢ P A V E D ▢ I D O L ▢ ▢
S C O R E R ▢ A C E S ▢ S O S
C A I R N S ▢ B U S H I E S T
A N N E ▢ U T I L E ▢ T R I O
L O T S ▢ R A D A R ▢ E V E R
P E S T ▢ E X E R T ▢ M E R E
```

58

```
S C R A P ▢ S L A B ▢ A F A R
N A I V E ▢ P O L L ▢ R A C E
I N T A N G I B L E ▢ I C E S
P E A ▢ N I C E ▢ W I S E S T
▢ ▢ B A B Y ▢ C O V E T ▢ ▢
A F L A M E ▢ G I V E S O U T
D R O N E ▢ C O V E S ▢ F R O
A I R S ▢ S L I E R ▢ S A G A
P A D ▢ S L A N T ▢ L A C E D
T R I F L I N G ▢ C O M E D Y
▢ ▢ T R I P S ▢ S A N E ▢ ▢
A V O I D S ▢ S I N G ▢ B O W
D I V E ▢ H O L D S F O R T H
E V E N ▢ O R A L ▢ O V A T E
N A R D ▢ D O P E ▢ R A Y O N
```

67

```
▢ ▢ S T O R M S ▢ S O B E R ▢
▢ S T E P O U T ▢ A M U L E T
L E A D U P T O ▢ V E N I C E
I C Y ▢ S E T U P O N ▢ C A D
S U C H ▢ D E T E R ▢ M I L D
T R A I L ▢ R E D ▢ H O T L Y
S E L D O M ▢ R A P I D ▢ ▢
▢ S M E A R S ▢ L A V I S H ▢
▢ ▢ O N S E T ▢ R E C T O R
B O G U S ▢ R A H ▢ S U R G E
A P E S ▢ M I T E R ▢ M U T E
T E N ▢ M A N T L E S ▢ T I L
O N E W A Y ▢ E M U L A T E S
N E V A D A ▢ R E S O L E D
▢ D A N E S ▢ S T E W E D
```

6

A	R	A	B		B	I	S	O	N		S	H	A	M
L	A	V	A		E	R	O	D	E		H	O	B	O
E	V	E	R		C	O	R	E	S		R	O	L	L
S	E	R	G	E	A	N	T		T	R	A	D	E	D
			A	R	M	Y		P	L	A	N			
S	Q	U	I	R	E		C	R	I	C	K	E	T	S
T	U	R	N	S		F	L	U	N	K		T	H	E
R	I	G	S		A	L	O	N	G		C	H	E	W
A	R	E		A	R	I	S	E		C	R	I	M	E
P	E	D	I	G	R	E	E		S	L	I	C	E	D
			D	E	E	R		R	I	O	T			
S	T	R	E	S	S		C	A	R	D	I	N	A	L
A	R	E	A		T	W	I	C	E		C	O	M	E
L	I	S	T		E	A	T	E	N		A	S	E	A
T	O	T	E		D	R	E	S	S		L	E	N	D

15

F	A	D	E		G	R	I	T	S		F	A	N	G
I	R	A	N		R	A	D	I	O		O	D	O	R
D	I	R	T		I	N	L	A	W		R	O	T	A
O	A	K	R	I	D	G	E		H	A	T	R	E	D
	H	A	R	D	Y		B	A	S	K	E	D		
P	R	O	P	E	L		S	A	T	I	N			
E	A	R		E	G	A	D		D	O	O	R	S	
R	I	S	K	S		R	U	G		E	X	P	E	L
K	N	E	E	L		I	C	E	S			P	E	A
			N	I	N	N	Y		N	O	B	O	D	Y
	P	O	T	T	E	D		F	A	V	O	R		
R	O	B	U	S	T		R	E	C	A	N	T	E	D
A	L	E	C		T	R	U	N	K		N	U	D	E
M	A	S	K		L	A	N	C	E		E	N	D	S
P	R	E	Y		E	G	G	E	D		T	E	A	K

24

B	L	A	N	K		C	E	D	E		S	T	A	Y
A	U	D	I	E		O	D	I	N		H	U	G	E
B	R	A	G	G		P	I	N	T		E	R	O	S
S	I	G	H		S	T	I	R	R	I	N	G		
	D	E	T	E	R		S	N	E	A	K			
		C	E	I	L		G	E	M		D	U	B	
S	W	E	L	L	F	I	S	H		P	H	O	T	O
T	A	B	U		E	T	H	A	N		E	L	A	N
A	D	O	B	E		T	E	L	E	P	A	T	H	Y
B	E	N		P	A	L		L	A	I	D			
			F	I	N	E	D		R	E	L	I	C	
	B	R	I	C	K	B	A	T		I	V	A	N	
S	E	A	S		L	E	N	A		A	N	O	D	E
O	A	T	H		E	A	T	S		C	E	R	E	S
B	U	S	Y		T	R	E	K		T	R	Y	S	T

33

M	A	P	L	E		B	O	M	B		F	A	D	E
A	L	L	A	N		O	P	A	L		O	N	E	S
C	O	A	S	T		O	U	T	O	F	S	T	E	P
A	N	Y		R	O	T	S		W	A	T	E	R	Y
W	E	A	S	E	L	S		L	O	R	E			
			T	O	A	D		B	E	V	E	R	A	G	E
S	P	R	A	T		H	I	V	E	S		S	E	E
L	A	I	R		F	I	N	E	R		S	T	A	R
A	R	C		S	I	N	G	E		C	A	R	R	Y
B	E	K	I	N	D	T	O		S	A	G	O		
			N	A	G	S		D	U	R	A	N	T	E
R	E	F	U	G	E		S	E	N	T		A	I	M
O	V	E	R	S	T	A	T	E		O	V	U	L	E
B	I	T	E		E	D	A	M		N	I	T	E	R
S	L	E	D		D	O	G	S		S	A	S	S	Y

41

```
B A L E   R A F T S   C H A P
A B E T   A D L A I   R I C E
B L A C K G U A R D   A G R A
Y E N   I L L Y   E S T H E R
    G N A T   S L U E S
A S S I G N   S P I N S T E R
G O L F S   S P U N K   R Y E
A L I T   S P I R E   C U R B
P O P   G I A N T   G E N I E
E N S C O N C E   C U D G E L
    T I N G E   D O L E
S U R G E S   L U M P   S U E
A S E A   I R I D E S C E N T
G E A R   N A M E D   O T I C
A R M S   G Y P S Y   B A T H
```

50

```
C H A F F   P E A   P A U L
L O I R E   N A S H V I L L E
O L D E R   A S S A I L A N T
D E S T R O Y S   V I S A S
    I N S   S P A N
P O N G E E   S H I N G L E S
A L I A S   S T I N T   A R T
G I G S   A T O M Y   S T O A
E V E   S C A R S   S E E D Y
S E R A P H I M   S T A R E S
    W E E D   D U E
C A B A L   R A M P A R T S
O V E R L A D E N   P L A I T
L O A D S T O N E   E L I D E
E N D S   E G O   S A L E M
```

59

```
B E E R   G O O P   S A L T
A C M E   E R N E   T W A I N
C H I L B L A I N   A F I R E
H O T E L   L O T   L U R E D
    A U K   N A T A L
L I N S E E D   N E G L E C T
E R I E   G O R G E   Y A L E
G O T   O I L   T A N
A N E W   E D G E D   W E R E
L Y R I C A L   S A T I N E T
    N A R E S   M I L
F A C E T   B E D   F L A R E
A B U S E   U N R U F F L E D
D E B A R   G N A T   U S E D
    T A P S   S A G E   L O L A
```

68

```
H A D J   O R G A N   A G A R
A R E A   C A I R O   F A R O
L I E S   T I L E S   F L I T
F A R M H A N D   T E R E D O
    I O N S   P R O A
A V E N U E   R A I N Y D A Y
G A S E S   B U R L   S A L E
A N T   E A R N E S T   V I A
P E E R   L E G S   E D I C T
E S S E N C E S   R A I S E S
    J O A D   T O R S
D E S E R T   C R U S A D E S
E R I C   R E L I T   V I V A
S I L T   A G A T E   O V E N
I N K S   Z O N E S   W A R D
```

7

```
POEM  RESTS  CASH
ABLE  EXTRA  RITA
TOSS  STEEL  URAL
  EASYCOMEEASYGO
    MAUL    SIT
LOCALE  TOMMYROT
IRATE  TIMES  ORE
TIRE  PAGAN  WADE
HOE  SUPER  RISEN
ENDANGER  PASTRY
    NUN   BASE
WILDGOOSECHASE
AVER  SPARK  CLIP
LANE  EAGLE  RARE
KNOW  SLEET  EWER
```

16

```
RIVAL  STAR  SLAM
ARISE  LIFE  LOBO
JACKOFALLTRADES
ANT  NOTE  RIVETS
  OVINE  RIFE
STRAND  DUEL  MAN
POISE  PULVERIZE
ALOE  TEPEE  ESTE
CLUSTERED  FAMED
ESS  ILKS  PIRACY
  ABLY  CANST
AVOCET  BALL  CPA
LIGHTASAFEATHER
ACRE  LURE  NIECE
SEES  EBBS  DESKS
```

25

```
 MUSIC  SPITE
MATURE  TEASING
AROMAS  UNCLESAM
RIP  NARRATE  CUE
SNIP  RUNTS  SODA
HEART  LIE  RANIN
  EATEN  WINCES
  LASSOS  SOLDER
VANITY  SHELL
ABIDE  POI  SOLES
SOME  PRONG  TORE
ERA  TEETERS  COW
SETFORTH  INVADE
  REUNITE  SOILED
  DRYLY  TWEED
```

34

```
SODA  APPAL  GULL
WART  NAIVE  ASEA
AHUM  SPEECHLESS
TUGOFWAR  TOASTS
   SLEW  CUP
PAUPER  FORECAST
ALPHA  SAVE  HULA
WIPE  SPIED  ORAL
EVER  LINT  SPATE
DERELICT  BOSSES
   APE  ROUT
HARASS  TOURISTS
OVERTHROWN  CHIP
SIAM  OILED  KOTO
EDDY  DOLLS  SOOT
```

42

```
TRAP  ELDER  SLAB
AONE  NOISE  PICA
RAND  TROTS  OVEN
TREACHEROUSNESS
    NOR    PLOD
QUATRAIN  TREMOR
ULT ELBOW  TEASE
ATLE LIRAS  SICS
FRANZ SMITH  NAT
FASTER STEELERS
    ESAU   ERA
PRINTINGPRESSES
LILT STILE  SORE
OGLE EIDER  ELSE
PASS DEEDS  NEED
```

51

```
GLOVE  CATS  SLED
RARER  OMIT  WILE
ANGER  DINE  EASE
SCARAB  DIAPERED
PEN  TOP  EMIT
   MILLER  EMBER
REJECTED  GREAVE
ORES EAGER  ABED
MISSED  ADAPTERS
ENTER  BRIDES
   NOSE TEA  HOT
GANGSTER  SCRAPE
ALOE ETON  HOVER
USER ALTO  EVENS
LOSS LEST  SENSE
```

60

```
 STIGMA  COPES
SEEDIER SIMILAR
CANASTA AGITATO
ETA HABITAT  TIP
NABS LINER  SERE
ELLEN ATE  SHRED
SEEPED  ONENESS
   TRAM  SEER
 CHEVRON LAMBDA
BRUTE SOP  DARED
OURS BARON  NOVA
RID SLIMMER  MIG
ISLAMIC AVARICE
SEERESS DENUDES
 DRAWS  ERASES
```

69

```
ALUM LAMAR  AVER
CASE INANE  RAGE
EVEN KENTUCKIAN
SARACENS  BRANDO
    CANT  SEEN
SPHERE  FINESSED
ERA PSALM  DANTE
VOLT SPOOR  SOUL
EVERS TONES  ODE
RESELLER  GLADES
   SEAR  PAIL
GASPER  WELTERED
REPATRIATE  PERU
IRIS URGER  PAID
DOTS PEERS  ORES
```

8

```
W O V E . S H R U B   I S M S
H O A X   H O U S E   M O I L
E Z I O   A L D E R   P O L O
T E N T A C L E   L I O N E T
      I N K Y   B I N S
P A R C E L   S A N C T I O N
A G E   W E L T S   H O R S E
R O A R   S A R A H   R A C E
I N L E T   T A L O N   D A D
S Y M P A T H Y   P O S E R S
      A L O E   D E N Y
S P A R K S   S A L E S M A N
W A L T   S E I Z E   T A P A
A C M E   U R G E S   E Y E S
B A S E   P E N D S   M A S H
```

17

```
C A R S   C R A B   P O L O
O M E N   C H A S E   A B E D
D A D O   H U N K S   R O A D
A H O W L I N G S U C C E S S
      B A L K   R U E
C R E A S E   S T E R L I N G
R I L L S   T H R O B   C U R
E V I L   S H E A F   W I D E
T A T   N E E D Y   B I N G E
E L E V A T E S   D A N G E R
      E B B   S I L K
T A K E S A D I M V I E W O F
A G A R   C O C O A   D A V E
M U L E   K N O T S   A G E E
S E E D   S A N E   T E N T
```

26

```
S K E T C H     A B L A Z E
A N X I O U S   C R O O N E D
L E C T U R E   R E S P I T E
V E E   P L A T E A U   M A N
E L L A   P O P   N C O
    R I P O S T E   A S P S
S H I M M E R S   M A N I L A
T O M   P A T   F E W   T O G
U N M A S K   L I N O T Y P E
B E E T   S W I N D L E
    D E W   I K E   E C R U
S A I   H O N E S T Y   H I P
E V A S I V E   S E A S O N S
R E T E N E S   E N L A R G E
B R E W E R     D E T E S T
```

35

```
P A G E D   C H I   S K I D
A Z A L E A   H O D   W I R E
C U M B E R S O M E   A W O L
E R I E   S T R E A M L I N E
D E N   O U T   S A L
    F O N D L Y   N O M A D
S A F A R I   E A T   W O R E
C U R T E S T   M I L I T I A
U T A H   T A T   T I N E A R
M O T E L   B O W L E G
    R O C   P E A   R A T
W E L L W I S H E R   D U D E
A G U E   S H O P K E E P E R
C A N S   C A L   S T E E P S
O D D S   O W E   A R E T E
```

43

52

61

70

9

```
C O T S . M O T O R . S H E D
O L E O . U T I L E . L A V A
B L A C K S H E E P . U N I T
B A L A N C E D . R I D D L E
. . L E A R . B O N G O . .
T A B L E T . P E A C E F U L
A R I E L . B O T C H . F R O
M I N D . S O U T H . L A I R
P E G . B U N N Y . C A T E R
A S C R I B E D . M U T E L Y
. . R O A M S . W I L T . .
B L O U S E . D I S T I L L S
L O S T . R A I S E S C A I N
A B B E . G I V E R . E D N A
B O Y S . E M E R Y . S E E P
```

18

```
R A M S . . A L M S . B E D E
E V I L . A B E A M . O X E N
S E C O N D B A S E . I C E D
T R A P E Z E . S A I L O R S
. . . P O E . F E R R E R . .
R A V E N . E L Y . K R I S S
A R I D . B A A . R E S A L E
M E N . P U R S U E D . T A W
P A D R E S . H S T . F E T E
S L I E R . S E E . C E D E D
. . C L O V E S . S A M . .
S A T A N I C . B E L A T E D
E X I T . S T R E A M L I N E
R I V E . T O U T S . E T O N
B L E D . A R M S . S O W S
```

27

```
H O O P . M A T E . C A K E S
A B L E . I V A N . H I N D U
R O A R . S O B S . A D A G E
D E V I L F I S H . R A V E D
. . . A I D . R A G . E R E
A S S E N T . W I L E S . .
S H O R E . M O N A S T E R Y
P O O R . D A M E S . E R A S
S E N O R I T A S . P R A T E
. . R A V E N . B A N T E R
B A R . T A R . S O S . . .
A L O F T . I D E N T I C A L
R E G A L . A R I D . B A R I
B R U T E . L I N E . I R I S
S T E E R . S P E D . S E A T
```

36

```
P R I M . S P E A R . D A I S
L O C O . E L O P E . U N D O
O V E N . C A N E S . S N O B
D E S S E R T S . P E T A L S
. . . T R E E . F O R M . .
D E S E R T . H A N G O V E R
A V E R S . B E N D . P A V E
L E T . B R A G S . L O W
E R O S . E A T S . B R O K E
S Y N O P S I S . S O A R E D
. . C O O N . S I T S . .
S C R I P T . P U S H C A R T
E R I E . T O L E T . A S E A
G I S T . E R O D E . L I N K
O B E Y . D E T E R . S A T E
```

44

53

62

71

45

M	A	T	E	D	■	B	E	S	S	■	H	E	W	S
A	L	A	M	O	■	U	R	A	L	■	E	X	I	T
S	I	M	I	L	A	R	I	T	Y	■	A	P	S	E
O	V	E	R	T	I	M	E	■	B	O	P	E	E	P
N	E	D	■	I	D	A	■	B	O	N	E	D	■	■
■	■	■	A	S	E	■	F	L	O	U	R	I	S	H
P	E	A	C	H	■	B	O	U	T	S	■	T	O	O
R	A	N	T	■	F	O	R	E	S	■	D	E	A	L
E	R	N	■	M	I	N	U	S	■	C	A	R	R	Y
P	L	A	T	I	N	U	M	■	B	A	Y	■	■	■
■	■	P	O	L	E	S	■	B	A	H	■	D	A	M
S	T	O	L	E	N	■	C	A	R	O	L	I	N	E
P	Y	L	E	■	E	V	I	L	D	O	I	N	G	S
A	R	I	D	■	S	I	T	E	■	T	R	E	E	S
S	O	S	O	■	S	P	E	D	■	S	A	D	L	Y

54

A	P	S	E	■	E	B	B	S	■	O	A	T	H	S
C	E	L	L	■	L	O	O	P	■	A	R	R	O	W
M	A	Y	F	L	O	W	E	R	■	R	O	U	T	E
E	R	A	■	O	P	E	R	A	S	■	U	S	E	D
■	■	S	A	V	E	D	■	W	H	I	S	T	L	E
M	O	A	N	E	D	■	P	L	A	C	E	■	■	■
U	N	F	E	D	■	D	A	I	R	Y	■	T	I	P
S	C	O	W	■	B	R	I	N	K	■	W	I	D	E
H	E	X	■	C	L	U	N	G	■	C	A	M	E	L
■	■	■	B	O	O	M	S	■	P	A	L	E	S	T
F	R	E	E	D	O	M	■	V	A	U	L	T	■	■
R	U	S	H	■	M	A	T	I	N	S	■	A	G	E
O	C	T	A	D	■	J	I	T	T	E	R	B	U	G
S	H	O	V	E	■	O	M	A	R	■	O	L	L	A
T	E	P	E	E	■	R	E	L	Y	■	W	E	L	D

63

■	H	A	R	P	O	■	S	P	O	D	E	■	■	■
O	C	A	L	A	■	A	P	A	N	A	G	E	S
B	U	T	T	E	R	■	R	U	N	A	B	O	U	T
I	D	A	■	A	S	S	O	R	T	S	■	T	R	I
D	I	E	T	S	■	P	U	N	S	■	V	I	O	L
E	N	O	W	■	F	U	S	S	■	G	A	S	P	E
S	I	N	E	C	U	R	E	■	N	A	N	T	E	S
■	■	■	A	I	R	S	■	D	O	L	T	■	■	■
B	R	A	K	E	S	■	B	A	D	L	A	N	D	S
L	E	V	E	L	■	S	A	N	E	■	G	A	I	T
E	G	A	D	■	C	A	R	T	■	S	E	I	N	E
A	R	T	■	D	O	U	R	E	S	T	■	L	E	W
T	E	A	D	A	N	C	E	■	T	E	N	E	T	S
S	T	R	A	N	G	E	R	■	A	V	E	R	T	■
■	■	■	S	N	E	A	D	■	G	E	E	S	E	■

72

D	I	C	T	U	M	■	R	P	M	■	D	A	M
I	N	H	A	L	E	■	D	E	L	U	S	I	V	E
S	T	A	N	C	E	■	E	N	A	M	E	L	E	D
C	O	R	N	E	T	I	S	T	S	■	C	U	R	D
A	N	G	E	R	■	D	I	E	T	■	T	E	A	L
R	E	E	D	■	M	O	R	S	E	■	I	N	G	E
D	D	S	■	D	E	L	E	■	R	I	O	T	E	D
■	■	■	P	U	N	S	■	P	E	O	N	■	■	■
S	T	R	A	N	D	■	T	E	R	N	■	D	A	W
I	R	E	S	■	I	D	E	A	S	■	R	I	V	E
L	A	D	S	■	C	A	N	S	■	H	O	V	E	L
V	I	N	A	■	A	N	T	E	C	E	D	E	N	T
E	L	E	G	A	N	C	E	■	E	M	E	R	G	E
R	E	S	E	N	T	E	D	■	D	A	N	G	E	R
Y	R	S	■	A	S	S	■	E	N	T	E	R	S	■

Challenging
IQ Test
ANSWERS

TEST ONE

1. TRIVIAL
2. 8. The top number is the product of the bottom numbers divided by 15.
3. TORRENTIAL
4. ALOUD, ALLOWED
5. The number of votes the winning candidate received was $(963 + 53 + 79 + 105) \div 4 = 300$. The second received $300 - 53 = 247$, the third received $300 - 79 = 221$, and the fourth received $300 - 105 = 195$.
6. REDEVELOP, PENTAGRAM
7. FINE AND DANDY
8. C. It is the only one that doesn't have an identical match.
9. FANCIFUL, SENSIBLE
10. E. ARIES : RAM
11. WEASEL
12. E. The lines of the third pentagon are determined by the lines of the first two. All lines are carried forward, but when two lines coincide in the same position in the first two figures they appear as a curved line in the final figure.
13. COCKATRICE, BASILISK
14. 44. The rule is multiplication and division before addition and subtraction.
15. AIM DRAG = DIAGRAM. The buildings are STADIUM, LIBRARY, HOSPITAL, and PAVILION.
16. HORN
17. E. LILY
18. 64. The bottom number is the top right number times the square root of the top left number.
19. LESSEE, LANDLORD
20. B

TEST TWO

1. 523377. All the others, when split into two three-digit numbers, add up to 1000. (For example, $586 + 414 = 1000$.)
2. BEAGLE
3. INSPECTS, EXAMINES
4. TIRELESSLY
5. B. Lines in the outer circle move 45 clockwise at each stage. Lines in the middle circle move 45 counterclockwise at each stage. The line in the inner circle moves 45 clockwise at each stage.
6. A. If a segment is folded on top of the opposite segment, numbers on top of each other total 10. (For example, the top segment folds onto the bottom segment so that the 8 covers the 2, the 5 covers the 5, and the 7 covers the 3.)
7. 151. The difference between two consecutive squares is the sum of the two numbers being squared. So this is simply $76 + 75$.
8. MARTIAL, MARSHAL
9. A. TAPERING TO A POINT
10. C. Each symbol alternates between black and white or black and gray. The circles on the right move from corner to corner, one clockwise, one counterclockwise.
11. Mixed fortunes
12. 13. Starting at 1 and moving two segments clockwise yields the series 1, 2, 3, 5, 8, ?, 21. Each term of the series is the sum of the previous two terms.
13. VIOLIN: This is a string instrument, the rest are wind instruments.
14. SPLENETIC, HAPPY
15. MILWAUKEE
16. B. ILLUMINATION : LIGHT
17. EGLANTINE, BRIER
18. TIE
19. E. The second number is the first digit of the first number times the second digit of the first number plus the third digit of the first number. $26 = 8 \infty 3 + 2$.
20. B. In each row and column, the third circle is the first and second circle superinmposed,

with overlapping parts removed.

TEST THREE

1. 17271. Each term in the series is the first two digits of the previous term times the last three digits of the previous term. So 17271 = 19 ∞ 909.
2. INVENTOR, DESIGNER
3. BROWN, ORANGE, BLUE
4. ACT
5. EQUESTRIAN
6. NAÏVE, SLY
7. E. It contains one large circle, three medium circles, two small white circles, and two small black circles.
8. RATIONAL
9. SAGACIOUS, FOOLISH
10. ALTER, ALTAR
11. B. In all the others, the top half is a mirror image of the bottom half.
12. C. NIZNAI = ZINNIA. The gems are ZIRCON, DIAMOND, SAPPHIRE, and JACINTH.
13. 7. The center number is the product of the top two numbers divided by the bottom number.
14. OXYGEN
15. WEAPON
16. SWIMMING: The others require a ball.
17. MAGNETIC, ALLURING
18. 1. Starting at the first 1 and moving one segment clockwise yields the series 1, ?, 2, 4, 7, 11, 16, 22. The difference between terms of the series increases by 1; that is, the differences are 0, 1, 2, 3, 4, 5, and 6.
19. D. SAPPHIRE : BLUE
20. B. It is the onlyone that doesn't have an identical match

TEST FOUR

1. D. The second and third numbers are 909 greater than the numbers to their left.
2. VOLUME: It has an alternating consonant and vowel arrangement.
3. COUNCIL, CONCLAVE
4. SON OF A GUN
5. F. Moving across, the letters jump two, then three places in the alphabet. Moving down, they jump three, then four places.
6. TANGO, WALTZ, RUMBA
7. ESCORTED, ATTENDED
8. D. ALPHA : OMEGA
9. B. All the others are the same figure rotated.
10. C. ADORNTO = TORNADO. The clouds are CIRRUS, ALTOSTRATUS, CUMULUS, and NIMBUS.
11. PITTANCE (small amount). All the others have to do with crime.
12. FRATERNITY
13. WINE
14. D. The figures move two corners clockwise at each stage and are being repeated, but black instead of white.
15. DEEP BLUE
16. 36. Starting at 4 and moving three segments counterclockwise yields the sequence 4, 9, 16, 25, ?, 49, 64. These are perfect squares: 2^2, 3^2, 4^2, 5^2, 6^2, 7^2, 8^2.
17. D. 2500 sq. yd. Each side is 50 yards.
18. OFF
19. COMMODIOUS, CRAMPED
20. C. The second circle is the first one rotated 180degrees.

TEST FIVE

1. RELEVANT, APPOSITE
2. STUBBORN, FLEXIBLE
3. 131. The center number is the sum of the squares of the outer numbers. $131 = 1^2 + 7^2 + 9^2$.
4. C. The total for C is 62. The total for both A and D is 60, and the total for both B and E is 147. C is the only one that doesn't have an identical match.
5. INCOMPETENT, ADEQUATE
6. D. The black dot moves two corners counterclockwise at each stage. The triangle moves two sides clockwise at each stage and alternates being inside and outside the pentagon. The rectangle moves one side counterclockwise at each stage and alternates being inside and outside the pentagon.
7. POSTPONE, ADVANCE
8. D
9. E. WOOL : ANGORA
10. MADISON
11. CUT FIGURE
12. REREDOS (a decorated wall in a church). All the others have to do with cooking.
13. MEMORABLE DATE
14. 41. The center number is the difference between the products of the two diagonals. $41 = (13 \infty 7) - (10 \infty 5)$.
15. ORIGINATOR
16. BAG
17. −21. The rule is parentheses first, then multiplication and division before addition and subtraction.
18. DRAGON
19. BEAT, BEET
20. E. Each circle is made by superimposing the two circles below it and removing overlapping parts.

TEST SIX

1. PAN
2. COSMIC (COMIC)
3. D. In each row and column, the third square is the first and second square superimposed, with overlapping parts removed.
4. ENTIRELY, SLIGHTLY
5. 55. Each number is the number above it times 3 plus either 2, 3, or 4, depending on which column it is. $55 = 17 \infty 3 + 4$. $169 = 55 \infty 3 + 4$.
6. BERNADETTE
7. SATURATE, DOUSE
8. STOWAWAY
9. A. The rectangle and square swap places and the center item in each stays on the side that it was on.
10. DIRECT
11. ONLOOKER
12. CHASTE, CHASED
13. PERSIMMON (fruit). All the others have to do with poetry.
14. 21. Starting at 6 and moving three segments clockwise yields the sequence 6, 7, 9, 12, 16, ?, 27. The difference between terms in the sequence increases by 1 each time.
15. 126. (9! (5! ∞ 4!)). n! = $1 \infty 2 \infty 3 \infty 4 \infty ... \infty$ n.
16. DEXTERITY, CLUMSINESS
17. Change of heart
18. C. LOWLIP = PILLOW. The trees are POPLAR, WILLOW, LARCH, and DEODAR.
19. E. The left halves of the second and third numbers are formed by adding the first and third digits of the previous number. The right halves are formed by adding the second and fourth digits of the previous number. $12 = 3 + 9$, $15 = 7 + 8$, $2 = 1 + 1$, $7 = 2 + 5$.
20. E

TEST SEVEN

1. E. The figures change ABCDEFG to FCEAGBD.
2. SIDE, SIGHED
3. LINEN
4. D. In each row and column, the third square is the overlapping parts of the superimposed first and second squares.
5. LICENSE TO MARKET
6. WORK
7. DIRT: All of the words have their letters in alphabetical order.
8. INTERMEDIATE
9. 74. The center number is the sum of the reversals of the outer numbers.
   $74 = 37 + 12 + 25$.
10. D
11. CLEMENT
12. 15. The center number is the sum of the top left number, the top right number, and the lower right number, minus the lower left number.
    $15 = 17 + 4 + 9 - 15$.
13. UP TO DATE
14. ASTRINGENT, SEPARATING
15. CHAFF
16. HEXAGON: It is a planar figure; the rest are solid figures.
17. INTIMATE, INDICATE
18. NELSON
19. COL, DEPRESSION
20. 2B

TEST EIGHT

1. SOUVENIR, KEEPSAKE
2. 3096. The center number in each row is the product of the digits on the left followed by the product of the digits on the right.
   $30 = 5 \times 2 \times 3$; $96 = 8 \times 2 \times 6$.
3. A. SCI SOAP = PICASSO. The composers are ROSSINI, COPLAND, WAGNER, and MAHLER.
4. C. It contains circles of three different sizes with a black dot in all of them.
5.
   | 30 |
   | 11 |

   The top number is the product of the two previous numbers. The bottom number is the sum of the two previous numbers.
   $30 = 6 \times 5$; $11 = 6 + 5$.
6. B. ABBREVIATIONS, UNDERSTOOD
7. ADVENTURER
8. 25622. All the others are three-digit numbers followed by their square roots. For example, 67626 is 676 followed by 26, which is the square root of 676.
9. EPHEMERAL, BRIEF
10. COB: This is a male animal; the rest are female.
11. CORD, CHORD
12. CHAPTER
13. 4. The center number is the difference between the sum of the left three numbers and the sum of the right three numbers.
    $4 = (6 + 11 + 2) - (5 + 9 + 1)$.
14. SOUP
15. DIMINUTIVE, GARGANTUAN
16. PAVANE
17. $\frac{5}{3}$ or $1\frac{2}{3}$.
18. SEAWEED
19. SAUERKRAUT (cabbage). All the others are sausages.
20. C. In each row and column, the third circle is the first and second circle superimposed, with overlapping parts removed.

TEST NINE

1. C. All the others are the same figure rotated.
2. D. SQUARE : OCTAGON. An octagon has double the number of sides of a square and a hexagon has double the number of sides of a triangle.
3. $3500 = 50 \infty 70$. $50 = 5 + 9 + 3 + 17 + 1 + 15$; $70 = 4 + 10 + 2 + 14 + 32 + 8$.
4. BOUND: The vowels A, E, I, O, and U are being repeated in order.
5. B. The large arc moves 90 counterclockwise at each stage. The middle arc moves 90 clockwise at each stage. The inner arc moves 90 clockwise at each stage.
6. 15. In each row and column, the third number is the product of the first two numbers divided by four.
7. DEMOCRATIC
8. CONFUSED
9. ROME WAS NOT BUILT IN A DAY.
10. REST
11. THRILL
12. $131\frac{5}{8}$. Each term is $-1\frac{1}{2}$ times the previous term.
13. MASTER
14. 26. Starting at 10 and moving three segments clockwise yields the series 10, 11, 14, 19, ?, 35, 46. The difference between terms in the series is the sequence of odd numbers, 1, 3, 5, 7, 9, 11.
15. DRAGOMAN, INTERPRETER
16. BEECH, BEACH
17. TANKER: It is engine driven; the rest use sails.
18. CHAT
19. D. TUBERT = BUTTER. The flowers are DAFFODIL, TULIP, GLADIOLI and PANSY.
20. A. Each part moves a fixed number of degrees clockwise, either 0, 90, or 180.

TEST TEN

1. C. It contains five small white circles and four black circles, while the rest contain four small white circles and five black circles.
2. VOLATILE, CONSTANT
3. B. 96. The numbers are successive perfect squares (1, 4, 9, 16, 25, 36, 49, 64) split into groups of two numbers.
4. SUGGESTION
5. MINIMAL
6. B. At each stage the black dot moves 45 counterclockwise, the small white circle moves clockwise 90, the medium size circle moves clockwise 90, and the large circle moves clockwise 45.
7. C. OROLOGY : MOUNTAINS
8. OVERWHELM
9. N. Starting with A, the sequence alternates between skipping two letters and one letter.
10. BUILD, BILLED
11. FILE
12. 9. The center number is the product of the upper left, upper right, and lower right numbers, divided by the lower left number. $9 = 9 \infty 3 \infty 4$ 12.
13. FAVEOLATE (honeycombed). All the others have to do with wind.
14. LANCINATE, MEND
15. D. GENORA = ORANGE. The vegetables are POTATO, CABBAGE, SPROUTS, and CARROT.
16. DULCIMER
17. There is a 50% chance that two coins will land heads up. It is a certainty that at least two coins will end up with the same side up. Thus it is just as likely that those two coins will be heads as it is that they will be tails.
18. FEMALE DONKEY
19. IRON
20. E. Each circle is made by superimposing the two circles below it and removing overlapping parts.

TEST ELEVEN

1. 11. The center number is the difference between the upper right number and the lower left number divided by the difference between the upper left number and the lower right number. 11 = (89 – 56) ÷ (21 – 18).
2. GOPHER
3. D. It is the only one that doesn't have an identical match. A is the same figure as B. C is the same figure as E
4. INTRINSIC, NATIVE
5. AUGUST: It has 31 days; all the other months have 30 days.
6. BOOK
7. 6. The sum of the numbers in each column decreases by one from left to right (24, 23, 22, 21, 20).
8. CALIPER (LIP)
9. D. At each stage an additional line is added, and the figure is reflected.
10. TELESCOPIC
11. Zero. There are three white socks and one black sock in the drawer. The chances are as follows:
    White pair = 0.5
    Mixed pair = 0.5
    Black pair = 0
12. D. RUTCK = TRUCK. The boats are CARAVEL, CANOE, LAUNCH, and CRUISER.
13. APPEASE
14. MEAD
15. KINGFISHER
16. HAND
17. NIPPON
18. PALPATES, EXAMINES
19. MEAT
20. E

TEST TWELVE

1. B doesn't fit.

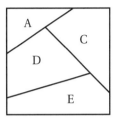

2. FELLOWSHIP
3. B. 71364259. The numbers move from the position ABCDEFGH to the position EGBDAHFC.
4. ARTISAN = SINATRA. The instruments are CORNET, BASSOON, PICCOLO, and ACCORDION.
5. PLETHORA, DEARTH
6. E. It contains a shaded part common to two figures. In all the others, the shaded area is common to only one figure.
7. 3. Starting at 0 and moving two segments clockwise yields the series 0, 1, ?, 6, 10, 15, 21. The difference between terms in the series is 1, 2, 3, 4, 5, 6.
8. OUST
9. DON'T TAKE CHANCES
10. MODULATE, REGULATE
11. 726. Each number is produced by adding the previous number to its reverse. For example, 33 = 12 + 21. 726 = 363 + 363.
12. Innocent (in O cent)
13. GIBUS (hat). All the others have to do with horse legs.
14. PILLAGE
15. SILK
16. WIND
17. E. RUGAS = SUGAR. The forms of transportation are TRAIN, OMNIBUS, CYCLE, and TRAM.
18. TRICKERY
19. TICK
20. E

TEST THIRTEEN

1. RUMINATE, CONSIDER
2. ON THE LOOSE
3. A. The second and third numbers are formed by adding the number in the middle of the previous number to the previous number.
   For example, $46 + 3469 = 3515$,
   and $51 + 3515 = 3566$.
4. PROFICIENT
5. SLIP
6. D. It is the only one that doesn't have an identical match.
7. LACE
8. VEILED
9. NEOPHYTE (novice). All the others have to do with the sky, space, and gas.
10. The smallest number has digits multiplying to 1 and summing to 2, namely 11. The next smallest has digits multiplying to 2 and summing to 4, namely 112. So the house number is 11 and there are at most 111 houses.
11. B. Each pentagon is made by superimposing the two pentagons below it and removing overlapping parts.
12. 8. Each square block of four numbers totals 20.
13. HORSE
14. CRISTATE, TUFTED
15. SELL, CELL
16. A. WALLSOW = SWALLOW. The fish are TURBOT, FLOUNDER, PLAICE, and HADDOCK.
17. HEART-SHAPED
18. SLUDGE
19. MAN
20. A. Each arm rotates a fixed amount at each stage.

Math & Logic Puzzle
ANSWERS

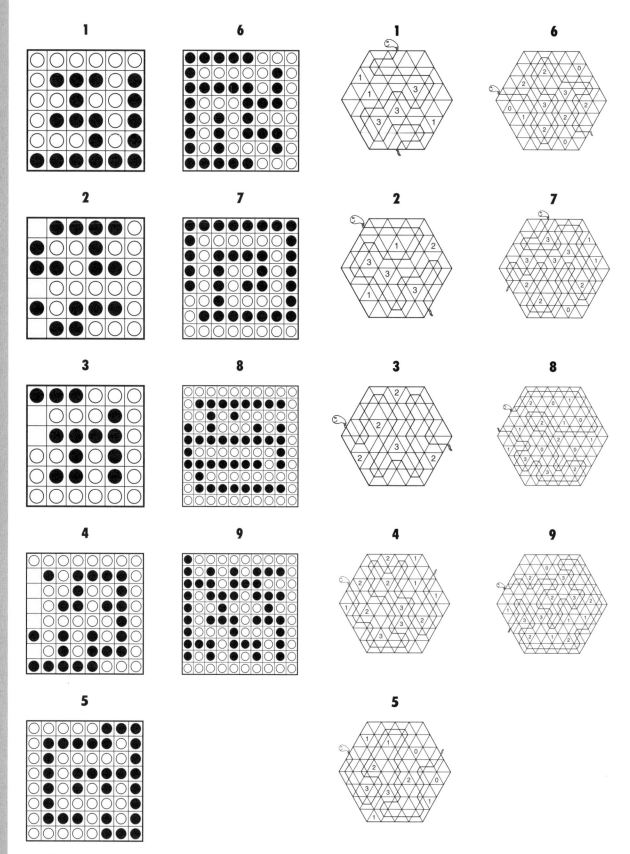

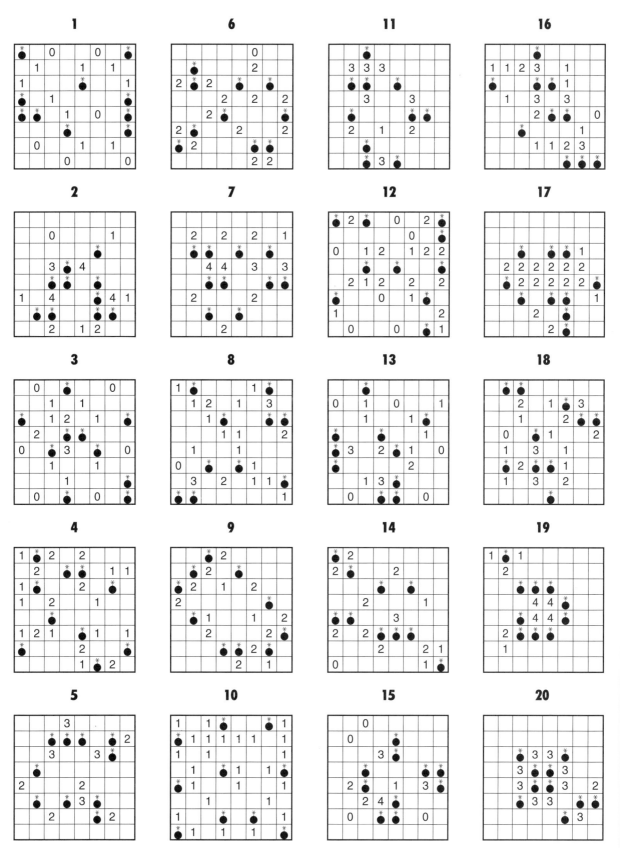

289

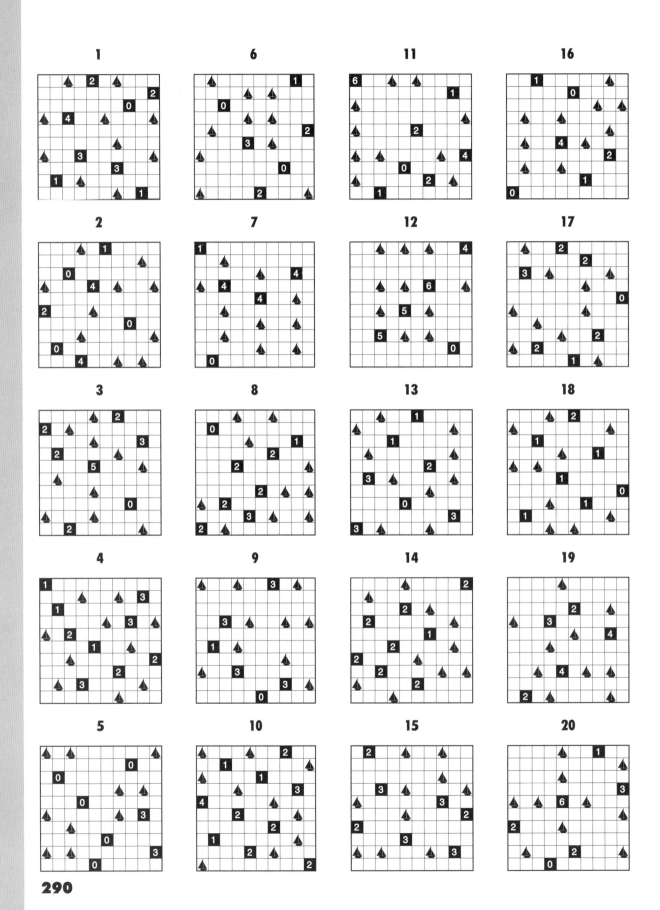

290

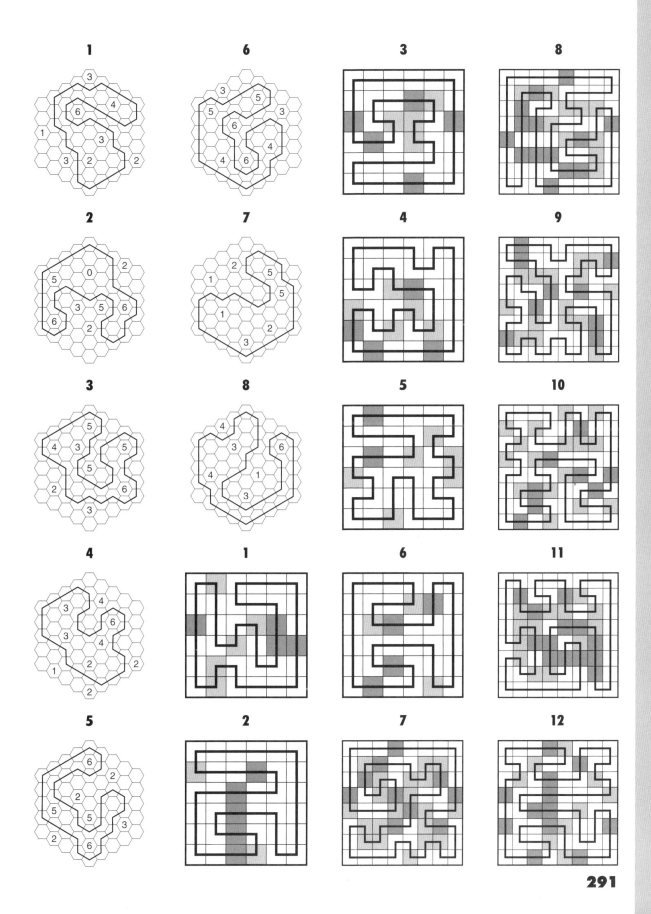

291

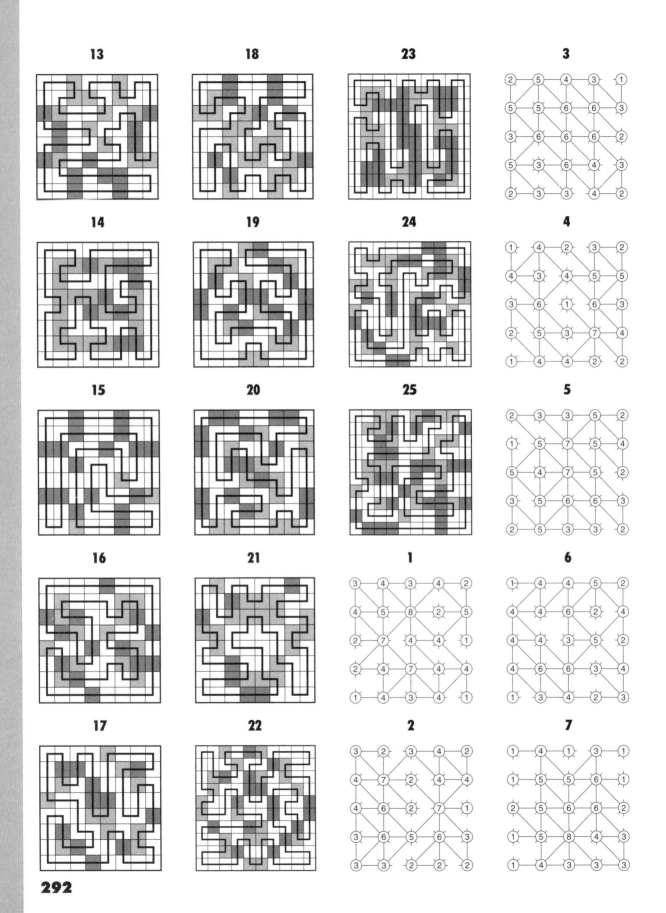

13

18

23

3

14

19

24

4

15

20

25

5

16

21

1

6

17

22

2

7

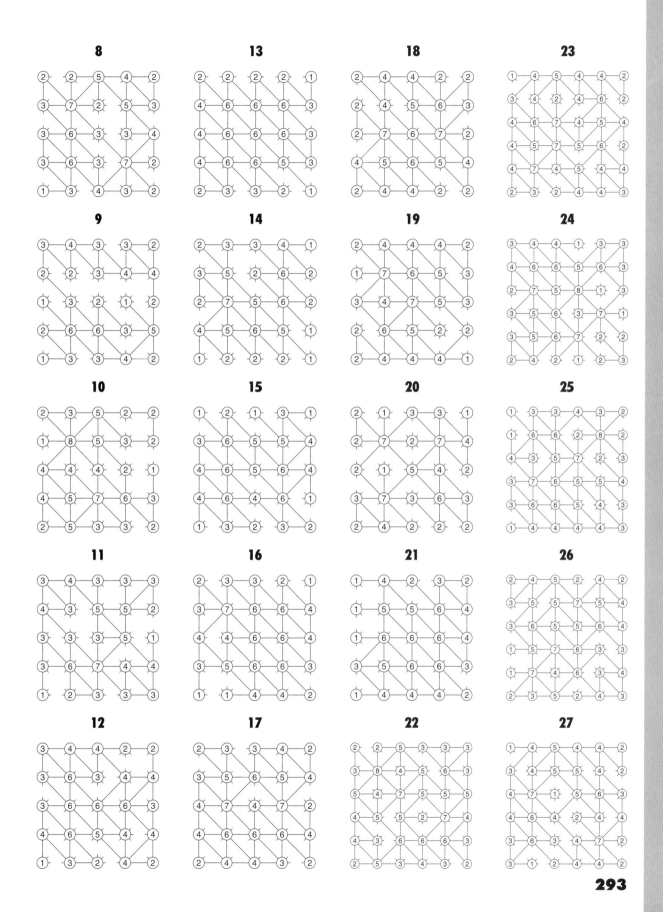

293

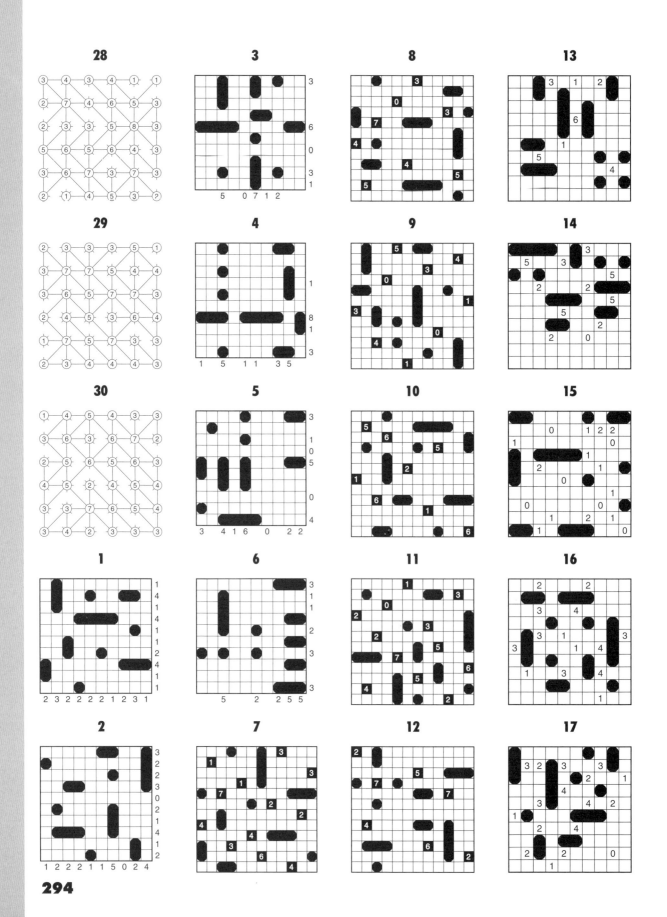

18

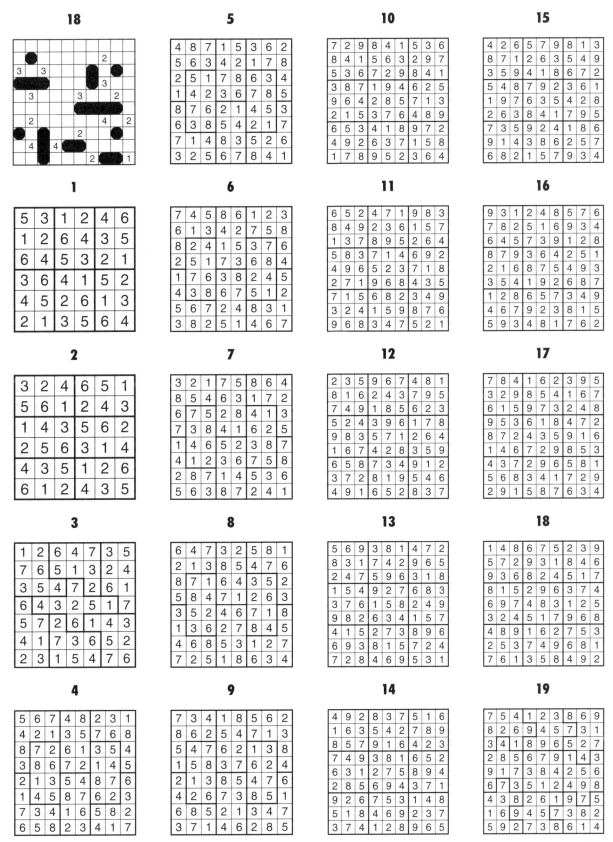

5

4	8	7	1	5	3	6	2
5	6	3	4	2	1	7	8
2	5	1	7	8	6	3	4
1	4	2	3	6	7	8	5
8	7	6	2	1	4	5	3
6	3	8	5	4	2	1	7
7	1	4	8	3	5	2	6
3	2	5	6	7	8	4	1

10

7	2	9	8	4	1	5	3	6
8	4	1	5	6	3	2	9	7
5	3	6	7	2	9	8	4	1
3	8	7	1	9	4	6	2	5
9	6	4	2	8	5	7	1	3
2	1	5	3	7	6	4	8	9
6	5	3	4	1	8	9	7	2
4	9	2	6	3	7	1	5	8
1	7	8	9	5	2	3	6	4

15

4	2	6	5	7	9	8	1	3
8	7	1	2	6	3	5	4	9
3	5	9	4	1	8	6	7	2
5	4	8	7	9	2	3	6	1
1	9	7	6	3	5	4	2	8
2	6	3	8	4	1	7	9	5
7	3	5	9	2	4	1	8	6
9	1	4	3	8	6	2	5	7
6	8	2	1	5	7	9	3	4

1

5	3	1	2	4	6
1	2	6	4	3	5
6	4	5	3	2	1
3	6	4	1	5	2
4	5	2	6	1	3
2	1	3	5	6	4

6

7	4	5	8	6	1	2	3
6	1	3	4	2	7	5	8
8	2	4	1	5	3	7	6
2	5	1	7	3	6	8	4
1	7	6	3	8	2	4	5
4	3	8	6	7	5	1	2
5	6	7	2	4	8	3	1
3	8	2	5	1	4	6	7

11

6	5	2	4	7	1	9	8	3
8	4	9	2	3	6	1	5	7
1	3	7	8	9	5	2	6	4
5	8	3	7	1	4	6	9	2
4	9	6	5	2	3	7	1	8
2	7	1	9	6	8	4	3	5
7	1	5	6	8	2	3	4	9
3	2	4	1	5	9	8	7	6
9	6	8	3	4	7	5	2	1

16

9	3	1	2	4	8	5	7	6
7	8	2	5	1	6	9	3	4
6	4	5	7	3	9	1	2	8
8	7	9	3	6	4	2	5	1
2	1	6	8	7	5	4	9	3
3	5	4	1	9	2	6	8	7
1	2	8	6	5	7	3	4	9
4	6	7	9	2	3	8	1	5
5	9	3	4	8	1	7	6	2

2

3	2	4	6	5	1
5	6	1	2	4	3
1	4	3	5	6	2
2	5	6	3	1	4
4	3	5	1	2	6
6	1	2	4	3	5

7

3	2	1	7	5	8	6	4
8	5	4	6	3	1	7	2
6	7	5	2	8	4	1	3
7	3	8	4	1	6	2	5
1	4	6	5	2	3	8	7
4	1	2	3	6	7	5	8
2	8	7	1	4	5	3	6
5	6	3	8	7	2	4	1

12

2	3	5	9	6	7	4	8	1
8	1	6	2	4	3	7	9	5
7	4	9	1	8	5	6	2	3
5	2	4	3	9	6	1	7	8
9	8	3	5	7	1	2	6	4
1	6	7	4	2	8	3	5	9
6	5	8	7	3	4	9	1	2
3	7	2	8	1	9	5	4	6
4	9	1	6	5	2	8	3	7

17

7	8	4	1	6	2	3	9	5
3	2	9	8	5	4	1	6	7
6	1	5	9	7	3	2	4	8
9	5	3	6	1	8	4	7	2
8	7	2	4	3	5	9	1	6
1	4	6	7	2	9	8	5	3
4	3	7	2	9	6	5	8	1
5	6	8	3	4	1	7	2	9
2	9	1	5	8	7	6	3	4

3

1	2	6	4	7	3	5
7	6	5	1	3	2	4
3	5	4	7	2	6	1
6	4	3	2	5	1	7
5	7	2	6	1	4	3
4	1	7	3	6	5	2
2	3	1	5	4	7	6

8

6	4	7	3	2	5	8	1
2	1	3	8	5	4	7	6
8	7	1	6	4	3	5	2
5	8	4	7	1	2	6	3
3	5	2	4	6	7	1	8
1	3	6	2	7	8	4	5
4	6	8	5	3	1	2	7
7	2	5	1	8	6	3	4

13

5	6	9	3	8	1	4	7	2
8	3	1	7	4	2	9	6	5
2	4	7	5	9	6	3	1	8
1	5	4	9	2	7	6	8	3
3	7	6	1	5	8	2	4	9
9	8	2	6	3	4	1	5	7
4	1	5	2	7	3	8	9	6
6	9	3	8	1	5	7	2	4
7	2	8	4	6	9	5	3	1

18

1	4	8	6	7	5	2	3	9
5	7	2	9	3	1	8	4	6
9	3	6	8	2	4	5	1	7
8	1	5	2	9	6	3	7	4
6	9	7	4	8	3	1	2	5
3	2	4	5	1	7	9	6	8
4	8	9	1	6	2	7	5	3
2	5	3	7	4	9	6	8	1
7	6	1	3	5	8	4	9	2

4

5	6	7	4	8	2	3	1
4	2	1	3	5	7	6	8
8	7	2	6	1	3	5	4
3	8	6	7	2	1	4	5
2	1	3	5	4	8	7	6
1	4	5	8	7	6	2	3
7	3	4	1	6	5	8	2
6	5	8	2	3	4	1	7

9

7	3	4	1	8	5	6	2
8	6	2	5	4	7	1	3
5	4	7	6	2	1	3	8
1	5	8	3	7	6	2	4
2	1	3	8	5	4	7	6
4	2	6	7	3	8	5	1
6	8	5	2	1	3	4	7
3	7	1	4	6	2	8	5

14

4	9	2	8	3	7	5	1	6
1	6	3	5	4	2	7	8	9
8	5	7	9	1	6	4	2	3
7	4	9	3	8	1	6	5	2
6	3	1	2	7	5	8	9	4
2	8	5	6	9	4	3	7	1
9	2	6	7	5	3	1	4	8
5	1	8	4	6	9	2	3	7
3	7	4	1	2	8	9	6	5

19

7	5	4	1	2	3	8	6	9
8	2	6	9	4	5	7	3	1
3	4	1	8	9	6	5	2	7
2	8	5	6	7	9	1	4	3
9	1	7	3	8	4	2	5	6
6	7	3	5	1	2	4	9	8
4	3	8	2	6	1	9	7	5
1	6	9	4	5	7	3	8	2
5	9	2	7	3	8	6	1	4

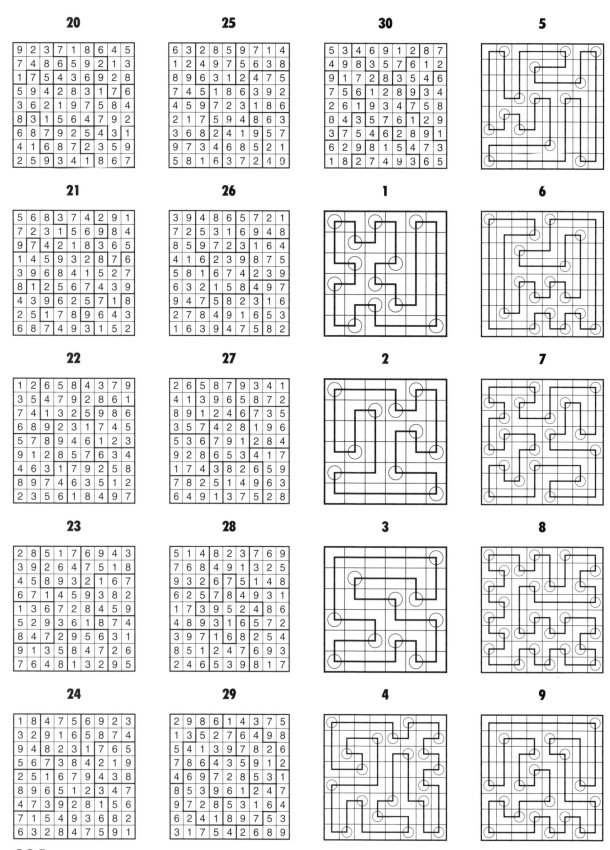

20

9	2	3	7	1	8	6	4	5
7	4	8	6	5	9	2	1	3
1	7	5	4	3	6	9	2	8
5	9	4	2	8	3	1	7	6
3	6	2	1	9	7	5	8	4
8	3	1	5	6	4	7	9	2
6	8	7	9	2	5	4	3	1
4	1	6	8	7	2	3	5	9
2	5	9	3	4	1	8	6	7

25

6	3	2	8	5	9	7	1	4
1	2	4	9	7	5	6	3	8
8	9	6	3	1	2	4	7	5
7	4	5	1	8	6	3	9	2
4	5	9	7	2	3	1	8	6
2	1	7	5	9	4	8	6	3
3	6	8	2	4	1	9	5	7
9	7	3	4	6	8	5	2	1
5	8	1	6	3	7	2	4	9

30

5	3	4	6	9	1	2	8	7
4	9	8	3	5	7	6	1	2
9	1	7	2	8	3	5	4	6
7	5	6	1	2	8	9	3	4
2	6	1	9	3	4	7	5	8
8	4	3	5	7	6	1	2	9
3	7	5	4	6	2	8	9	1
6	2	9	8	1	5	4	7	3
1	8	2	7	4	9	3	6	5

5

21

5	6	8	3	7	4	2	9	1
7	2	3	1	5	6	9	8	4
9	7	4	2	1	8	3	6	5
1	4	5	9	3	2	8	7	6
3	9	6	8	4	1	5	2	7
8	1	2	5	6	7	4	3	9
4	3	9	6	2	5	7	1	8
2	5	1	7	8	9	6	4	3
6	8	7	4	9	3	1	5	2

26

3	9	4	8	6	5	7	2	1
7	2	5	3	1	6	9	4	8
8	5	9	7	2	3	1	6	4
4	1	6	2	3	9	8	7	5
5	8	1	6	7	4	2	3	9
6	3	2	1	5	8	4	9	7
9	4	7	5	8	2	3	1	6
2	7	8	4	9	1	6	5	3
1	6	3	9	4	7	5	8	2

1

22

1	2	6	5	8	4	3	7	9
3	5	4	7	9	2	8	6	1
7	4	1	3	2	5	9	8	6
6	8	9	2	3	1	7	4	5
5	7	8	9	4	6	1	2	3
9	1	2	8	5	7	6	3	4
4	6	3	1	7	9	2	5	8
8	9	7	4	6	3	5	1	2
2	3	5	6	1	8	4	9	7

27

2	6	5	8	7	9	3	4	1
4	1	3	9	6	5	8	7	2
8	9	1	2	4	6	7	3	5
3	5	7	4	2	8	1	9	6
5	3	6	7	9	1	2	8	4
9	2	8	6	5	3	4	1	7
1	7	4	3	8	2	6	5	9
7	8	2	5	1	4	9	6	3
6	4	9	1	3	7	5	2	8

2

23

2	8	5	1	7	6	9	4	3
3	9	2	6	4	7	5	1	8
4	5	8	9	3	2	1	6	7
6	7	1	4	5	9	3	8	2
1	3	6	7	2	8	4	5	9
5	2	9	3	6	1	8	7	4
8	4	7	2	9	5	6	3	1
9	1	3	5	8	4	7	2	6
7	6	4	8	1	3	2	9	5

28

5	1	4	8	2	3	7	6	9
7	6	8	4	9	1	3	2	5
9	3	2	6	7	5	1	4	8
6	2	5	7	8	4	9	3	1
1	7	3	9	5	2	4	8	6
4	8	9	3	1	6	5	7	2
3	9	7	1	6	8	2	5	4
8	5	1	2	4	7	6	9	3
2	4	6	5	3	9	8	1	7

3

24

1	8	4	7	5	6	9	2	3
3	2	9	1	6	5	8	7	4
9	4	8	2	3	1	7	6	5
5	6	7	3	8	4	2	1	9
2	5	1	6	7	9	4	3	8
8	9	6	5	1	2	3	4	7
4	7	3	9	2	8	1	5	6
7	1	5	4	9	3	6	8	2
6	3	2	8	4	7	5	9	1

29

2	9	8	6	1	4	3	7	5
1	3	5	2	7	6	4	9	8
5	4	1	3	9	7	8	2	6
7	8	6	4	3	5	9	1	2
4	6	9	7	2	8	5	3	1
8	5	3	9	6	1	2	4	7
9	7	2	8	5	3	1	6	4
6	2	4	1	8	9	7	5	3
3	1	7	5	4	2	6	8	9

4

6

7

8

9

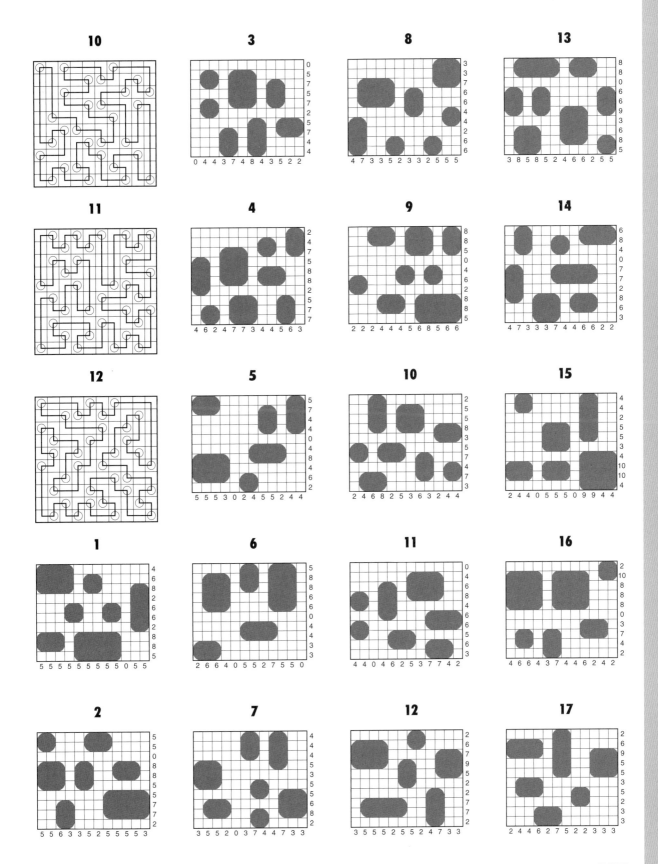

297

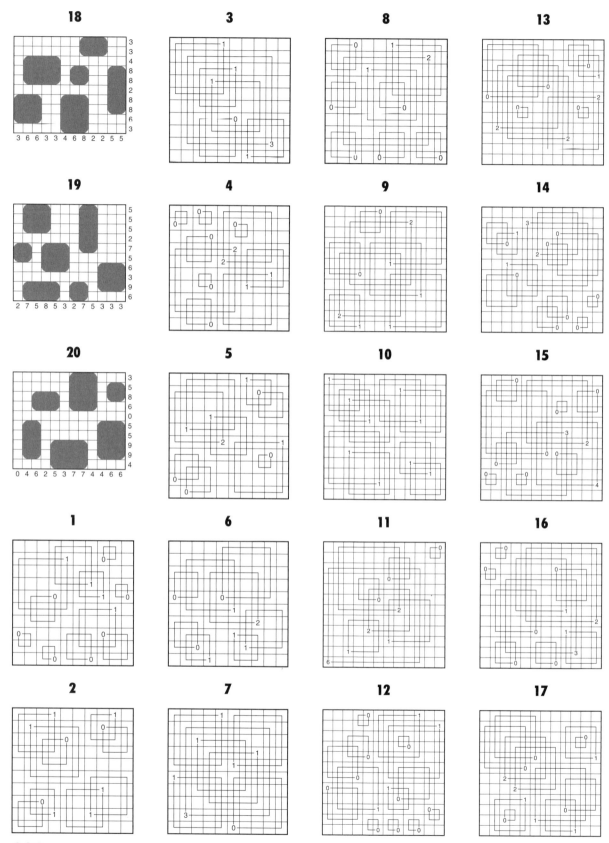

298

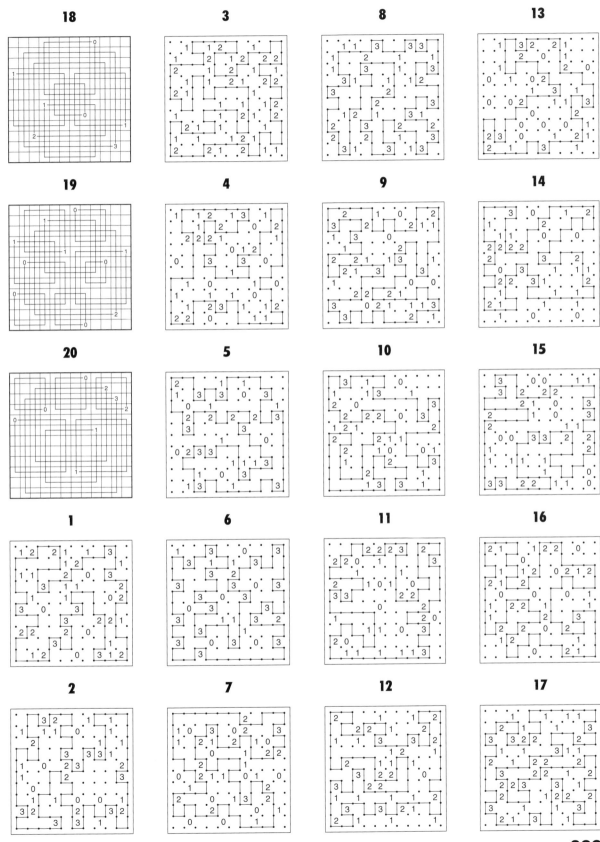

299

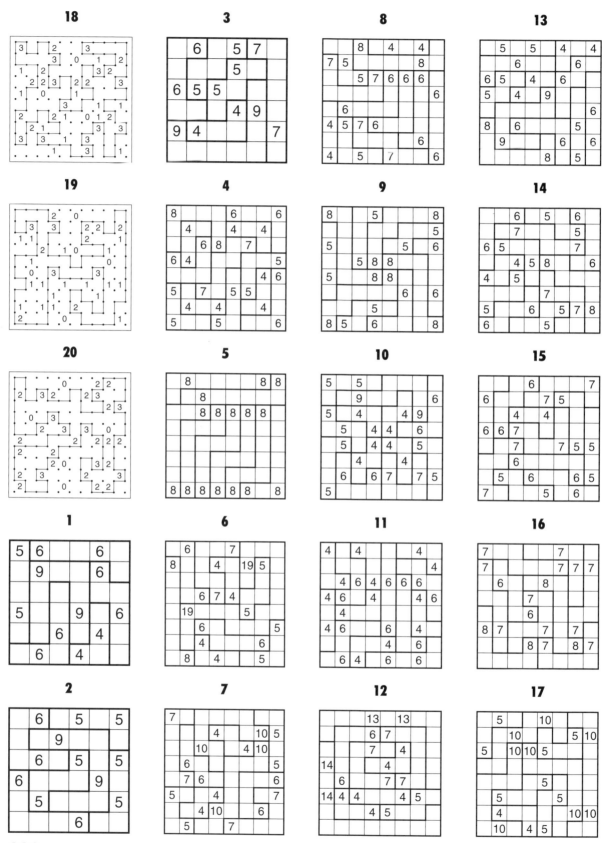

18

3

8

13

19

4

9

14

20

5

10

15

1

6

11

16

2

7

12

17

300

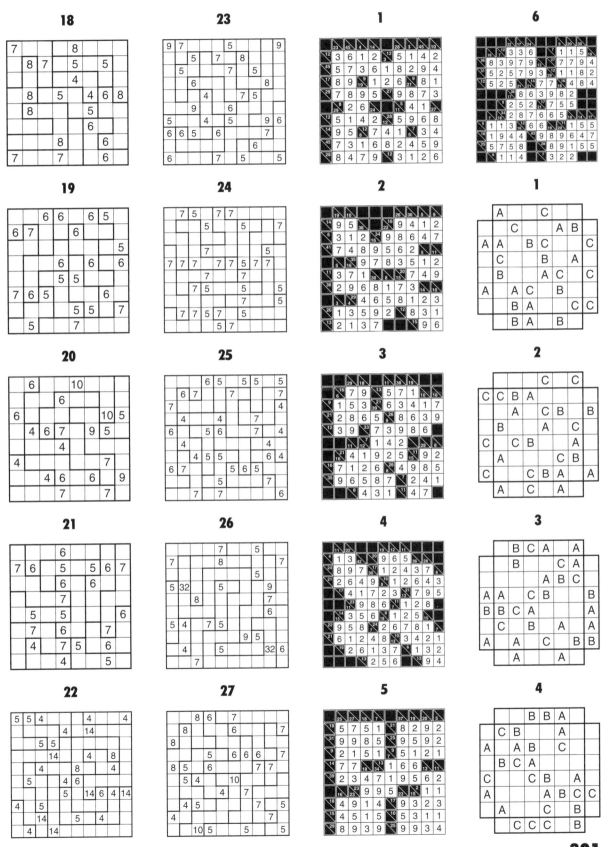

301

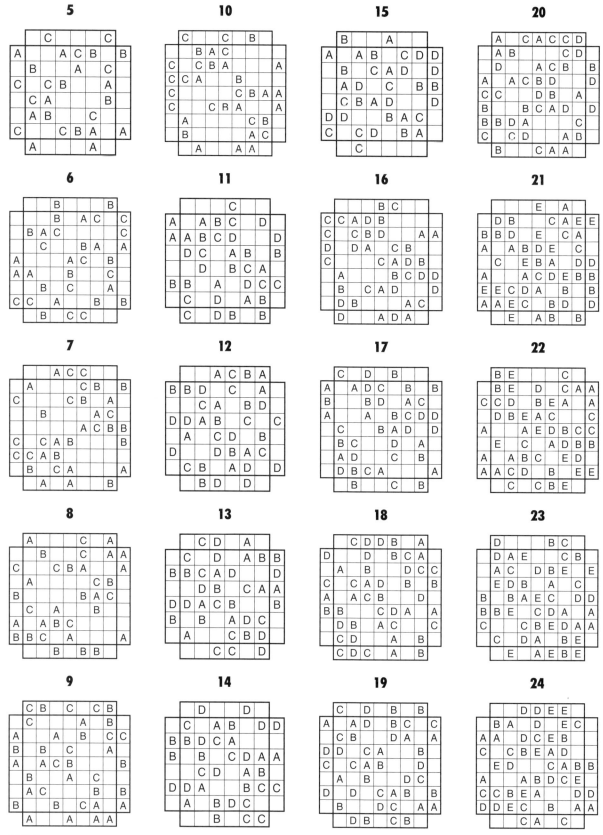

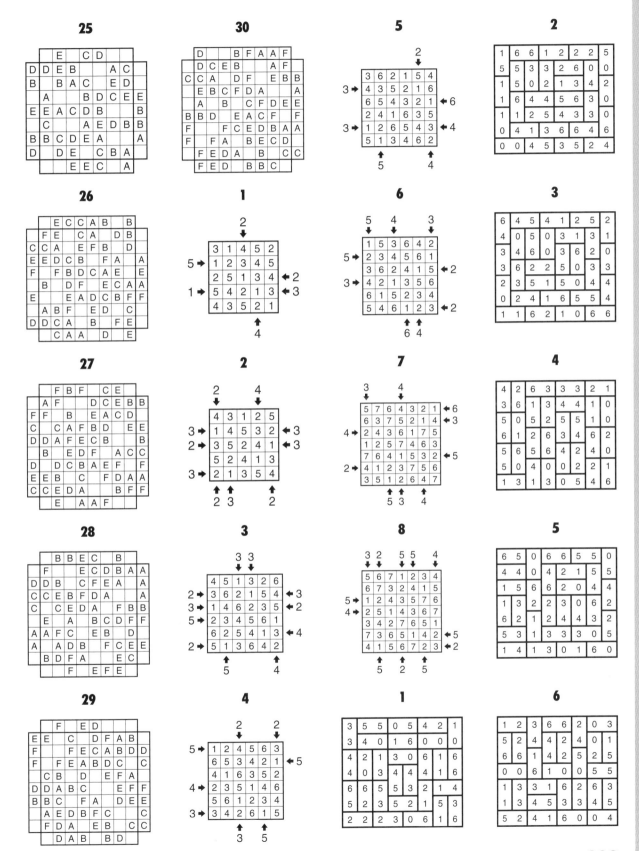

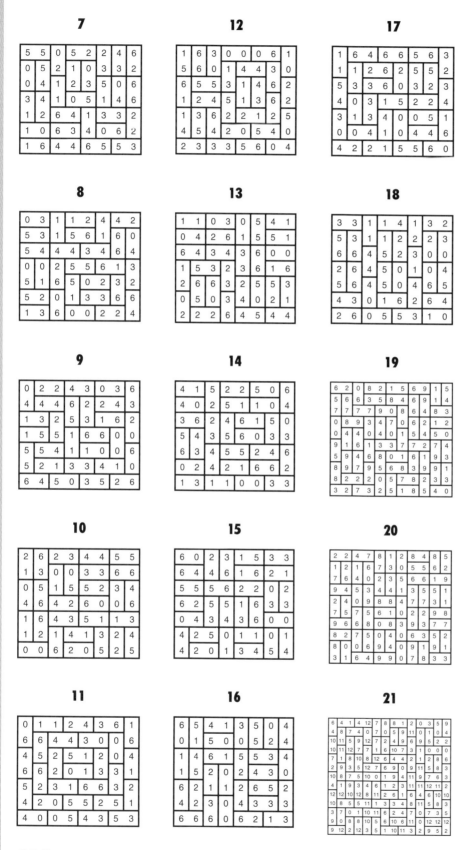

7

5	5	0	5	2	2	4	6
0	5	2	1	0	3	3	2
0	4	1	2	3	5	0	6
3	4	1	0	5	1	4	6
1	2	6	4	1	3	3	2
1	0	6	3	4	0	6	2
1	6	4	4	6	5	5	3

12

1	6	3	0	0	0	6	1
5	6	0	1	4	4	3	0
6	5	5	3	1	4	6	2
1	2	4	5	1	3	6	2
1	3	6	2	2	1	2	5
4	5	4	2	0	5	4	0
2	3	3	3	5	6	0	4

17

1	6	4	6	6	5	6	3
1	1	2	6	2	5	5	2
5	3	3	6	0	3	2	3
4	0	3	1	5	2	2	4
3	1	3	4	0	0	5	1
0	0	4	1	0	4	4	6
4	2	2	1	5	5	6	0

8

0	3	1	1	2	4	4	2
5	3	1	5	6	1	6	0
5	4	4	4	3	4	6	4
0	0	2	5	5	6	1	3
5	1	6	5	0	2	3	2
5	2	0	1	3	3	6	6
1	3	6	0	0	2	2	4

13

1	1	0	3	0	5	4	1
0	4	2	6	1	5	5	1
6	4	3	4	3	6	0	0
1	5	3	2	3	6	1	6
2	6	6	3	2	5	5	3
0	5	0	3	4	0	2	1
2	2	2	6	4	5	4	4

18

3	3	1	1	4	1	3	2
5	3	1	1	2	2	2	3
6	6	4	5	2	3	0	0
2	6	4	5	0	1	0	4
5	6	4	5	0	4	6	5
4	3	0	1	6	2	6	4
2	6	0	5	5	3	1	0

9

0	2	2	4	3	0	3	6
4	4	4	6	2	2	4	3
1	3	2	5	3	1	6	2
1	5	5	1	6	6	0	0
5	5	4	1	1	0	0	6
5	2	1	3	3	4	1	0
6	4	5	0	3	5	2	6

14

4	1	5	2	2	5	0	6
4	0	2	5	1	1	0	4
3	6	2	4	6	1	5	0
5	4	3	5	6	0	3	3
6	3	4	5	5	2	4	6
0	2	4	2	1	6	2	0
1	3	1	1	0	0	3	3

19

6	2	0	8	2	1	5	6	9	1	5
5	6	6	3	5	8	4	6	9	1	4
7	7	7	7	9	0	8	6	4	8	3
0	8	9	3	4	7	0	6	2	1	2
0	4	4	0	4	0	1	5	4	5	0
9	1	6	1	3	3	7	7	2	7	4
5	9	4	6	8	0	1	6	1	9	3
8	9	7	9	5	6	8	3	9	9	1
8	2	2	2	0	5	7	8	2	3	3
3	2	7	3	2	5	1	8	5	4	0

10

2	6	2	3	4	4	5	5
1	3	0	0	3	3	6	6
0	5	1	5	5	2	3	4
4	6	4	2	6	0	0	6
1	6	4	3	5	1	1	3
1	2	1	4	1	3	2	4
0	0	6	2	0	5	2	5

15

6	0	2	3	1	5	3	3
6	4	4	6	1	6	2	1
5	5	5	6	2	2	0	2
6	2	5	5	1	6	3	3
0	4	3	4	3	6	0	0
4	2	5	0	1	1	0	1
4	2	0	1	3	4	5	4

20

2	2	4	7	8	1	2	8	4	8	5
1	2	1	6	7	3	0	5	5	6	2
7	6	4	0	2	3	5	6	6	1	9
9	4	5	3	4	4	1	3	5	5	1
2	4	0	9	8	8	4	7	7	3	1
7	5	7	5	6	1	0	2	2	9	8
9	6	6	8	0	8	3	9	3	7	7
8	2	7	5	0	4	0	6	3	5	2
8	0	0	6	9	4	0	9	1	9	1
3	1	6	4	9	9	0	7	8	3	3

11

0	1	1	2	4	3	6	1
6	6	4	4	3	0	0	6
4	5	2	5	1	2	0	4
6	6	2	0	1	3	3	1
5	2	3	1	6	6	3	2
4	2	0	5	5	2	5	1
4	0	0	5	4	3	5	3

16

6	5	4	1	3	5	0	4
0	1	5	0	0	5	2	4
1	4	6	1	5	5	3	4
1	5	2	0	2	4	3	0
6	2	1	1	2	6	5	2
4	2	3	0	4	3	3	3
6	6	6	0	6	2	1	3

21

6	4	1	4	12	7	8	8	1	2	0	3	5	9
4	8	7	4	0	7	0	5	9	11	0	1	0	4
10	11	5	9	12	7	2	4	9	6	9	5	2	2
10	11	12	7	7	1	6	10	7	3	1	0	0	0
7	1	8	10	8	12	6	4	4	2	1	2	8	6
2	9	3	5	12	7	6	9	0	9	11	5	8	3
10	8	7	5	10	0	1	9	4	11	9	7	6	3
4	1	9	3	4	6	1	2	3	11	11	12	11	2
12	12	10	12	8	11	2	6	1	6	4	6	10	10
10	8	5	5	11	1	3	3	4	8	11	5	8	3
3	7	0	1	10	11	6	2	4	7	0	7	3	5
9	0	8	8	10	5	6	10	6	11	0	0	12	12
9	12	2	12	3	5	1	10	11	3	2	9	5	2

Critical Thinking Puzzle

ANSWERS

Balance

First, use the balance to divide the 80 grams into two piles of 40 grams. Then divide one of the 40-gram piles in half. Now balance the 20 grams against the 7 grams produced by the two masses. The 13 grams that are removed from the balance form one pile. The 7 grams added to the 40 grams + 20 grams produces the larger pile of 67 grams.

Big Magic

The sum of the side is thirty-four, and the square looks like this:

1	11	6	16
8	14	3	9
15	5	12	2
10	4	13	7

Break It Up!

Nine toothpicks need to be removed as shown below.

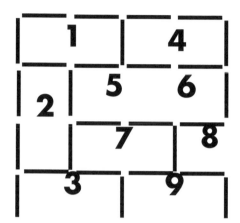

Breaking the Rules

Two inches. Each chalk piece will advance only half the distance covered by the ruler.

Breaking Up Is Hard to Do... Sometimes

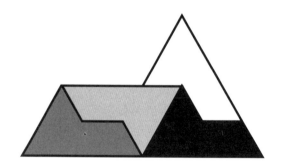

Bridge, Anyone?

The sticks below are arranged so that they support each other in a central triangle formed by over- and underlapping supports.

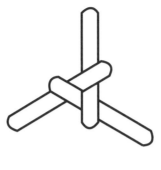

Cards, Anyone?

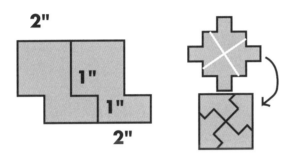

Change of Pace

a. either 5 pennies ($.05) + 4 nickels ($.20)
+ 1 quarter ($.25) = $.50; or 10 nickels ($.05) = $.50

b. 25 pennies ($.25) + 1 nickel ($.05)
+ 2 dimes ($.20) + 2 quarters ($.50) = $1.00

Check It Out

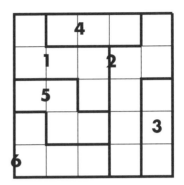

A Class Act

Seven students play only keyboards. A diagram helps illustrate and solve this problem.

Coin Roll

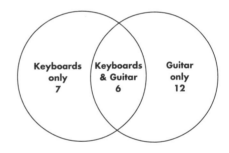

The coins maintain their relative position to each other as they move along the track. What changes is the direction in which the coin images point.

Cool Cut

Make the cut from one corner straight across to the corners as shown below. Each side of this regular triangle that is formed is equal in length to the diagonal of the square.

Doing Wheelies

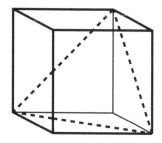

Wheel A would be spinning at five revolutions per minute. Wheel B would be spinning at twenty revolutions per minute. The difference in speed results from the "gearing up" and the "gearing down" from the first wheel set to the second wheel set. The belts between the second and third wheel sets do not affect the spin.

Don't Stop Now

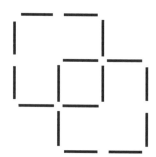

Exactly... Well, Almost

E. It is the mirror image of the other repeating (but rotating) design.

Face Lift

a. Eighteen faces.

b. Twenty-six faces.

c. Twenty-two faces.

A Game for Losers

By placing your "O" marker in either of the boxes indicated below, you are ensured a victory no matter where your opponent places his or her "X"s.

Get Set. Go!

150 miles long. In order to complete 30 miles of distance, the faster cyclist requires

1 hour of time while the slower cyclist needs 1.20 hours. Therefore, the time difference per 30 miles of travel is .20 hours. In order to increase the difference to 1 hour, multiple the 30 miles by 5.

Give Me Five

1111. Easy, unless of course you forget all it takes to solve this problem is to divide 5555 by 5!

Going Batty

The number of beetles captured on each successive night were 8, 14, 20, 26, and 32.

Good Guess

Forty-eight gumballs. Since two guesses were off by seven and no guesses were repeated, these values had to refer to numbers at the opposite extremes of the spread. The two extremes are 41 and 55. If you add 7 to one and take 7 away from the other, you arrive at the middle number of 48.

Here, Art, Art, Art

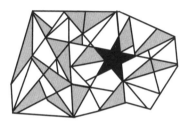

Here, Spot, Spot, Spot

Iron Horse Race

The trains will be tied 3 hours after the faster train (or $4^1/2$ hours after the slower train) begins the race. For example, if the trains travel 60 mph and 90 mph, the $4^1/2$-hour journey for the slower train covers 270 miles, while the 3-hour journey for the faster train also covers 270 miles.

Keep On Tickin'

First you'll need to find out what each section needs to add to. To get this number, add up every number on the clock's face (1 + 2 + 3 + 4 + 5 + 6 + 7 + 8 + 9 + 10 + 11 + 12 = 78). Divide 78 by 3 and you'll get 26—the sum that each section must add to. The next part is relatively easy, since the numbers are already laid out in a ready-to-add pattern.

Keeping Time

Six hours. In 6 hours, the slow clock will be exactly 30 minutes behind while the fast clock will be exactly 30 minutes ahead of time.

Lasagna Cut

Each person gets one large and one small triangular piece.

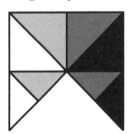

Here's a slightly different pattern that produces four similar-shaped slices (if we assume the connecting points between the triangle pairs remain uncut).

Look Over Here

The direction of the look is based upon the number of neighboring eyes that are in contact with the eye's circumference. Eyes that "touch" three other circles (such as the circle in question) have a pupil that points to the right.

Magic Star

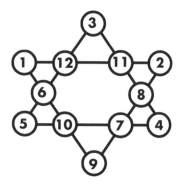

Main Attraction

Take either bar (it doesn't matter which one) and touch one end of the bar to the middle of the other bar. If the bar you are holding is a magnet, then its pole will cause the nonmagnetized bar to move. If, however, you've picked up the nonmagnetized bar, no attraction will occur. That's because neither of the poles is being touched.

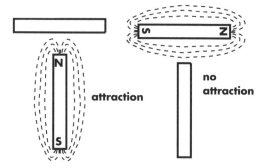

Melt Down

The level of water will not change. Although the top of the cube floats above the surface of the water, the amount of water in the entire ice cube can fill a space equal to the dimensions occupied by the part of the cube that is under the water's surface. In other words, as the ice cube turns to water, it produces the same amount of water as the space occupied by the submerged part of the cube.

Mind Bend

Place three parallel cuts in the card. Two of the cuts should be positioned on one side, while a single central cut should be made on the opposite side (as shown below). Then place a twist in the card so that half of the upper surface is formed by the "bottom-side" of the card. For extra fun, you might want to tape the folded card by all of its edges to the desk (making it more difficult to uncover the baffling "twist").

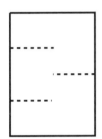 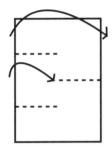

More Cheese

No. Six cuts are the fewest number of cuts needed to produce the twenty-seven smaller cubes. Stacking doesn't result in fewer cuts. Think of it this way: that innermost cube of the twenty-seven must be formed by a cut on each of its six sides.

Mind Slice

The angle of the cut will not affect the shape at all. All cuts will produce faces that are perfect circles. The feature that does change with the cutting angle is the circle size.

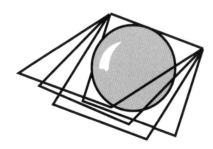

More Coinage

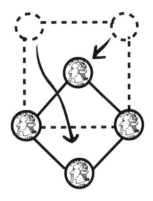

More Wheelies

480 revolutions. Since wheel B's rim is four times longer than wheel A's rim, it spins at one-fourth the speed (4 rps). Likewise, wheel B's rim is twice as long as wheel C's rim. Therefore, wheel C's rim spins twice as fast (8 rps). In 1 minute, C wheel will complete 60 x 8 revolutions, or 480 revolutions.

Number Blocks

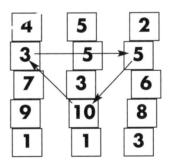

One Way Only

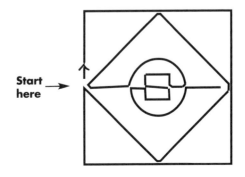

Parts of a Whole

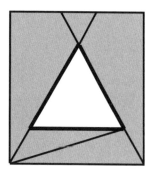

Puzzle Paths

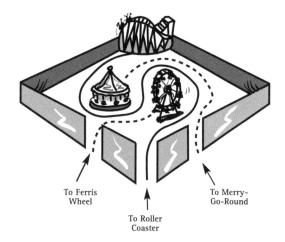

To Ferris Wheel

To Roller Coaster

To Merry-Go-Round

Oops, 1 Wasn't Concentrating

It is weaker than the original solution. In order have the original concentration, Anthony would have to add grape juice that is $2\frac{1}{2}$ times the regular strength.

Raises and Cuts

They are now both earning the exact same amount. To prove this, let's take a sample first-week salary of $100 for both Moe and Bo. After the first adjustment, Moe earned $110 while Bo earned $90. During the second adjustment, Moe was cut by $11 to $99. At the same time, Bo was increased by $9 to $99.

Runaway Runway

Six intersections as shown below.

Roller Coaster Roll

Young Ed. The car that travels along the curved slope accelerates faster. This extra speed results from the quick drop in the path that allows the car to quickly pick up speed as the car moving down the straight slope accelerates at a slower and more uniform rate.

Satellite Surveyor

80 square miles. If you examine the dissected grid, you'll uncover that the composite shapes include side-by-side pairs that can be joined to form four squares. The total area is 20 X 20, or 400 square miles. Each of the five identical squares contains one-fifth, or 80 square miles.

Say Cheese

Make three cuts that divide the cube into eight smaller but equal cubes. Each of these eight cubes has a side length of 1 inch to produce a surface area of 6 square inches. The sum of the eight cube surface areas is 48 square inches.

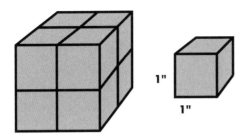

Screws in the Head

As the threads turn, they will produce a counterclockwise motion in the gear of the tuning post. This motion will decrease the tension in the string to produce a note of lower pitch.

Screwy Stuff

The threads of screw A form a spiral that would "go into" the wood block. In contrast, the opposite spiral of screw B would result in this screw moving out of the wooden block.

Separation Anxiety

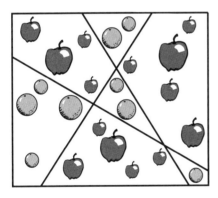

Sequence Grid

Triangle. The grid is filled by a series of number sequences. The first sequence consists of only one member—a square. The second and adjoining sequence includes a square + circle. The third sequence expands to include a square + circle + triangle. The complete sequence from which the "?" can be determined is square + circle + triangle + triangle + circle + circle.

Some Things Never Change

7 + 49 + 343 + 2401 + 16,807 = 19,607.

Spiral^2

The complete path from entrance to center is 5,000 feet. To obtain this distance, determine the total area of the structure (10,000 square feet). Now mentally unroll the spiral. Divide the 10,000-square-foot area by the area associated with one foot of forward travel. Since the corridor is 2 feet wide, the area for a single foot of forward motion is 2 square feet. Dividing 10,000 by 2, we arrive at the total distance of 5,000 feet.

The Race Is On

The wheel with the centrally placed lead will accelerate fastest. This behavior reflects a property of physics that ice skaters execute during their moves. As a skater spins, the speed of the spin can be adjusted by altering his or her distribution of weight. As the arms extend, the spinning skater slows. As the arms draw in, the spin accelerates.

Another Ant Walk

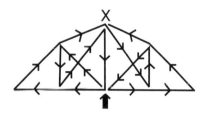

Surrounded By Squares

Thirteen squares.

Take 'em Away

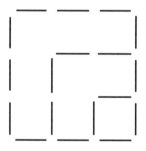

Take Your Pick

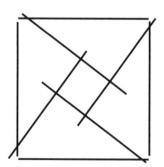

Thick as a Brick

Sixty bricks. You don't have to count all of the bricks. Just count the bricks in the uppermost layer (twelve) and multiply by the number of layers (five) so that you arrive at a total number of sixty bricks.

Time on Your Hands

7:22. For each given time, the minute hand advances a quarter of a complete counterclockwise rotation, while the hour hand advances three-eighths of a complete counterclockwise rotation. The final arrangement looks like this:

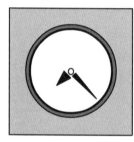

Togetherness

The computer weighs 16 pounds and its monitor weighs 32 pounds.

Trying Times

Eight unique triangles as shown below.

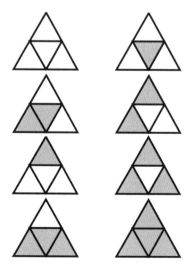

Turn, Turn, Turn

F.

Weighty Problem

120 pounds. If she needs to add "half of her weight" to get her full weight, then the weight that she does tell (60 pounds) must be half of her total. Therefore, 60 pounds is half of her weight. 60 + 60 = 120 pounds. If this doesn't seem right, just work it backwards starting with the 120 pounds.

What's the Angle?

a. Three copies of this shape are positioned as shown here.

Whale of a Problem

Two minutes. The amount of time needed to catch the seals doesn't change. Since two whales can catch two seals in 2 minutes, it is logical to assume that a single whale can catch one seal in that same period of time. Likewise, three whales can catch three seals in 2 minutes. As long as the number of whales is equal to the number of seals, the time doesn't change. Therefore, ten killer whales will also take 2 minutes to catch ten seals.

Wrap It Up

d. Here's what you see as you unwrap the folds.

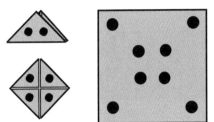

And a Cut Below

Eight pieces as shown below:

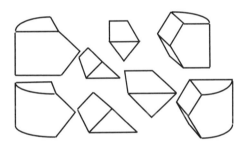

Egg Exactly

Simultaneously turn over the five and three minute timers when you begin to boil the water.

When the three minute timer runs out, put the egg into the boiling water. When the five minute timer runs out, the egg is done. Two minutes have elapsed.

Losing Marbles?

Start spinning the marble along the bottom of the cup so that it pushes against the inner wall.

When the spin is fast enough, the force overcomes the pull of gravity and the cup can be turned upside down.

A Puzzle of Portions

There are several ways to divide the juice. Here's one of the quickest:

Vessel size	24	13	11	5
To start	24	0	0	0
First	8	0	11	5
Second	8	13	3	0
Third	8	8	3	5
Fourth	8	8	8	0

Mixed Up?

There is the same amount of root beer in the cola as there is cola in the root beer.

For every drop of root beer that is in the cola cup, a drop of cola has been displaced and is in the root beer cup.

Toothpick Teasers

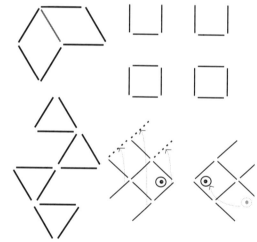

Going to the Movies

Tracing, counting, and remembering each step would drive you crazy. To make things easier, just write down the possible paths to each circle. The number of paths to the next circle is equal to the sum of the paths that connect to it.

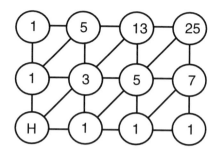

Now Seating?

1. There are ten possible combinations: BBGGG, BGBGG, BGGBG, BGGGB, GBBGG, GBGBG, GBGGB, GGBBG, GGBGB, GGGBB.

2. The chances for two boys being on the ends are 1 in 10.

3. The chances for two girls being on the ends are 3 in 10.

Weighing In...

The weight of the jar doesn't change. In order to fly, the insects must produce downward air currents that are equal in force to their weight. Therefore, whether standing or in flight, the insects push down with the same force.

The Strangest Eyes

Unfortunately, you will need to check this one by tracing over the pattern. As you do, you'll discover a single loop on the left and a double loop on the right.

Monkey Business

Both the crate and the chimp go up.

Head Count

Although this type of problem is perfect for algebra, let's do it visually. If all of the thirty heads belonged to two-legged birds, then there'd be only sixty legs. If one of the animals has four legs, then there'd be sixty-two legs. If two animals are four-legged, there'd be sixty-four legs.

By continuing in this pattern until we reach seventy legs, we will get a combination of twenty-five birds and five lizards.

Möbius Strip

The shape you get from dividing the Möbius strip is one large continuous loop with four twists.

Ant Walk

Nine centimeters. One basic pattern is illustrated below. Although there are other turns, they cover the same total length.

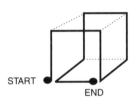

Cubic Quandaries

There is a total of 27 cubes. There are six cubes with one red side, twelve cubes with two red sides, eight cubes with three red sides, and one cube with no red sides.

Squaring Off

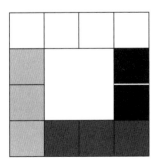

Saving Face

1. The face should have a circle design.

2. The pattern folds into a cube that looks like this:

3. Folding the creases would produce this final version:

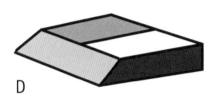

Cut the Cards

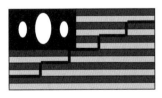

Stripped Stripe

Here is the cut pattern....

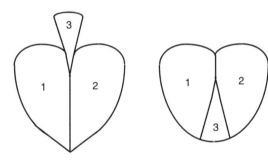

and here is the reassembly.

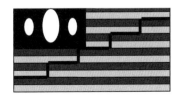

Missing Square

There isn't an extra block. The area making the new block was "shaved off" from some of the other blocks. The loss of each block's area is so small that it's not easy to observe.

Tipping the Scales

Snake Spread

The snakes will fill their stomachs and not be able to swallow anymore. The circle will then stop getting smaller.

Falcon Flight

The falcon's total distance is determined by the amount of time he was aloft and the speed he maintained.

The speed is given. The time is derived from the two cyclists. Since the cyclists are 60 miles apart and drive towards each other at 30 mph, the total time elapsed is 2 hours. The bird flying at 45 miles per hour will cover 90 miles in this 2-hour period.

A Question of Balance

It has to do with friction, balance, and the weight of the yardstick.

As you move your fingers towards the middle of the yardstick, the balance of the yardstick shifts. The finger that is closer to the middle will support more weight, making it easier for the other, more distant finger to "catch up" and move closer to the middle as well. This "catching up" flip-flops between the two fingers until they both arrive at the middle of the yardstick.

The finger that moves first from the middle immediately bears less of the ruler's weight, which makes it easier for this finger to keep moving. The farther it moves, the easier sliding becomes.

Well-Balanced Plate

You must mirror your opponent's placement of the plate. This way, as long as he has a place for his plate, you have a place for yours.

Robot Walkers

The robots follow a path that forms a continually shrinking and rotating square. Eventually, the robots will meet in the middle of the square.

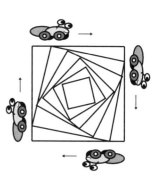

Chain Links

Select the chain with three links. Break open one of the links and use it to connect any two of the other sections. Break another of its links and use it to connect two other sections. Break the third and final link and use it to make a complete loop.

Rope Ruse

Fold your arms as shown above. Then, pick up the free end of the rope while your arms are already crossed. As you uncross your arms, the rope will automatically knot itself.

Money Magic

The clips will lock together and drop off the bill. A paper clip isn't a complete loop. It has two stretched openings through which the clip can slip off the bill. As the two sections of the bill move by each other, the clips slip through their openings and are pushed together to "reclip" onto each other's loop.

Revolutionary Thoughts

Four and a half hours. In order to be in a straight line the satellites must travel either one full revolution or one-half revolution. In 4¹/2 hours, they'll look like this:

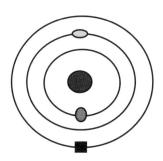

Baffling Holes

Fold the card in half so that the circular hole is also folded in half. Then slightly twist the paper as you pass the quarter snugly through the hole.

A Fair Solution

1. Either teenager can cut the slice, but the other person selects who gets which slice.

2. The four removed toothpicks leave the word "TEN."

Sock It to Me

Four socks. In a worst case scenario, if you draw three socks, each of a different color, the next sock you draw guarantees a matching color.

Nuts!

1. As you rotate each screw in a clockwise direction, they come together.

2. City-owned bulbs have opposite threads so that they won't screw into the standard light sockets that people have in their homes. Therefore, this discourages theft.